GÜLEN

Gülen

*The Ambiguous Politics of Market Islam
in Turkey and the World*

Joshua D. Hendrick

NEW YORK UNIVERSITY PRESS

New York and London

NEW YORK UNIVERSITY PRESS
New York and London
www.nyupress.org

References to Internet websites (URLs) were accurate at the time of writing. Neither the author nor New York University Press is responsible for URLs that may have expired or changed since the manuscript was prepared.

LIBRARY OF CONGRESS CATALOGING-IN-PUBLICATION DATA
Hendrick, Joshua D.
Gülen : the ambiguous politics of market Islam in Turkey and
the world / Joshua D. Hendrick.
pages cm
Includes bibliographical references and index.
ISBN 978-0-8147-7098-6 (hardback)
ISBN 978-1-4798-0046-9 (paperback)
1. Islam—Economic aspects—Turkey. 2. Turkey—Politics and government.
3. Gülen Hizmet Movement. I. Title.
BP173.75.H46   2013
297.2'73—dc23   2013006919

New York University Press books are printed on acid-free paper, and their binding materials are chosen for strength and durability. We strive to use environmentally responsible suppliers and materials to the greatest extent possible in publishing our books.

Manufactured in the United States of America
10 9 8 7 6 5 4 3 2 1

To NBR,
thank you

Contents

Acknowledgments

Primary funding for the research that led to this book was provided by the U.S. Fulbright "Islamic Civilization Special Initiative" (2006–2007) and by the Department of Sociology at University of California, Santa Cruz (UCSC). I began fieldwork in the United States in the fall of 2005, and continued in Istanbul, Turkey, in the summer of 2006 through the summer of 2007. Additional research was conducted in the United States during the summer of 2008, and intermittently between 2009 and early 2012. At the outset, it is important to extend my sincere sense of gratitude to the dozens of research participants in Turkey and in the United States who took part in this project as interviewees, conversationalists, and coworkers. First and foremost, I am forever grateful for the hospitality shown to me, and for the access granted to me, by my colleagues at Akademi and by the workers and executives at the array of institutions in Turkey who agreed to participate in this project. Considering their efforts in publishing, community development, journalism, dialogue, and education, and considering their identities as dedicated followers of Fethullah Gülen, it is very important to me that these men know how much I appreciate their willingness to participate in this project. I ask for their forgiveness if and when they disagree with my interpretation of their collective organization and impact.

I view the purpose of social scientific inquiry in general, and cultural analysis in particular, as an effort to critique social and cultural life as fervently as possible so as to better understand how social actors interpret their thoughts and actions, and how those thoughts and actions affect local, national, and global societies. Since the completion of my fieldwork in Istanbul in August 2007, the topic of the Gülen Movement (GM) has emerged as more divisive than ever in the Turkish context, and since early 2010, as an increasingly more divisive topic of discussion in the U.S. context as well. Although I am intellectually critical of the GM's mobilization, I implore all those who read the pages that follow to view this work as an *interpretation* of collective action, and as an account anchored on the academic necessity to treat all social phenomena with a skeptical eye, and with a focus on critique. This means that although I present the collective thought and practice of the Gülen Movement from a perspective rooted in critical theory, I do not view the Gülen Movement as inherently threatening to the structural integrity of Turkish society, to U.S. education, or to Turkey–U.S. relations. Although one's personal worldview might be at odds with the views and organization that is collectively exemplified by the Gülen Movement, in a free and open society enmity and hatred accomplish nothing but the continuation of intercultural miscommunication.

Notwithstanding, I am also of the opinion that inclinations toward ambiguity on the part of Gülen Movement actors when describing their aims and organization, regardless of how rational such practices might be in the Turkish context, invite suspicion and social criticism. Unfortunately, however, such criticism far too often treads into the waters of conspiratorial fantasy and xenophobic alarmism. My only hope is that the narrative presented in this volume will contribute to a more sophisticated and nuanced debate about the role of faith and social power in Turkish society in particular, and world society in general.

I am thankful for the support (scholastic and financial) and encouragement offered to me by the Department of Sociology at UCSC, whose faculty, staff, and graduate students all played significant roles in my intellectual and professional development. I am specifically grateful for the guidance and critique offered by Paul Lubeck, Terry Burke, and Walter Goldfrank. In their own way, each of these scholars provided me with valuable perspective, and without their contributions, I would not have succeeded in carrying out this project. In Turkey, I extend a very warm thank-you to Haldun Gülalp, who invited me to participate as a resident fellow at the Center for Global Studies at Yıldız Technical University in Istanbul from October 2006 to July 2007, and who offered very useful and thoughtful comments while I was in the field. Also in Turkey, I am forever indebted to Özge Yağiş, Didem Ikizoğlu, and Deniz Keskin, whose assistance during the research phase of this project was essential for its successful completion. Thank you to all. Notwithstanding the contributions offered by each of the above-mentioned individuals, the present volume is entirely my responsibility, as are any inconsistencies, theoretical or logical errors, and general lapses in narrative coherence.

Other scholars who shared their thoughts with me about this work, and without whose comments I would not have succeeded in producing this volume, are too many to list. Nonetheless, I would be remiss if I did not extend my gratitude to Brandon Wolf-Hunnicut, Hakan Yavuz, Nancy Gallagher, William Martin, Carsten Vala, and Erdem Çipa for their thoughtful criticisms of earlier drafts of various chapters. I am also forever grateful for the attentive comments offered by the four anonymous readers who reviewed earlier versions of the full text, as well as to Jennifer Hammer, Senior Editor at New York University Press, for her guidance, patience, and good nature during the revision process. Lastly, I am very thankful for the warm welcome and support extended to me by new colleagues at Loyola University Maryland, specifically Barbara Vann, Mark Peyrot, Lovell Smith, Betsy Schmitt, Carsten Vala, Michelle Gawerc, and Marianne Ward.

On a personal note, I am forever grateful for the support and encouragement extended to me by those I hold dearest in my life, a group of remarkable people that includes Norma Rosen, Lisa Mertz, Lauren Moret, Anne Hendrick, Jann Besson, Sarah Cousins, Erick Mertz, Damon Vance, Wendy Vance, and Tommy and Barbara Dunn. Foremost, I would not have been able to successfully carry out a long-term field research project or to complete a book project if it were not for the uncompromising support extended to me by my life partner and best friend, Leah Hendrick. From the bottom of my heart, thank you all!

Note on Turkish Transliteration

The modern Turkish alphabet was standardized in 1924 in accordance with a revolutionary language reform initiative, and is written in Roman script in an A-to-Z alphabet with the exception of the letters "x" and "q." The English letter "c" is pronounced like the English letter "j," and the English letter "j" is pronounced like its equivalent in French (i.e., as in the French name "Jacques"). In addition, modern Turkish uses five additional letters to connote common sounds in spoken Turkish:

Ö   This vowel signifies a sound that resembles as soft "er" in English. An "o" without the dots above it resembles the sound "o" when saying the letter in English. Example: "top" ("ball") is pronounced "t-o-p" with a clear pronunciation of the "o." "Döst" ("friend/pal") is pronounced "d-er-st," but with a *very* soft "r."

Ü   This vowel signifies a sharp "ew" in English. A "u" without the dots above it resembles the sound signified by "oo" in English. Example: "süt" ("milk") is pronounced "sewt." "Su" ("water") is pronounced "soo."

I   This vowel sound, an "ı" without a dot, signifies a sound similar to soft "i" in English (and "i" with a dot signifies a long "e" in English). Example: "Mısır" ("Egypt") is pronounced "misser" (*not* "M-ee-sir"). "Git" ("go") is pronounced "g-ee-t."

Ç   This consonant sound signifies a "ch" sound in English.

Ş   This consonant sound signifies a "sh" sound in English.

Ğ   This vowel, which is silent in itself, signifies an elongation of the preceding vowel sound, and thus always follows a vowel. Example: "Ağaç" ("tree") is pronounced "a-a-ch."

Also, when reading a Turkish word, the reader should pronounce every letter according to its sound. Example: "ayakkabı" ("shoe") is pronounced "a-yak-ka-bı," with the "ı" pronounced like the "i" in the English world "sir." Lastly, the Turkish suffix "lar/ler" indicates the plural form. Example: more than one "ayakkabı" (shoe) connotes "ayakkabılar" (shoes).

Abbreviations

AKP	Adalet ve Kalkınma Partisi (Justice and Development Party)
ANAP	Anavatan Partisi (Motherland Party)
AOYEV	Akyazılı Orta ve Yüksek Eğitim Vakfı (Akyazılı Foundation for Middle and Higher Education)
AP	Adalet Partisi (Justice Party),
BA	Bank Asya (Bank Asia)
BDP	Barış ve Demokrasi Partisi (Peace and Democracy Party)
CHA	Cihan Haber Ajansı (Cihan News Agency)
CHP	Cumhuriyet Halk Partisi (People's Republican Party)
CMO	Charter School Management Organization
DYP	Doğru Yol Partisi (True Path Party)
GIS(s)	Gülen-Inspired School(s)
GM	Gülen Movement
GNA	Turkish Grand National Assembly
GYV	Gazeticiler ve Yazarlar Vakfı (Journalists and Writers Foundation)
IP	Turkçe Işçi Partisi (Turkish Worker›s Party)
MEB	Milli Eğitim Bakanlığı (Ministry of Education)
MGH	Milli Görüş Hareketi (National Outlook Movement)
MHP	Milliyetçi Hareket Partisi (Nationalist Action Party)
ÖKS	Ortaöğrentim Kurumları Giriş Sınavı (High School Entrance Examination)
ÖSS	Öğrenci Seçme Sınavı (University Selection Exam)
PASIAD	Pasifik Ülkeleri İle Sosyal ve İktisadi Dayanışma Derneği (Association for Social and Economic Cooperation in Pacific Asia)

RNK   *Risale-i Nur Külliyatı* (*Epistles of Light*)
RP   Refah Partisi (Welfare Party)
TLO   Turkish Language Olympics
TSK   Türk Silahlı Kuvvetleri (Turkish Armed Forces)
TÜSIAD   Türk Sanayicileri ve İşadamları Derneği (Turkish Industrialists' and Businessmen's Association)
TUSKON   Türkiye İşadamları ve Sanayiciler Konfederasyonu (Turkish Businessmen and Industrialists Confederation)
TZ   *Today's Zaman* (Newspaper)

Introduction

The World's Most Influential Public Intellectual

Truth can be established and supported in many ways . . . if
a place of worship rouses its community with thoughts of
eternity, if a school awakens hope and faith in its pupils, they
are serving their purpose and therefore are sacred. If this is
not the case, they are no more than devilish traps divert-
ing us from the truth. We may apply the same standards to
unions, trusts, political institutions, and societies in general.
—M. Fethullah Gülen

In a 2005 poll administered to determine "the world's most influential public intellectual," the U.S. political magazine *Foreign Policy* (*FP*),
together with its British affiliate, *Prospect*, published an unranked list
of one hundred people whom their editors believed to be the most
impactful opinion makers, political leaders, policy advisers, activists,
and scholars in the world. Included on the 2005 list were two Turkish
citizens, the best-selling fiction writer Orhan Pamuk, and the longtime World Bank and United Nations economist and former Turkish
parliamentarian Kemal Derviş. After twenty thousand votes were cast,
Pamuk finished fifty-fourth, Derviş sixty-seventh. Self-critiqued as
unscientific, the poll was hailed as a thought-provoking exercise concerning "the grand tradition of oppositional intellectuals." When the
critical philosopher Noam Chomsky won by more than 4,800 votes, the
FP/Prospect editors concluded that even in the "post-ideological" era of
globalization, there was still very much a market for fervent social critique and oppositional public debate (Herman 2005).

Revising their methods for generating an unranked list of one hundred influential public intellectuals, in 2008 *FP* and *Prospect* administered their poll for a second time. In his introduction to the publication

of the 2008 list, the British political commentator Christopher Hitchens (fifth on the 2005 list), offered his advice for selection as follows:

> An intellectual need not be one who, in a well-known but essentially meaningless phrase, "speaks truth to power." (Chomsky has dryly reminded us that power often knows the truth well enough.) . . . The attitude towards authority should probably be skeptical, as should the attitude towards utopia, let alone to heaven or hell. Other aims should include the ability to survey the present through the optic of a historian, the past with the perspective of the living, and the culture and language of others with the equipment of an internationalist. In other words, the higher one comes in any "approval" rating of this calling, the more uneasily one must doubt one's claim to the title in the first place. (Hitchens 2008)

Orhan Pamuk won the Nobel Prize for Literature in 2006, which assured him a repeat appearance on the top one hundred in 2008. Among the changes to the list, however, was that Kemal Derviş was out. In his place from Turkey was a retired religious functionary named M. Fethullah Gülen. Knowing little about Gülen, the poll organizers were taken by surprise when after one week of online voting tens of thousands of votes were registered in his favor, propelling him well past Pamuk, Hitchens, Chomsky, and ninety-six others. After four weeks and more than five hundred thousand votes, Fethullah Gülen was named "the world's most influential public intellectual" by a wide margin (Nuttal 2008). The July 2008 edition of *Prospect* magazine subsequently published a series of articles asking the question—who is Fethullah Gülen?

The "Esteemed Teacher"

Called "Hocaefendi" (esteemed teacher) by the hundreds of thousands, if not millions, of Turks who devote themselves to his teachings, Fethullah Gülen is the most widely known, and most controversial, religious personality in contemporary Turkey. Known by many names, what is hereafter referred to as the "Gülen Movement" denotes to a transnationally active, Turkish and Muslim-identified education, media, and business network whose actors and institutions span well over one hundred countries. The GM first emerged as a social network of young men who were inspired by Fethullah Gülen's applied articulation of the teachings of a preceding Turkish faith-community leader, Bediüzzaman Said Nursi (1877–1960). With modest beginnings that date back to the late 1960s in the western Turkish city of Edirne, Gülen first attracted a following when he worked as a religious functionary in Turkey's Presidency of Religious Affairs (Diyanet). By the late 1970s, Fethullah Gülen was attracting increasingly larger crowds to his public sermons. Motivated by his oratory skills, passion, and projected wisdom, Gülen's early admirers were moved by his ability to intellectually link an applied understanding of Nursi's teachings with the challenges of late-industrial Turkey.

Instructed to focus their attention on educating Turkey's youth in mathematics and in the natural/physical sciences, throughout the 1970s GM affiliates established a number of student dormitories, summer camps, and afterschool programs in Turkey's largest cities. They also began to disseminate Gülen's teachings via audiocassettes, print publications, and VHS recordings. In the context of a military junta in 1980–1983, followers of Fethullah Gülen found opportunity in a nationally underdeveloped private education sector. Throughout the 1980s, students at what are now most commonly referred to as "Gülen-inspired schools" (GISs) began to score noticeably higher than their counterparts on nationwide high school and university placement exams, and began to earn countrywide recognition by winning national scholastic competitions with regularity. In the same period, GM affiliates also became active in publishing, light manufacture, construction, and media. In all sectors GM activities became increasingly more reliant on the support of an expanding cohort of socially conservative entrepreneurs who emerged in the context of a transformative period of Turkish liberalization.

In the early 1990s, GM-affiliated actors seized on opportunities to expand their education, media, and business initiatives abroad, initially to the newly independent countries in Central Asia and the Balkans, and later to Russia, Australia, Southeast Asia, and Africa. Also at this time, affiliated business interests consolidated into a number of regionally defined trade associations, and in 1996 a small group of affiliated business leaders opened Turkey's first 100 percent Turkish-owned interest-free "participation bank." By the late 1990s, GM affiliates operated schools and had business interests in more than eighty countries. Paralleling these moves were efforts to advertise the GM's activities to a wider audience through the mechanism of mass media, public relations, and interfaith outreach. By the mid-2000s, approximately one thousand GISs were open for business in more than 120 countries, as were dozens of interfaith/intercultural "dialogue" institutions whose task was to promote Gülen's teachings throughout Europe, Australia, the United States, and elsewhere. Not surprisingly, this was also when GM initiatives around the world started to receive regular praise from international media outlets for allegedly offering the world a "mild" brand of Islam-inspired collective action.[1]

In an interview setting in Istanbul, a first-generation student of Gülen's explained that Hocaefendi's ability to wield social power amazes as much as it confuses:

> The subject I want to emphasize is the person, *Hocaefendi* [Fethullah Gülen], . . . Once a sociologist said . . . "What kind of man is this? He says a word in Istanbul and it turns into a school in Africa!" (Field Interview, Winter 2007)

Opening a private education institution in a foreign country requires coordinated effort in investment capital, negotiation, and marketing. It also requires a significant degree of political lobbying by investors who promise to assist host governments with their national educational goals. If GM affiliates can easily embark on such a venture, organizing an Internet campaign to sway the results of an online poll comes into clearer perspective. And although there is little reason to believe that Gülen had anything personally to do with his *FP/Prospect* victory, his overwhelming triumph provides a useful piece of data from which to speculate about the extent to which he inspires Turkish Muslims to act with coordinated intent.

Indeed, as they struggled to figure out how and why Gülen won their poll, *FP/Prospect* editors learned that shortly after the May 2008 publication of their unranked list of one hundred influential public intellectuals, Gülen's candidacy was announced on the front page of the GM-affiliated *Zaman* newspaper, Turkey's most widely circulated newspaper and the flagship brand under the larger GM-affiliated media corporation Feza Gazetecilik (Feza Media Group). The poll was also widely publicized on each of Feza's three television stations, on its national radio station, and on the pages of Feza's numerous other print publications,[2] as well as on each of the GM's twenty-five "official" websites,[3] and on dozens of other open-source web forums. On the Yahoo! e-mail groups "Fethullah Gülen" (*fethullah_gulen*, 1,751 members), "Turkish schools" (*turk_okulları*, 25,438 members), and "*Zaman* readers" (*zaman_okurları*, 886 members), for instance, mass e-mails asking people to vote for Gülen were common.[4] What *FP* and *Prospect* soon realized was that "Hocaefendi" Fethullah Gülen won their poll because the networks that link Islamic activists in Turkey were well organized, had a high degree of technological savvy, and perhaps most important, were deeply invested in the praise and promotion of their leader.

Skepticism, Criticism, and Inquiry

Following World War I, the once powerful and multi-ethnic Ottoman Empire was defunct and a new Republic of Turkey emerged in its wake. To "protect" Turkish society from competing nationalist forces, Turkey's young republican regime vested the Türk Silahlı Kuvvetleri (Turkish Armed Forces, TSK) with semi-autonomy and powers of political oversight. Over time, the TSK strengthened its role in Turkey's power structure, which produced a series of five actual or threatened military-led coups since the founding of the Republic in 1923 (1960, 1971, 1980, 1997, 2007). This is significant because in addition to being a religious community leader, Fethullah Gülen has long been associated with allegations of conspiracy in Turkey. Fears about "Fethullahcılar" (Fethullahists) infiltrating Turkey's civilian and military bureaucracies in an effort to patiently "Islamicize" the secular republic are common. For instance, in the context of Turkey's second military-led coup in 1971, when Fethullah Gülen was still an employee for the Diyanet, he was charged with the crime of leading a secret religious community that threatened the integrity of the secular Turkish state. After seven months in prison, he was released but was temporarily barred from public speaking.

In 1980, Turkish social tensions again reached a boiling point, and again, Turkey experienced a penetrating military-led coup. Gülen was again detained and questioned about the activities of his community before being released. Nearly two decades later, Gülen faced more serious charges about the aims of his organization, and in 2000 he was indicted in absentia after having fled to the United States the previous year. The primary piece of evidence used to mount the case against him was a purportedly leaked video excerpt that was published widely in the Turkish press, wherein Gülen allegedly instructed his community as follows:

> You must move in the arteries of the system, without anyone noticing your existence, until you reach all the power centers. . . . You must wait until such time as you have gotten all the state power, until you have brought to your side all the power of the constitutional institutions in Turkey. . . . Until that time, any step taken would be too early—like breaking an egg without waiting the full forty days for it to hatch. It would be like killing the chick inside. The work to be done is [in] confronting the world. Now, I have expressed my feelings and thoughts to you all—in confidence . . . trusting your loyalty and sensitivity to secrecy. I know that when you leave here—[just] as you discard your empty juice boxes, you must discard the thoughts and feelings expressed here.[5]

When this clip aired on Turkish television in the spring of 1999, Gülen had already moved to the United States. Although he cited health reasons, skeptics lambasted Gülen for pre-emptively leaving the country instead of confronting the allegations against him. Gülen responded to his critics as follows:

> I have never thought of taking over the state; if people think that I have such a desire they should remember that people are judged on their deeds not their intentions. . . . Today, because of conversations which were edited and intentionally misquoted in written articles, I am facing execution without trial. ("Gülen" 1999)

In 2006, a lower court acquitted Gülen of conspiracy charges, a verdict that was reaffirmed by Turkey's 9th Branch of the Supreme Court of Appeals in June 2008. Despite legal vindication, however, Gülen remained in the United States, eventually settling down in the Pocono foothills in Pennsylvania. In 2001, he began to actively seek permanent U.S. residency. In November 2008, lawyers on his behalf convinced a federal judge to grant Gülen a green card based on the fact that he was "an alien of extraordinary abilities in the field of education." Despite his vindication in the Turkish and U.S. legal systems, however, Gülen's critics continued to insist that the faith leader was more accurately understood as either a "radical Islamist" who instructs his followers to indoctrinate schoolchildren, or as a social movement leader who coordinates with Turkey's ruling "Islamist roots" Justice and Development Party (2002–) to slowly overhaul the secular institutions of the Turkish state (Çetinkaya 2007; Krespin 2007, 2009; Rubin 2008; Schwartz 2008; Yanardağ 2006). Over the years, GM loyalists became quite adept at anticipating such claims and thus developed a sophisticated system of refutation and denial.

Today, both domestically and abroad, GM affiliates regularly counter their critics by arguing that, without equivocation, their leader and the "civic movement of volunteers" he inspires are interested in nothing more than the promotion of worldly knowledge, tolerance, and dialogue with others. Now Turkey's largest and most influential Islamic identity community, the GM's significance extends well beyond Turkey's borders. This is important for the world community because in the context of a rapidly emerging Turkey (e.g., it is projected to become the world's fifteenth-largest economy in 2013), GM loyalists control one of the country's largest media conglomerates, a number of the country's most globally linked companies, and approximately one thousand math- and science-focused GISs in more than one hundred countries. Following their leader across the Atlantic, loyalists in the GM network have expanded their operations in the United States, where they are now active in intercultural outreach, commerce, construction, IT solutions, political lobbying, and charter school education. Indeed, access to public funding via the expanding "school choice" system in the United States has produced an environment whereby, with approximately 130 schools as of March 2012, the United States hosts more GISs than does any country in the world outside Turkey.

As a political ethnography, this book explains the GM's emergence as evidence of rationalized charisma in contemporary Turkey, and as the institutionalization and marketization of Muslim-inspired collective action. By building private schools instead of public mosques, the GM reframes "secular" education in science and math as "moral" education in the ways of creation. By educating future bankers, investors, accountants, and lawyers, the GM reframes the spiritual requirement to follow God's path as a social requirement to realize white-collar success and elite-level influence. By investing religiously motivated donations (*himmet*) as start-up capital for profit-driven enterprises, the GM's expansion illustrates the ways that piety has become rationalized in Turkey, and how the politics of global participation has, in many ways, secularized Muslim identity politics in the interests of material expansion.

Questions

Three analytical questions focus our discussion: (1) What factors explain the shift from "overtly political" (i.e., open protest, partisan mobilization) to "passively political" (i.e., private education, media, and business) Muslim politics in late twentieth-century Turkey? (2) What factors explain the GM's emergence as the go-to example for scholars and analysts in the United States, Europe, and Australia who seek to promote a phenomenon they refer to as "mild," "moderate," "liberal," or "peaceful" Islam? (3) Does the GM case provide the world with an alternative understanding of the relationships that exist between modernity and Islam in the global era?

The above questions are answered by presenting the GM as an example of rationalized Islamic sensibility. The GM case, therefore, illustrates not only the degree to which traditional Islam and liberal modernity are compatible, but that modernity reframes tradition in its image. Based on fourteen months of extensive ethnographic fieldwork in Turkey and the United States, this book argues that in conjunction with its expanding media and financial holdings, the GM has emerged as Turkey's most influential nonpartisan, nonmilitary social force and thus constitutes a primary player in what Tuğal (2009) has rightfully termed Turkey's ongoing "passive revolution." As a primary collective actor in Turkey's passive revolution, the community of Fethullah Gülen offers an indicative case by which to observe the "post-political" turn in twenty-first-century Muslim politics in general, and an illustrative case by which to observe Turkey's political, economic, and cultural transformation in particular.

Rather than calling on pious Turks to seize the Turkish power structure, however, "organic Muslim intellectuals" close to the GM employ a sophisticated discourse to advocate for patience and diligence in a long-term effort to increase the "Muslim share" in the administration of Turkey's political economy. In this regard, the case of the GM forces scholars and policy analysts alike to reconsider static dichotomies that posit "Islamists" versus "secularists" by calling for a closer examination of Muslim experiences with contemporary globalization and the opportunities provided therein. In this context, this book's primary objective is to emphasize that although its goals are anchored on a conservative, faith-based social identity, and although its methods are often nontransparent, GM actors are reliant on the market for their continued expansion and are thus best presented as *products of, rather than as a fundamentalist reactions to, the processes of neoliberal globalization.*

1

Approaching Muslim Politics in Turkey

Those who understand politics as political parties, propaganda, elections, and the struggle for power are mistaken. Politics is the art of management, based on a broad perspective of today, tomorrow, and the day after, that seeks the people's satisfaction and God's approval.
—M. Fethullah Gülen

This book focuses on a particular case of Muslim politics in late modern Turkey, a diverse Muslim majority country that is distinguished as much by its conservative Anatolian culture as it is by its history with secular state authoritarianism. For the purposes of this analysis, *Muslim politics* refers to the employment of categories historically associated with the faith and culture of Islam by social actors who express aspirations for political and economic reform or revolution (Eickelman and Piscatori 1996, 4).

Approaching Muslim Politics

In Sunni Islam, modern Muslim politics emerged under the auspices of the Salafiyya,[1] an ideologically fervent but organizationally undeveloped social movement that was spearheaded by the Egyptian scholar Muhammad Abduh (1849–1905) and his disciple, Rashid Rida (1865–1935). Responding to the social, political, and economic ills associated with European colonialism, Abduh and Rida published *al-Manar* (The Lighthouse), which became the most widely circulated Muslim identity journal of its time (1898–1935). In so doing, Abduh, Rida, and their intellectual circle in Cairo and beyond marked the discursive and ideological birth of the modern Muslim intellectual, the secularly educated, religiously devout, and politically motivated social theorist who called for social and political reform in line with an emerging "Islamic identity" in the Maghreb, the Levant, Anatolia, and elsewhere. Although a failed project in the long term, the Salafiyya laid a foundation on which would-be social critics in the middle and late twentieth century mounted their projects of *tajdid* (renewal) and *islah* (reform) in nationalizing Muslim majority polities. Adapting to local conditions, the middle decades of the twentieth century witnessed the maturation of modern Muslim politics from a project of political and social critique to an organizationally mobilized project for political and social change.

The institutionalization of modern Muslim identity occurred under the leadership of an Egyptian schoolteacher, Hasan al-Banna (1906–1949), and a Pakistani journalist, Sayyid Abul a'la-Maududi (1903–1979). Banna founded the Egyptian Ikhwan Muslimin (Muslim Brotherhood) in 1928, and Maududi founded the Jamaat-i Islami (Islamic Community/Party) in 1941. According to Banna, "Because of the political stages through which they have passed, the social influences which have passed through them, and under the impact of Western civilization . . . [Muslims] have departed from the goals of their faith" (quoted in Mitchell 1969, 6). Echoing Banna, Maududi (1984, 77–78) argued that because of Western intrusion, "[Muslims] have moved away from God, towards man's exploitation by man and towards moral degeneration and cultural pollution." By institutionalizing cultural, social, and political alternatives to the policies of postcolonial national development, both Banna and Maududi inspired an international project to offer "Islam as the solution" to modern social, political, and economic ills.

Focusing on the incompatibility arguments presented by Banna, Maududi, and their emulators around the world, a number of scholars and the majority of media in the United States and western Europe came to understand Islam as a unique civilization whose majority was either unable or unwilling to coexist with the civilization of the modern West. Proponents of this approach assumed that within Islam there existed no separation between faith and politics, which led them to suggest that pious Muslims could not appreciate the secular order of the

politics + culture

modern world system. Scholars the likes of Bernard Lewis (1993, 2002 [1990]), Samuel Huntington (1993, 1996), Daniel Pipes (2002), and others insisted that in the post–Cold War era (i.e., the "post-ideology" era) "politics" and "culture" fused to define the primary contours of twenty-first-century political contest. As such, "Islam" and "the West" were presented as culturally determined social formations that, in the absence of an intermediary ideology to compete with free market liberalism (i.e., socialism), were destined for enmity. The geo-political result was a "Muslim world" that existed in a constant state of tension between "modernizing" (i.e., secularizing, Westernizing) states and "traditional" (i.e., Muslim) societies, and a "Western world" where Muslim migrants who displayed their religious beliefs were understood to constitute a cultural, social, political, and economic challenge to "Western" values.

This phenomenon has led to a troubling rise in "Islamophobia" in many non-Muslim majority societies (Ali et al. 2011). Indeed, as this manuscript goes to press, public opinion regarding Muslims in the United States is too often guided by a mass media establishment that presents cultural incompatibility between "the West" and Islam as self-evident. Some consumers of this approach have framed their critique of the GM's successes in U.S. charter school education as evidence of what they designate "education jihad" in that country.[2] To the contrary, this book argues that these concerns are not only unfounded, they are often preposterous and achieve little more than stoking a growing blaze of hatred in an increasingly xenophobic U.S. public sphere.

Beyond "Culture Talk"

Because those who adhere to the incompatibility thesis equate "the modern" with that which is "Western," they fall into the trap of what Mamdani (2004) calls "culture talk," a discursive phenomenon that assumes every culture to have a tangible essence that defines it, and that frames politics as reducible to essential cultural qualities. This approach often leads its consumers to view Muslims first and foremost as Muslims, and only secondarily as parents or children, women or men, wealthy or working class, progressive or conservative. Culture, as expressed in fashion, taste, and other consumption habits, becomes a rational means by which to presuppose someone's politics before actual opinions, experiences, or worldviews are ever discussed. When presenting Muslim politics from a perspective that champions "culture talk," therefore, analysts, journalists, and laypeople alike pose questions that ponder whether Islam is a religion of peace or violence, whether Islam is for or against democracy, or whether Islam represses or liberates women. In each case, "Islam" is treated as an agential category with causal power. This means that if Islam is assumed to repress democracy, then one's Muslim identity (e.g., as observed by the wearing of a head scarf) is believed to signify one's disbelief in democratic governance. By default, "good Muslims" are understood to favor moderation, democracy, peace, and the liberation of women. To prove that they hold such values, these "good Muslims" are expected to repress their tradition by embracing "the modernity" of secular liberalism and the cultural habits associated therein (e.g., taking off their head scarves and shaving their beards). By contrast, "bad Muslims" are understood to project their identities in accordance with their cultural traditions, which is evident by their adornment in what one popular U.S. journalist termed "Muslim garb."[3] When they do so, they signify that their primary political allegiance is to Islam, and by default, to a political and social world that is inherently antithetical to modern life. This approach, therefore, views Islam as a divided cultural signifier that is either "fundamentalist" (and potentially "radical") or "moderate" (and potentially peaceful). The moods, beliefs, and behaviors of nearly two billion people are quickly reduced to subjective interpretations of secular or pious, "good" or "bad" (Mamdani 2002, 2004).

An alternative approach to the study of Muslim politics attempts to analyze political and social action as evidence of cultural diversity, rather than cultural incompatibility. Indeed, scholars and analysts who apply this approach view Islam as an adapting collection of cultural codes, and thus as an internally competing and contradictory amalgam that varies in different contexts. Critiquing the cultural incompatibility thesis, analysts who operate from what I call the "symbolic authority" approach strive to explain the observable variation of Muslim politics by analyzing the discourses disseminated by influential Muslim opinion makers who draw on symbolic Islamic categories to expound on the challenges of modern political, economic, and social recognition (Eickelman and Piscatori 1996; Eickelman and Anderson 2003; Göle 1997, 2002; Hefner 2004; Mamdani 2002, 2004; Mandaville 2001, 2006;

Mardin 1989; Sayyid 1997; White 2002; Yavuz 1999, 2003a). Political agency, in this regard, is viewed less as something embedded in Islam, than it is as something embedded in the consciousness of individual humans. Islam is understood as a malleable cultural system that *has the potential* to inform (or not inform, as the case may be) the modern identities of billions; and moreover, that has the potential to inform the actions of relief workers, doctors and surgeons, schoolteachers, and businesspeople, as much as it does the actions of would-be politicians, social movement activists, and armed insurrectionists (Hendrick 2007). Viewing Muslim politics from such an interpretive lens allows observers to see "the competition and contest over both the interpretation of symbols and control of the institutions, formal and informal, that produce and sustain them" (Eickelman and Piscatori 1996, 5). What comes into focus is a complex and competing marketplace of ideas that range from overtly political antagonism to passively political civil debate. Indeed, this book presents the charisma and community of Fethullah Gülen as one variation amid a range of possibilities that emerge when Muslim politics interacts with local particularity to produce an effective project for social change.

A third and more recent trend in the study of Muslim politics builds on the symbolic authority approach but incorporates the vocabulary of social movements to focus more specifically on strategies of collective mobilization, recruitment, and political opportunity (Baker 2003; Bayat 2007; Beinin 2005; Beinin and Stork 1997; Clark 2004; Gülalp 2001; Lubeck 2000; Wiktorowitz 2004; Yavuz 2003a). In addition to analyzing the cultural framing mechanisms employed by Muslim intellectuals (i.e., symbolic authority), emphasis is placed on the "opportunity structures" that emerge in the context of global integration, on the strategies of power used to recruit followers, and on the tactics used to engage in locally defined contentious projects. There is thus an effort to "move beyond the explication of texts and the biographies of intellectual figures to examine the local circumstances and historical particularities of each movement, which often turn out to be more substantial than a simple conception of 'Islam' in opposition to secular politics" (Beinin and Stork 1997, 7). An undercurrent focuses on the resourceful use of social networks that facilitate the movement of people, finances, information, and ideas with collective intent.

Of particular salience for our purposes is that evidence from social movement research indicates that as organizations, it is simply incorrect to posit that all Islamic activist movements are fundamentally at odds with the Western-centric modern world system, "because, in contradictory ways, Islamism appeals to both the losers and the winners of global neo-liberal economic restructuring" (Beinin 2005, 113). In Turkey this is very much the case. Described in ethnographic detail, this book explains how neo-liberal economic restructuring in the 1980s provided new actors with greater access to wealth accumulation, and subsequently, with increased ability to affect the development of public opinion in a privatized marketplace, which facilitated a shift in Turkish Muslim politics from the politics of revolution to the politics of participation.

Muslim Politics in Turkey

In Turkey's republican period (1923–1950), the policies of secular nationalism took an especially rigid form. Framed in terms of Turkish Kemalism (the political doctrine of Turkey's first president, Mustafa Kemal Atatürk), Turkey's mid-twentieth-century development model was implemented in accordance with a political discourse that legitimized the domination of a small circle of elites whose supporters spent much of the twentieth century marginalizing Turkey's periphery in the interests of state centralization. Established in terms of "six arrows" (populism, nationalism, republicanism, secularism, reformism, and state planning), a primary goal of Turkey's Kemalist regime was to suppress Anatolia's Ottoman–Islamic tradition by taking control over the definition and application of faith, education, and law in Turkish society. Centuries of tradition became subordinate to a state-driven project of European-oriented, import-substitution industrialization that was managed by a vanguard group of party officials, state bureaucrats, select industrialists, and military leaders. Islam's symbolic authority was uniformly suppressed in Turkey's public sphere from the time of the Republic's founding in 1923 until its shift to a plural party polity in 1950. From a symbolic authority perspective, Göle (1997, 173) explains that Muslim politics in Turkey emerged as an effort "to rename and reconstruct Muslim identity by freeing it from traditional interpretations and by challenging assimilative forces of modernism."

When the Demokrat Parti (Democratic Party, DP) emerged as modern Turkey's first partisan alternative to Kemal's original Cumhuriyet Halk Partisi (People's Republican Party, CHP), Islam became a channel for DP operatives to cultivate support throughout Anatolia. Notwithstanding, the DP was less centrally defined by its Muslim identity than it was by its populism, and thus it was not until the formation of the Milli Görüş Hareketi (National Outlook Movement, MGH) in 1970 that a specifically "Islamic" coalition of partisans mounted an opposition to Turkey's oligarchic elite. Under the leadership of Necmettin Erbakan, the MGH formed the Milli Nizam Partisi (National Order Party) to compete in Turkish elections. Between 1970 and 2001, Turkey's Islamic movement under MGH's leadership steadily increased its electoral percentage, to which the Turkish state reacted by routinely closing MGH-affiliated political parties, and by routinely jailing or politically barring MGH leaders from political participation. In the early 1990s, the MGH adapted; its leaders began to passively voice their acceptance of Turkish political and economic liberalization, and they began to reframe their "Islamic identity" in comparatively liberal terms. By 2001, the representative Fazilet Partisi (FP) gave up on the MGH's longtime call for Islamic Law (Shariah, Turkish: Şeriat) as a viable political goal, thus signaling the final "absorption" of Turkey's Islamist opposition (Tuğal 2009).

What explains the reform of Muslim politics in Turkey? Throughout the 1980s and 1990s, hundreds of small-to-medium-sized enterprises emerged to capitalize on new opportunities to export their products to an expanding global marketplace. In addition to equal rights, equal representation, and a chance to express their collective identity (i.e., a symbolic authority argument), however, Turkey's Islamic activists began to seek greater access to the overall material benefits of modernity, to a "Muslim share," so to speak. This book presents the charisma and community of Fethullah Gülen as a success story in this effort. Because the economic base that emerged as the GM's underwriting sector was first and foremost interested in its own reproduction, whom its organizational leaders supported politically was contingent on policies that expanded Turkey's export economy, and that expanded the diversification of the Turkish elite. The market actors who constituted the cohort of socially conservative, economically liberal patrons of the

GM, therefore, were many of the same actors who supported the coming to power of Turkey's currently governing Adalet ve Kalkınma Partisi (Justice and Development Party, AKP) in 2002. Having marketed itself as being both "progressive" (evidenced by its initiative to speed up Turkey's reform in line with the EU's Copenhagen criteria) and "traditional" (evidenced by the party's focus on "conservative values" and its leaders' history with the MGH), the "Islamist roots" AKP fused progressive globalism with traditional conservatism, which, coupled with the self-destruction of Turkey's left-of-center partisan alternatives, allowed the AKP to mobilize "a coalition that [was] able to keep together both the winners and the losers of the neo-liberal globalization process" (Öniş 2009, 24). As the most powerful "winner" in the AKP's "new Turkey coalition," in the 2000s the GM matured to become a profoundly effective actor in Turkey's political economy, a nonpartisan social and economic network whose organizational capacity to invest material and social capital has become second to none in Turkish civil society. Indeed, when considering the GM's impact as the AKP's most important collective partner, a common question in contemporary Turkish politics is whether the AKP–GM alliance will last, and if so, for how long.[4]

A Middle Way?

Among the primary ethnographic critiques presented in this study is that GM affiliates consistently and ubiquitously assert that their initiatives are indicative of a "nonpolitical" effort to facilitate dialogue and cooperation in Turkish (and world) society. If this is true, is it accurate to situate the GM's mobilization in the field of Muslim politics? This book asserts that the answer is most certainly yes. This is because when GM actors discuss their impact, they employ the term "political" in a very narrow sense, reserving it to connote either political party mobilization or state-directed protest/confrontation. Expanding the realm of the political, this book presents the GM as a transnational advocacy network that uses "nonpoliticism" as an alternative strategy to influence reform. It is a *network* because it is "[a] form of organization characterized by voluntary, reciprocal, and horizontal patterns of communication and exchange" (Keck and Sikkink 1998, 8). It is an *advocacy network* because it organizes collectively to express a shared set of values and meanings with an ultimate goal of establishing influence and affecting policy.

The GM's "pro-systemic" stance in terms of Turkish national identity, EU integration, and neo-liberal structural adjustment, however, inhibits any inclination to designate it either as a "social" movement," in the ideal typical sense of the term, or as "progressive," in the universal sense of left-leaning critique. This is because social movements are specific collective phenomena that share specific constitutive criteria. Indeed, according to Tilly (2004), in order for collective action to be designated a social movement, its actors must systematically make collective claims on "target audiences," they must organize collective protests, demonstrations, and other "claim making performances," and they must advertise their "worthiness" in the public sphere.

Does the GM make claims on target audiences? Yes, but it does so according to the established standards of the Turkish state and in accordance with the universal norms of market competition. The GM's method of engagement is thus only *passively* confrontational. Its actors organize their publications, their schools, their media, and their business endeavors according to Turkish and host country laws and in harmony with the logic of global capitalism. *Does the GM organize collective protests, demonstrations, and other "claim making performances"?* Yes and no. The GM does not organize demonstrations, marches, or protests, but its actors do form organizations and associations in an effort to put Gülen's teachings into action (*aksiyon*). But again, these actions are only passively contentious. Instead of directly confronting the Turkish state through claim making, GM loyalists seek to passively overhaul the principles of state–society relations by persuading the Turkish public that piety and modernity are compatible—that Islam and secularism, Islam and markets, and Islam and human rights are not conceptually antithetical. In this way, the GM is neither anti-systemic, nor is it antagonistic. Rather, its actors posit themselves as representative of the "pluralization and moderation of the Turkish Islam" in general (Yavuz 1999, 126). *Does the GM advertise its "worthiness" in the public sphere?* Yes! GM actors spend a great deal of time and money advertising their worthiness to the Turkish and international public. They do so, however, to advance their own interests, not to advance the interests of some larger public good (however much they might frame the former using language of the latter). Indeed, favorable public reception is understood to be of primary importance for the GM's continued expansion, which has led to an extensive public relations campaign that spends enormous amounts of resources promoting Gülen as Turkey's (and the world's) answer to so-called "radical Islam." Since 2001, the GM has expanded exponentially, which, depending on the source, is evidence of the network's credibility, its ulterior motives, or its grace.

If its efforts to affect social change are not realized via revolutionary assault or via direct political engagement (e.g., party mobilization, protest mobilization, armed resistance), how are observers of the Turkish case expected to understand the GM's organizational aims and collective impact? Adapting and updating the teachings of his predecessor, Said Nursi, toward a twenty-first-century project for social change, Gülen claims to offer Turkey (and the world) a "middle way" between secularism and piety (Kuru 2003). Citing Gülen's "middle way" as evidence of a general trend in political culture, White (2004) contends that individual and group identities as either "secularists" or "Islamists" in Turkey have given way to varying senses of "Muslimhood." By this, White suggests that despite one's personal piety, Islam has become normalized as an accepted public identity in contemporary Turkish society, and is conceived as existing in harmony with Turkish secularism. Operating from a symbolic authority approach, White argues that "Muslimhood" in Turkey underscores two general trends: (1) a classical Islamist confrontation against the state in Turkey is increasingly less viable, less realistic, and less appealing; and (2) individual expressions of piety, and individual yearnings for social mobility and advancement, have taken the place of religiously motivated political protest.

The idea of a "middle way" between state-enforced secularization (Kemalism) and Şeriat-focused antagonism (Islamism) provides a useful lens through which to observe the recent transformation of Turkey's political public. From a social movement perspective, however, it is impossible to view the GM's "middle way" as indicative of society-wide reconciliation. Indeed, in her critique of what Giddens (1999) termed the "third way" in twenty-first century political discourse, Mouffe (2005) argues that "dialogue" between individuals who share a constant necessity to make "life choices" in an open and free public sphere presupposes class equality. Mouffe critiques Giddens's assumption that globalization can produce real "dialogue," because in her view, the global era is not defined by a context wherein everyone has a stake in the continued and uninterrupted integration of the world economy. Quite the contrary, such a post-political world does not compute with the reality of global risk, and with the world's increasingly more uneven experiences with it:

> [According to the third way] . . . society is viewed as basically composed of middle classes; the only exceptions are a small elite of very rich on one side, and those who are "excluded" on the other. . . . This of course chimes with the tenet that "post-traditional" societies are no longer structured through unequal power relations. By redefining the structural inequalities systematically produced by the market in terms of "exclusion," one can dispense with the structural analysis of their causes, thereby avoiding the fundamental question of which changes in power relations are needed to tackle them. . . . This is how a supposed renewal of social democracy has produced a "social democratic variant of neoliberalism." . . . [The notion of a dialogic democracy] *makes clear the refusal to acknowledge that a society is always hegemonically constituted through a certain structure of power relations, [which] leads to accepting the existing hegemony and remaining trapped within the configuration of forces.* (Mouffe 2005, 62–63; emphasis added)

Applying Mouffe's critique to the case of the GM, it is necessary to analyze the GM's effort to distance itself from politics within the context of global neo-liberalism, a hegemonic narrative that presupposes the inevitable collapse of political antagonism in the wake of matured democratic institutions. In this way, the GM has adapted Giddens's notion of dialogic politics to position its actors at the vanguard of an imagined post-political order in Turkey. The GM and the governing AKP converge on this topic, as both promote a shift to conservative populism by uniting Islam and Turkish ethnic pride as equally constituent of twenty-first-century Turkish national identity (Hendrick 2011b).

Similar to all promises of neo-liberal inclusion, the GM's articulation of the "middle way" is marred with contradiction. Despite the community's stated goals to cultivate "dialogue," "tolerance," and "compassion" (*hoşgörü*) in the public sphere, it is important to note that in GM media, antagonistic politics and subaltern resistance are either muted, or presented in terms of the Turkish status quo. Kurdish separatists who attack military instillations continue to be labeled "terrorists," Alevi groups that insist on their rights as religious minorities continue to be labeled "Muslims" (and thus as non-distinct from other Sunni Turks), and claims made by the Armenian Diaspora continue to be designated as either self-serving or outlandish. In this context, this book presents the GM neither as a nonpolitical force for dialogue and tolerance, nor as an Islamist organization hiding a secret agenda. Rather, in the chapters that follow, I argue that the GM seeks to passively increase "the Muslim share" in the production and reproduction of social power in Turkey, and that its "post-political" identity is illustrative of the fact that Turkey's Islamic actors have internalized the neo-liberal notion of "third way" political pluralism. That is, its goals focus less on seizing the state and implementing Islamic law, and more on capturing the imagination of Turkish society by becoming a market leader in the production of a new "post-Kemalist," "post-Islamist" national identity. This book, therefore, presents the GM not quite as a social movement, but certainly as representative of collective social action in the field of Turkish Muslim politics in general,[5] and a transformative force in Turkey's political economy in particular.

Market Islam

Originally developed as a critique of secularization theory, the literature on "religious economies" uses economic vocabulary to describe the successes and failures of varying religious groups in a given society (Davie 1999; Innaccone 1998; Introvigne 2006; Jelen and Wilcox 2002). Its practitioners start with the assumption that religious sects, communities, and groups compete for the allegiance of potential "consumers" in a crowded and competitive marketplace of religious ideas. Similar to goods and services markets, "producers" (e.g., movements, sects, groups) and "buyers" (e.g., individuals who choose which movement, sect, or group to join or to participate in, and at what level) together constitute the actors in a religious market. And just as is in any marketplace, "providers of religious goods must engage in what might be termed 'product differentiation.' That is, if religious producers seek to attract consumers, they must provide reasons why their particular products are different from (and superior to) those offered by their competitors" (Jelen and Wilcox 2002, 13).

Modern Turkey's religious market is cross-class and "intra-band" (i.e., in competition within Sunni Islam), and developed its current dynamics as a result of three overlapping foundations laid during the Ottoman period: (1) The Ottoman state maintained an "official Islam" that was codified and regulated by the Ottoman ulema. The Turkish state took over this function with the formation of the Republic and the subsequent establishment of the Turkish Presidency of Religious Affairs (Diyanet). (2) Anatolian Sufi brotherhoods (*cemaatler*) organized extensive networks throughout the Empire that garnered allegiance to particular teachings of particular sheikhs who were often members of the ulema, and who were thus in no direct conflict with the state's official version of Islam. (3) "Heterodox Islam," which incorporated *shi'a*, pre-Muslim, and non-Muslim influences in the Anatolian countryside, persevered and survived to the twenty-first century despite state repression (Introvigne 2006, 38–39).

Until the 1980s, the Turkish state was Turkey's sole legal producer of Turkish Islam. Muslim politics thus emerged as a collection of protest movements led by new Muslim intellectuals who expressed themselves through new media. Actors took advantage of universal education and advances in communication technologies to produce and disseminate a counter-narrative to Turkey's development project that called into question the legitimacy of Kemalist social engineering. Following the 1980 coup, an economic shift toward global integration led to the implementation of social liberalization policies, and to a revival of competition in a more competitive religious marketplace. Promoted by a post-1982 policy that sought to use religion as a sedative for Turkey's left–right divide, "Turkish Islam" (Anatolian Islam) was then, and is now, promoted as being more peaceful, more mystical (i.e., "Sufi"), more conducive to dialogue, and more apt to lead Turkey (and the entire Muslim world) into the twenty-first century.

By presenting the GM as an example of collective action that seeks to play a more active role in the legitimizing processes of Turkey's neoliberal integration, this book introduces the charisma and community

Market Islam

of Fethullah Gülen as a particular case of post-political, market Islam. Market Islam has two meanings. First, by focusing its efforts in education and in media, the GM has cultivated an entire generation of loyal supporters. In so doing, the GM has collectively established itself as the leading *private* producer of "Turkish Islam" for the twenty-first century religious marketplace. Second, market Islam also refers to the fact that in addition to producing goods and services for religious consumption (ideas, messages, media, books, videos, music, and other cultural goods that identify with, or that promote, Fethullah Gülen, Said Nursi, and "Turkish Islam"), the GM produces goods and services in the value-added marketplace of global capitalism. That is, the business, education, and media networks affiliated with the GM create economic value in money markets, capital markets, and labor markets; they provide professional opportunities; and they create the conditions for their own reproduction. Discursively linking economic and scholastic success with religious mobilization, GM enterprises expand because of their abilities to produce high-quality products that are just that—*high quality*. Although GM affiliates might view their personal and professional lives as elements of a larger "Islamic project," thousands, if not millions, of consumers tied to the GM network view their products and services as the best available for the prices offered.

Increasing the Muslim Share

This book builds on the assertion that in the post-1971 global era liberalized flows of information, finance, and people within and across national borders created new opportunities for actors to challenge the traditional authority of modern states. In Turkey, such restructuring led to a crisis of social hegemony, wherein previously marginalized groups took advantage of newfound opportunities to force their way into the civil sectors of Turkey's social institutions in the state and in the market. Tuğal (2009, 239) makes a parallel argument and contends that these recent transformations were characterized by the coming to power of former Islamists who moderated their worldviews in favor of a "market-oriented, liberal, and individualist direction . . . [that encourages] the accumulation of wealth and luxury." Epitomized by the coming to power of the AKP, "political society and civil society [in Turkey] . . .

[have] merged to build bourgeois Islamic ethics through preaching that working hard and privatization are an integral part of religion" (249). What resulted was a "passive revolution" in favor of a new elite whose leaders were defined, in large part at least, by their piety-informed reformulation of the modern Turkish experience and of modern economic well-being. This book presents the GM—as the largest and most influential collective actor in the AKP's Turkey—as the most influential player in the AKP-led passive revolution.

Only briefly theorized by Antonio Gramsci, a "passive revolution" refers to an episode of transformative social change that occurs gradually, without a violent overthrow of an existing social and political order, and without the destruction of the state apparatus. Rather than a rapid social revolution, a Gramscian "passive revolution" signifies the slow reform of a society's dominant social paradigm, a shift in the discursive structure of norms, values, and beliefs in the realm of education, the arts, and media that gradually leads to a reform of a society's political and economic social structures without open rebellion. Spearheading the passive revolution are new "organic intellectuals," whose role is to create the conditions for the production, deployment, and reproduction of legitimated social discourse. On the pages of mainstream newspapers, in popular books, magazines, and journals; on television screens and on the Internet, the role of the organic intellectual is to change the conversation about what is, and what is not, considered fair, just, equal, and moral in a given social and political culture. The social contest for power, therefore, happens at the level of discourse, rather than at the level of street protest or on a battlefield. For this reason, Gramsci contends that passive revolutions occur only *after* antithetical, "subaltern" social groups slowly and passively work their way through the hierarchy of institutions that constitute the production centers of a society's "superstructure" (i.e., education system, the system of arts and culture, the media), and subsequently, *after* they make the same march through the institutions of coercive political power (the military, the local and national police forces, and the local and national state bureaucracies). In this way, the AKP–GM coalition divides Turkey's passive revolution; the AKP leads the "political march" through Parliament, the presidency, and the state apparatus, while the GM carries out the "civilian march" through education, business, media, and public relations. Both groups, however, rely on each other to continue their project to cultivate a "conservative democratic" Turkey that unites a new elite in faith, nation, and material prosperity (Hendrick 2009).

Finally, a strictly Gramscian view of Turkey's recent transformation warrants some adjustment. That is, it is necessary to point out that although GM-affiliated individuals and institutions are primary actors in Turkey's ongoing passive revolution, as a whole, the GM *does not* derive from Turkey's "subaltern" classes. Although its leader and his closest students employ the language of conservative populism to frame their efforts, with exceptions, they do not recruit from Turkey's working class, from the disenfranchised, or from the downtrodden. Quite the contrary, followers of Fethullah Gülen hail from Turkey's upwardly mobile middle class, and from an increasingly wealthy and influential upper class of conservative elites. Sharing a number of similarities with the Spanish Catholic "personal prelature" Opus Dei and the increasingly influential Church of Latter Day Saints in the United States, in this regard, the GM increases its influence by integrating its activities with Turkey's market economy.[6] Unlike these former institutions, however, the GM is not organized as a centralized bureaucracy, and its hierarchy is not organized under the direct leadership of Fethullah Gülen. Rather, the GM's organizational strategy is "flexible," "networked," and "lean." Moreover, as explained in greater detail later, the GM's objectives, as well as its preferred tactics, are *strategically ambiguous*. Its ability to form alliances, to recruit sympathizers, and to market its identity is both highly malleable and increasingly more difficult to define. Nonetheless, the GM's remarkable rise in secular Turkey is second to none. What took the Mormons 150 years to accomplish in the United States the GM accomplished in less than forty years in Turkey. And while the founder and leader of Opus Dei was ultimately made a saint in the Catholic Church, his "secular institution" continues to provoke both awe and skepticism (and in some cases fear) the world over. By contrast, Gülen's handlers frame their leader's agenda as a "movement for world peace," not as a movement to realize "Muhammadan truth" (however much they might equate the two). Indeed, although the results were skewed and the polling unscientific, Fethullah Gülen was voted "the world's most influential public intellectual," and according to a number of hopeful insiders he should be a future candidate for the Nobel Peace Prize (Field Notes, Spring and Summer 2007).

Toward a Political Ethnography of a Post-Political Actor

How does one go about studying the political impact of a social and economic network whose leaders identify their efforts as "nonpolitical"? How can a non-Muslim, non-Turkish researcher establish the trust necessary to study an organization that mobilizes itself as an ambiguous network connecting thousands of institutions and hundreds of thousands of individuals in more than one hundred countries? Accepting the limits of a smaller sample size, as well as the challenge posed by reliability in qualitative research, this book presents the findings of ethnographic research that was conducted at several central organizational nodes in the GM's Turkish and U.S. networks.

In this context, ethnography refers to "social research based on close-up, on-the-ground observation of people and institutions in real time and space, in which the investigator embeds herself near (or within) the phenomenon so as to detect how and why agents on the scene act, think, and feel the way they do" (Wacquant 2003, 258). As a *political* ethnography, this book approaches the GM from three overlapping vantage points:

1. Studying politics, defined as events, institutions, or actors that are normally considered "political" (e.g., social movements, or states), but in an ethnographic way: at a smaller scale and as they happen. We call this version *ethnographies of political actors and institutions*

2. Studying routine encounters between people and those institutions and actors, encounters normally invisible in nonethnographic ways (e.g., the encounter between organized social movements and nonparticipants; or the encounters with state agencies or welfare agencies). We refer to this version as *encounters with formal politics*

3. Studying other kinds of events, institutions, or actors together, that while invisible from nonethnographic vantage points, are of consequence to politics in some way (e.g., apathy, or nonparticipation in social movements). We call this the *lived experience of the political*. (Baiocchi and Connor 2008, 140)

First, *politics as they happen*—how does the "nonpolitical" mobilization of GM actors and institutions affect the organization of social power in contemporary Turkey? Second, *encounters*—for what purpose does the GM engage with non-GM actors, with individuals and institutions in the Turkish government, in Turkish business, and in host countries around the world? Third, *consequence of politics*—how does the individual in the GM conceptualize "nonpolitical" social change, and subsequently, how do "volunteers" in the GM's "nonpolitical project" explain the GM's political impact in Turkish and world society?

My ethnographic access began when I first made contact with GM volunteers in the United States. After attending a conference that was sponsored and organized by GM loyalists at a prestigious U.S. university, I learned that an academically critical analysis of the GM was long overdue. This was because although it was advertised as an academic forum, although it included nearly two dozen presentations, and although many of those presentations (but by no means all of them) were delivered by practicing academicians, neither contentious politics, nor collective mobilization (i.e., social movement studies) were topics of discussion. Moreover, there was no mention of the controversy that surrounds Gülen in Turkey, and subsequently no discussion about the ways in which GM actors respond to the accusations levied against them. That is to say, there was no *critical* discussion about the GM at all. Further, after speaking with more than a dozen presenters, volunteers, and Turkish audience members in attendance, I realized that over a two-day period, most of my conversations with GM "volunteers" focused on individual scholastic success, professional employment, and world travel. After reviewing my notes, I realized that by viewing the GM's collective mobilization as the rational outcome of dedicated, upwardly mobile Turkish citizens, I could appreciate how the charismatic teachings of a faith leader were being applied to realize rational (i.e., secular) goals.

Soon after my experience at this conference, I sought to "plug in" to the GM's transnational network, a nonlinear path that over the course of four years led me to nearly every neighborhood in Istanbul, and to three U.S. cities. In Istanbul, I spent a significant amount of time at the GM's Akademi, an all-in-one publishing house, think tank, library, theology center, meeting center, school, and mosque. Functioning as a central ideational mode for the production and reproduction of the GM's collective identity, Akademi was a subsidiary of a medium-sized

Turkish holding company whose executives were all first- and second-generation admirers of Gülen's teachings. Most of these men (and they were all men) enjoyed a certain sense of prestige in the GM community as a whole; they were *hocalar* (teachers), who in addition to translating, editing, and publishing the teachings of Fethullah Gülen, were also responsible for managing the GM's many periodical journals and its twenty-five "official" websites. All of these men had long histories with the GM, either as former students at GISs in Turkey, as former teachers and administrators at GISs around the world, or as former contributors to GM-affiliated news media. In exchange for permission to observe the day-to-day activities at Akademi, and to interview editors, teachers, writers, and executives, I offered my services as an English language editor in Akademi's Department of Foreign Editions, a task that I performed free of charge (with the exception of a regular cafeteria lunch with my colleagues, and a whole lot of tea). Instead of payment in money or gifts (both of which I had to decline on a number of occasions over a seven-month period), I was granted an opportunity to learn how a self-described "nonpolitical" charismatic leader attempted to influence the hearts and minds of thousands, if not millions, of Turkish citizens. As a participant observer in the production and dissemination of the GM's collective identity, I was able to analyze "the lived experience of the political" firsthand.

Above the culturally focused publishing subsidiary was a larger Turkish holding company that was involved in a wide variety of education-oriented production ventures—from academic and nonacademic publishing to paper manufacturing, from educational furniture and classroom equipment to IT solutions, and from media-oriented retail to textile manufacture and international trade. Entertaining the invasive curiosity of a qualitative researcher from the United States, GM actors at Akademi were very gracious with their time and their patience. After several months in residence as an English language editor, I began to explore the personal and social connections that defined the GM community as a whole. From the Akademi, I traversed through the GM's Istanbul-wide social and professional network, connecting with individuals at the GM-affiliated Bank Asya, PASIAD (Pacific Asia Businessmen and Industrialists Association), *Zaman gazetesi* (*Zaman* newspaper), FEM Dershanesi (supplemental educational institution), Fatih

University, the Gazeteciler ve Yazarlar Vakfı (Journalists and Writers Foundation), and TUSKON (Confederation of Businessmen and Industrialists in Turkey). I also spent time with four university-age students from Central Asia who were studying in Istanbul, and who were living at a GM *ışık evi* ("house of light," or student apartment). To supplement, I conducted additional interviews with seven former students at GM schools, as well as with a high-ranking official in the AKP government, an operative in the center–left Democratic Left Party (DSP), and a senior editor at a high-circulating non-GM-affiliated Turkish newspaper.

I attended five conferences that were all sponsored by a different GM-affiliated outreach/public relations/"dialogue" institution, as well as a GM-sponsored Middle East policy luncheon in Washington DC. Also in the United States, I collected a large sample of media data that focused on the ways the U.S. public received the GM message, and how non-Turkish, non-Muslim Americans interpreted the GM's mobilization in charter school education in that country. I conversed at length with three acting or past directors at three separate GM-affiliated, U.S.-based cultural and dialogue institutions, and with a U.S.-based, GM-affiliated trade representative. I also interviewed ten "recruited sympathizers" in U.S. academia (i.e., people who were either courted by GM affiliates to participate in one of their promotional conferences, or people who worked for the GM at an affiliated institution). Finally, I corresponded with twelve self-identified "concerned parents" whose children attended (or used to attend) a GM-affiliated charter school in the United States, two former teachers at GM-affiliated charter schools in the United States, two labor organizers who assisted teachers at several GM-affiliated charter schools in their attempt to form unions, and a U.S. county school board director who was leading an investigation into the management of charter funding at a GM-affiliated charter school under his supervision.

In total I conducted fifty-five career history interviews with GM "loyalists" (*hizmet insanları*), "friends" (*arkadaşlar*), and "sympathizers" (*yandaşlar*), took part in more than a hundred informal conversations, and conducted approximately one thousand hours of participant observation. Participants in the research that led to this book trusted me with their career histories, their personal stories and concerns,

and their experiences as students, teachers, parents, loyalists, and critics. In return, even if they insisted on the contrary, I employed the use
of pseudonyms to protect anonymity. Although the institutions I discuss throughout this book are, for the most part, places of for-profit
and not-for-profit business in Turkey and in the United Stated (and are
thus publicly accessible), all identifying information about individuals including names, places of employment, gender, and age, has been
changed.

Organization of the Book

The presentation that follows is structured in accordance with my
own experiences with the GM. First, because any analysis of the GM
must be situated in the context of twentieth-century Turkish political
and economic development, chapter 2 provides a brief overview of the
social, political, and economic power structure that gave rise to the
GM's collective mobilization. As an introduction to the Turkish case,
this chapter's primary purpose is to situate the GM in its proper milieu
by explaining how Turkey's Kemalist regime led a mid-century development project that engineered Turkish society in favor of a very particular understanding of progress and modernization. Readers already
familiar with modern Turkey may wish to skim this chapter, if not skip
it entirely. Notwithstanding, it is of central importance to consider that
in accordance with a strong state apparatus, the traditional secular elite
in twentieth-century Turkey managed to organizationally outflank
competing (and would-be competitive) social forces by entrenching
an oligarchic state/class as both the pilots and beneficiaries of national
development. After the military seized the state apparatus for a third
time in 1980, a period of economic liberalization followed and new
leaders emerged to navigate Turkish development in the global era.
During this period, capital markets opened, and new economic actors
took advantage of new opportunities, which led to the emergence of
new interest groups, and ultimately, to the organizational development
of an alternative elite within Turkey's bourgeoisie. Over the course of
the 1980s and 1990s, socially conservative, economically liberal factions
in Turkish politics continued to gain ground, until finally the AKP rose
to single party rule in 2002. Coinciding with the AKP's rise to power

was the full maturation of the GM, a transnationally active, nationally focused advocacy network whose far-reaching influence in contemporary Turkey is, excluding the TSK, second only to the AKP itself.

Chapter 3 focuses specifically on the charismatic leadership of M. Fethullah Gülen, a religious community leader whose followers recognize as a mentor and sage. After first introducing readers to the impact of his predecessor, "Bediüzzaman" Said Nursi, Fethullah Gülen is presented from the perspective of those who love him the most, his students. In order to understand Gülen's impact on the collective consciousness of this very loyal inner community (*cemaat*), this chapter begins an analysis that continues throughout the book on the effectiveness of ambiguity as an organizational strategy. The GM's strategic employment of ambiguous language to describe its organization begins with Gülen himself, a figure who is at once credited as a recluse and as a leader, as powerful but removed. Although not an organic intellectual in Gramscian terms, Gülen has become an authority to which a growing cadre of Turkish Muslim intellectuals looks for validation and legitimacy.

Chapter 4 presents the GM as a social organization that creates and reproduces community in a composite of vertical, horizontal, diagonal patterns of authority. These patterns are rationalized via an articulated system of "applied Sufism," which is anchored on a foundation of patrimonial respect, duty, and service. The result is a complicated regime of affiliation that begins with a small and loyal community, that extends outward to a once removed strata of "friends," and that extends again to a further removed strata of "sympathizers." This chapter concludes by emphasizing that the GM's transnational reach and sustained social legitimacy is most dependent on a final stratum of "unaware consumers" who participate in GM activities as patrons, clients, and students in a globally connected marketplace of goods and services.

Chapters 5–7 survey the organizational strategies and impact of the GM as a whole. Focusing on different sectors of the GM's organizational model, these chapters are sequenced in the order I studied them. If the reader so desires, she can read these chapters according to the topic that interests her. Notwithstanding, chapter 5 provides a brief history of education in Turkey in order to illustrate how the GM managed to rise to the top of the field in private education and test preparation. Chapter 6 answers the elusive question "Değirmenin suyu nereden geliyor?" ("Where does the water for the mill come from?") This chapter explains the GM's strategies to accumulate investment capital, to tax followers, to create and invest profits, and to increase its collective representation in Turkey's political economy. Chapter 7 presents the ways in which the GM has successfully mobilized in the Turkish media and how it strives to persuade Turkish society via the mechanism of manufactured consent (i.e., by being "the most trusted name in news").

As a case study of its transnational mobilization, chapter 8 introduces readers to the GM's activities in the United States. Although the organization is conducive to rapid expansion, research findings presented in this chapter illustrate that the GM's reliance on ambiguity as a mobilizing strategy seems to have reached its limits. This is because for an increasingly xenophobic U.S. public, allegations of financial mismanagement, unfair hiring practices, discriminatory policies against women and minorities, and denials of social and economic affiliation have all culminated in a backlash against the GM's collective mission that threatens the public support of more than 130 charter schools in twenty-six U.S. states. Forced to deal with a public relations image that, on the one hand, emphasizes dialogue and transparency; and, on the other hand, favors denial and secrecy, GM actors in the United States are forced to respond to critics from three sectors in the U.S. public. As employers, GM actors face disgruntled teachers who demand their rights as public workers to collectively bargain and to access advancement in the workplace free from discrimination. As administrators, they face public education boards that demand transparency concerning the management of charter funding, the hiring and retention of qualified teachers, and the efficient and fair functioning of institutional governance. As Turkish Muslim immigrants, they face a growing mass of fearful U.S. citizens who feel threatened by the GM's rapid expansion, and who point to regular denials of GM-affiliation by administrators at publicly funded GISs as "proof" of what some of the more outlandish of these critics refer to as an "education jihad."

This volume concludes by arguing that despite the assertions of both its adherents and its critics, the GM is best presented as a collective mobilization whose actors seek to normalize neo-liberal wealth accumulation with aspirations for faith-based social change. Rather than a battle between "secularists" and "Islamists," therefore, the current conjuncture in Turkey pits rival bourgeois interest groups—oligarchic isolationists versus pious integrationists—against each other in an intra-class "war of position" between old and new. The GM is a primary actor in this contest, and its increasing influence is indicative of deep transformation still underway.

2

The Political Economy of Muslim Politics in Turkey

Today, I speak with the same faith and assurance that, within
a short period of time, the whole civilized world will once
again recognize that the Turkish nation, moving unified
toward the national ideal, is a great nation.
—Mustafa Kemal Atatürk

When assessing the GM's transnational mobilization, the unique context
of twentieth-century Turkey cannot be understated. Like in many other
countries, in Turkey the institutions of mid-twentieth century development suppressed the social forces of Islam in favor of particularly rigid
understandings of progress and modernization. Alienated by these processes, many Muslims viewed their faith in Islam as "a channel through
which persons who had failed to become integrated into the secular system
[began] . . . their own project of boundary expansion, and search for freedom" (Mardin 1989, 83–84). In this way, the GM's emergence in Turkey can
be seen as a dialectical synthesis between Anatolian Muslim culture and
secular nationalist social engineering. The result is a particularly Turkish
"brand" of faith-inspired collective action that links modern republicanism with neo-Ottoman faith revivalism and free market accumulation.

The Turkish Republic: Islam, Secularism, and
the Problem of National Authority

In 1914, the once vast Ottoman Empire was reduced to its Anatolian
heartland, the Tigris–Euphrates River Valleys, and the Arabian Hijaz.

By the end of the First Word War, the Ottomans had lost the Hijaz, Iraq, Syria, and Jerusalem, and the Treaty of Serves (1920) divided what was left of the Empire in favor of Britain, France, and their allies. Facing a British- and French-occupied Istanbul, an Italian-administered Mediterranean coast, a newly independent Armenia to the east, and a French-administered southeast, a rogue Ottoman commander named Mustafa Kemal led a multifront "War of Independence" (1919–1923) against what were perceived as occupying forces. On July 24, 1923, in Lausanne, Switzerland, the Allies of World War I succumbed to Kemal's efforts by formally recognizing the demise of the Ottoman Empire, the creation of the Turkish Republic, and Kemal himself as Turkey's undisputed national leader (Berkeş 1998; Lewis 1961; Zürcher 2004). Following Lausanne, a new capital city was recognized in Ankara, and a new republican form of government eventually took the place of Islam's last great imperial order.

After four years of turbulent transition from empire to republic, Kemal's political doctrine, Kemalism, was outlined in a thirty-six-hour Nutuk (Great Speech) in 1927. The Nutuk was the founding text that informed Turkish national lore, whereby "the myth of sacred territory and the myth of nation-as-family were intertwined in the presentation of Anatolia as motherland of the Turks and the Independence struggle as synonymous with the quest for the establishment of the Turkish Republic" (Adak 2003, 517). Although often presented at face value, the interpretation and implementation of what were eventually dubbed "the six arrows of Kemalism" were, since their first utterance, significant points of contention between Kemal, the single-party regime that emerged under his leadership, and the diverse peoples of Anatolia. Indeed, Kemal, who later renamed himself "Atatürk" (father of the Turks), employed an evolutionary perspective of social development to unite Anatolia's diverse populations as citizens of a new *Turkish* nation. In this regard, the Turkish state was promoted as a universal institution that was at once equally distant, and equally close, to all Turkish citizens. But despite such a "nonpolitical" discourse, in reality the Turkish state emerged to become both a powerfully revolutionary, and a highly repressive, institutional apparatus (Heper 1985, 1987, 1991; Jacoby 2004; Mann 2004; Parla and Davidson 2004; Yavuz 2003a; Zürcher 2004). After a few years of domestic political contest and economic openness,

Atatürk consolidated power under the authority of a state class who, in coordination with a powerful military bureaucracy and under the umbrella of the Cumhuriyet Halk Partisi (People's Republican Party, CHP), managed Turkey as a single-party regime until 1950.

As a political philosophy, Kemalism emerged ad hoc as a composite of quasi-reactive stipulations designed to speed up Turkey's modernization. By centralizing the power of the state at the expense of regional, ethnic, and religious authority, the goal of the Kemalist regime was not to shackle Turkish society within the confines of a closed political and economic system, but to engineer a new society in the mold of northwestern Europe. The CHP thus vested itself with the powers of a vanguard. For instance, to protect the state from perceived opponents who might use Anatolia's Muslim culture to mount a critique of Turkish secular republicanism, the CHP regime established the Diyanet İşleri Bakanlığı (Turkish Presidency of Religious Affairs) in 1924. Organizationally dominating the production and dissemination of Turkish Islam, the Diyanet's task was to consolidate culture under the authority of the state, and thus to institutionalize a particular brand of Turkish Islam that would harmonize with Kemalist reforms. The closing of *tarikatlar* (Sufi orders) and the outlawing of *cemaatler* (religious communities; brotherhoods) in 1925 were arguably the most significant of the early moves to enforce French-modeled *laiklik* (Fr. *Laïcité*), a particularly rigid variation of secularism that sought less to "separate church from state" than it did to bring religion under the control of the state. Unlike U.S.-style secularism, which sought to liberalize the movement of religious communities to ensure their free mobilization without oversight or regulation, Turkish *laiklik* permitted the CHP regime to inhibit religion in the public sphere, to suppress the traditional authority of religious brotherhoods, and to cultivate a national society that promoted ethno-linguistic identity above all other subject positions (e.g., confession, class).

The sociological technology of Turkish laiklik was as deeply penetrating as it was deeply alienating. This was because under the Ottomans, Islam existed at two levels—at the level of the high court under the authority of the ulema (council of religious scholarship), and at the level of the masses under the authority of cemaatler and tarikatlar. According to Erik Zürcher (2004, 192), "on a psychological level [cemaatler and tarikatlar] offered a mystical, emotional, dimension that was lacking in the high religion of the ulema and at the same time they served as networks offering cohesion, protection, and social mobility." It was because of the potential for these pre-existing allegiances to challenge the authority of the Kemalist regime that its leaders found it necessary to consolidate Islam under the administration of the Diyanet. While not exactly a state church, the Diyanet fulfilled a dual role of *public utility*, by providing religious knowledge, service, and authority, and *political instrument*, by defining what were and what were not appropriate and acceptable expressions, uses, and interpretations of Islam in Turkey.[1] Although acknowledging Islam as part of Turkish national culture, state-produced textbooks traced Turkey's ethnic heritage back thousands of years before its contact with "Arab Islam," which was framed as an alien import "that corrupted and stifled the secular genius of the Turkish people" (Kaplan 2006, 80).

Kemal's Legacy

The tension between the Atatürk's aspirations for Turkey to "Westernize" and the regime's focus on the necessity to consolidate power in the hands of a vanguard led to the development of corporatism in Turkey. Corporatism, in this context, "[opposed] the central categories of liberalism and Marxian models of society. . . . It [viewed] individualism in the former as overly atomistic and consequently disruptive of social equilibrium, and it [viewed] the struggle and warfare, if not the sheer presence, of classes in the latter as detrimental to the maintenance of the social system" (Parla and Davidson 2004, 28). Thus was the Kemalist contradiction. On the one hand, a liberal democracy in the mode of northwestern Europe required the existence of competing interest groups whose members would carve out a vibrant and democratic civil society. As a populist, however, Atatürk believed that in order to cultivate a "collective consciousness" anchored on an ethnic understanding of Turkish identity, the whole of Anatolian society needed to "emerge" in the postwar period as a society without social classes. Indeed, in a speech before the Izmir Economic Congress in 1923, Atatürk contended that Turkish society had no social groups whose members would "pursue interests that [were] very different from each other and [who] [would], accordingly, come into a state of struggle with one another" (Atatürk quoted in Biancchi 1984, 101). The contradiction between an ethnically determined national identity that was imagined alongside a fiction of social "classlessness" led to the emergence of a state–society relationship that was destined for conflict.

Beginning in the early 1930s, the regime began to cement its authority through publicly managed media and through the mechanism of universal education. In the late 1920s, all opposition newspapers were closed down. In 1931, new media laws stipulated that the government could monitor or close any press organ that "published anything contradicting the 'general policies of the country'" (Zürcher 2004, 180). It was also during this time when Atatürk's persona shifted from being the country's first president to being an awe-inspiring secular prophet:

> He was presented as the father of the nation, its savior, and its teacher. Indoctrination in schools and universities focused on him to an extraordinary degree. The fact that he was not associated with a very definite ideology that could be discredited, as fascism, national socialism, and Marxism–Leninism have been, means that his personality cult could survive changes in the political climate. (Zürcher 2004, 182)

To this day, Atatürk's likeness is portrayed in nearly every park and every city center in Turkey. His picture hangs over the counter at every bank and at nearly every business. His face is depicted on all currency, and all schools take pride in their "Atatürk corners," where Turkey's eternal leader reminds its youth of their duty to serve the nation.

Turkey's first president became its father figure, a technology of national solidarity that allowed the Kemalist regime to frame its goals as synonymous with the goals of the nation as a whole. In so doing, the regime developed into a semi-authoritarian managerial state whose strong bureaucratic apparatus was able to suppress the forces of Turkish civil society, to stagnate the growth of competing interest groups, and to organize the country's political economic development in the interests of a state-class elite.

Incomplete Democratization: 1923–1960

Turkey's development project started out as one defined by liberal integration but quickly morphed into a state-managed project of import-substitution industrialization (ISI). The 1920s were thus a period of

Bronze statue of Mustafa Kemal Atatürk teaching children the script and rules associated with the Turkish language reform. (Author's original photograph, Istanbul, March 2007)

maturation for the young CHP regime. Shackled by economic stipulations embedded in the Lausanne Treaty, the Turkish republic initially implemented an economic strategy that promoted free trade, foreign investment, and export-oriented comparative advantage (Jacoby 2004, 98). In 1929, however, a more powerful CHP was able to abolish the Lausanne stipulations and to assume full control over the economy (Celâsun and Rodrik 1989). The 1930s, therefore, brought an end to Turkey's liberal experiment, and ushered in an era of one-party consolidation.

Kemalist populism in the 1930s and 1940s included only those sectors of the Turkish economy that were deemed essential for economic development, and did not include the Kurdish southeast, which experienced a series of uprisings in protest to what was perceived as the forced exclusion of an entire population (McDowell 1992; Olson 1989, 2000). The prevailing rationale was that "discrimination against non-Turkish identities was part of a search for greater social cohesion within the ideological framework of industrial-capitalist advance" (Jacoby 2004, 102). In other words, the "non-Turkishness" of Anatolia's Kurdish populations, together with its populations of non-Sunni minority Alevi, Zaza, Laz, Circassian, Pomak, and Bosniak groups, was viewed less as a potential threat to Turkish ethnic purity, than it was as a potential obstacle to efficient industrial development. Indeed, because a strong national identity was viewed as essential for the larger project of economic modernization, the efforts of Kemalist-led industrialization concentrated in the core of the Turkish economy, in Istanbul, in the Western provinces, on the Mediterranean coast, and in a few select areas in central Anatolia. Jacoby (2004, 103) explains the economic impact of the CHP's policies as follows:

> In the tradition of Ottoman governance, the republican state, perhaps wary of Austrian and Russian fragmentation during industrialization, placed political integration before economic development as its primary policy aim. . . . While this may have succeeded in preventing comprador commercial groups from gaining autonomy, it could not provide the necessary "penetrative strength" to pursue the Western model of capitalist development.

Throughout the 1930s, Turkey focused on a growth strategy based on extensive government regulation (Ütkülü 2001). This path continued (interrupted briefly by a liberalization period from 1950 to 1953) until the late 1970s. And with two brief exceptions, the CHP enjoyed single-party rule until 1946, when President Ismet Inönü approved the formation of the DP.[2] In July of that year, the DP won sixty-five seats in Parliament, and the groundwork was laid for a reversal of power.

In the same year, Turkey lifted its ban on the organization of collective associations. Much of these reforms were conscious on the part of President Inönü, who felt the political winds shift and who wanted to forestall a potential DP victory in the 1950 national elections by preempting its agenda with his own liberal reforms (Zürcher 2004, 217). These attempts proved insufficient. In 1950, the DP added to their previous gains by wining an impressive 53 percent of the electorate, which equated to 408 seats in Parliament (compared to the CHP's 69) (Zürcher 2004, 217). The new party came to power on the promise of expanded democratic populism, religious sensibility, and free enterprise (Keyder 1988). In reality, however, the DP's political and economic philosophy closely resembled that of the CHP, which was rooted in heavy state involvement in a planned economy based on ISI protection schemes.

The DP's comparative difference from the CHP was less noticeable in its economic development policies than it was in its leaders' appeal to Islam and to the integrity of Anatolian faith and culture as constituent of Turkish national identity. Jacoby (2004, 104), quoting Sunar and Sayari, explains, "The DP was able to gain peasant support by promising lower taxes, less state intervention, and 'by rewarding regional cliques, kinship ties, religious demands, and personal influence networks.'" In other words, the DP sought support from peasant and small merchant capital, small traders, farm workers, and local patronage networks. The role of local culture, Islam specifically, proved successful. In 1954, Fethullah Gülen's predecessor, Said Nursi, announced his official support (and subsequently the support of the entire Nur community) for DP rule. The overwhelming support for the AKP observed in the GM's *Zaman* newspaper, and its continuous lambasting of the opposition CHP and of the "pro-establishment" media, played a similar role to the AKP victories in 2002, 2007, and 2011.[3]

Governing with a mandate following the 1954 elections, the DP sought to increase its leverage over Turkey's civilian and military bureaucracies. Its deputies first implemented a policy of early retirement for civil servants who served more than twenty-five years in their post. They then moved to increase their control over Turkish universities, and in 1956 the DP government revived an old law to increase Parliament's control over Turkish media. In the same year, the DP outlawed political organizing outside authorized electoral campaigning (Zürcher 2004, 230–231, 238). Its critics, as well as many of its supporters, viewed the DP's loss of seats in 1958 as the result of a change in the political winds, in response to what was viewed as the party's authoritarian tendencies. This was compounded by an economic crisis that struck in 1958, which was followed by an IMF-stabilization program. After ten years of economic turbulence, increased political centralization, and increased fears concerning a perceived attack on Turkish laiklik, the DP was forced out of power in a military coup in May 1960. The official explanation of the military-led overthrow of the DP was delivered as follows: "The popularity of the DP was not 'real,' but derived from the exploitation of religious feelings, excessive regard to the agricultural interest and from their bolstering of undemocratic patron–client relationships" (quoted in Heper 1985, 85).

Critics of the military's perspective, and of the coup in general, contended that what transpired in 1960 was a reversal of power back to the Kemalist vanguard; and although the 1961 constitution discursively normalized the participation of opposition parties, the reality of the 1960s and 1970s was that "the evolution of a liberal society did not follow" (Yeşilada 1988, 348). Instead, Turkey experienced consistent political instability, reoccurring economic collapse, and general social insecurity for the next forty years. This led to an environment whereby "political party policy preferences became rigid in the extreme, interest associations developed among militant ideological lines, and the pattern of interaction among party elites became hostile." Such extreme partisanship coupled with a continued increase in state power during the 1960–1980 period led the former Turkish president Celal Bayar (1950–1960) to proclaim that in the 1960s and 1970s, Turkey ushered in an era of "constitutional legitimation of the bureaucracy and the intellectuals" (Heper 1985, 89).

Social Unrest and the Emergence of Political Interest Groups: 1961–1983

DP opposition to the CHP represented a coalition that included peasant farmers, aspiring small traders and businesspeople, increasingly vocal religious communities, and a new cohort of occupational groups in medicine, law, and education. After coming to power, the DP's restrictions on the Turkish press, and a general intellectual social climate that defined DP policies as contradictory to the party's populist rhetoric, led to an erosion of its coalition and ultimately to its dissolution. Politically, the 1961 constitution brought to fruition new political parties that were free to mobilize and compete in public elections. The DP regrouped under the banner of the Adalet Partisi (Justice Party, AP), and a month later, the Turkçe Işçi Partisi (Turkish Worker's Party, IP) formed to represent an increasingly vocal Turkish left. In the absence of a legal communist party, the IP promoted itself as the voice of university professors, journalists, and students who subscribed to the postulates of Marxian political thought. Zürcher (2004, 246) explains that the IP's existence "forced the other parties to define themselves more clearly in ideological terms." The left was thus met with an increasingly vocal right that was represented by a reformed and reorganized Milliyetçi Hareket Partisi (Nationalist Action Party, MHP). Responding to leftist mobilization at Turkish universities, the MHP formed a youth organization, the Bozkurtlar (Grey Wolves), who, treading in the waters of fascism, "received paramilitary training in specially designed camps and, like Hitler's SS, their mission was to conquer the streets (and the campuses) on the left" (Zürcher 2004, 257).

Although religious communities survived that state's initial assault by going underground, their political mobilization was stunted until the 1970s. This was due, in part, to a state policy that sought to increase the visibility of Islam in the context of an ideologically divided political public. New mosques were built, Sufi shrines were restored, and new courses on religion were offered at public school (Zürcher 2004, 247). Foreshadowing a policy that was broadened following the coup of 1980, in the 1960s an effort was made to consciously appease more piously minded actors who viewed CHP policies as contrary to their religious/cultural sensibilities. This was also a time when the military firmly entrenched itself into the civil and political administration in Turkey, and when the so-called *derin devlet* (deep state) emerged behind the scenes to preserve the integrity and interests of the country's state-class elite. Discussed in more detail later, the existence of a derin devlet is a widely articulated conspiracy theory in Turkish society. Believed by some to be an elite remnant from Ottoman times, and by others to be a Turkish Gladio program created to stymie left mobilization during the Cold War, the existence of a derin devlet is a ubiquitous discursive formation in contemporary Turkish society. Allegedly comprising a shadow network of military, bureaucratic, business, media, and entertainment elites who mobilize secretly in the interests of "status quo" manipulation and power hoarding, Turkish media and politicians erupt with conversations about derin devlet whenever a Turkish journalist is assassinated (e.g., Hrant Dink in January 2007), whenever a foreigner is murdered (e.g., three Christian missionaries in Malatya in April 2007), or whenever a random act of violence disrupts a public event (e.g., the five judges shot by a lawyer in May 2006).[4]

Crisis of Development

By the 1960s, Turkey had affirmed its alliance with the United States and western Europe, but it did so in the context of the early Cold War, which allowed the regime to implement more cautious initiatives toward global integration. Increasingly more reliant on geostrategic aid, and consistently unable to diversify its development model, Turkey's agricultural sector was vanquished when a detrimental crop failure hit in 1977 (which exacerbated an already steady decline in international demand for Turkish agricultural goods). The percentage of the workforce in agriculture declined from 77 percent in 1962 to 61.8 percent in 1977, while the manufacturing sector rose from 7.2 percent to 11 percent, and services from 15.1 percent to 25 percent, respectively (Çeçen, Dogruel, and Dogruel 1994). Despite expansion in these sectors, however, Turkish manufacturing and services were unable to absorb the influx of urban migrants and the coming of age of Turkish youth. This resulted in increased unemployment, which reached 15 percent in 1979 (Economist Intelligence Unit 1995). These problems were compounded by the fact that neither the public nor the private sector satisfactorily invested in education schemes, which directly affected Turkey's ability to absorb the global shockwaves that resulted from rising oil prices and a transforming global economy:

> Because the production of high technology and the use of highly skilled labor, the deficiencies in labor training, technology adaptation, and management had very strong negative effects on efficiency and productivity growth . . . the sharp drop in total factor productivity growth from 3.2% (1963–67) to –1.18% (1973–76) in manufacturing is, beyond the oil-price shocks of this period, attributable to the characteristics of this new phase of import substitution. (Çeçen, Dogruel, and Dogruel 1994, 47)

Turkey's neglect of its education system played a significant role in the development of a private education market in the 1980s and 1990s. The GM's success in private education and its focus on science and technology are direct results of the state's failure to meet the needs of its growing urban youth population.

Economic and demographic turmoil in the 1970s led to political turmoil, which began with a second military intervention in 1971, and which ended with a third in 1980.[5] Economic and political insecurity led Turkish business to consolidate under an umbrella institution that was organized to better mitigate the economic risks of political turbulence. The Türk Sanayicileri ve İşadamları Derneği (Turkish Industrialists' and Businessmen's Association, TÜSIAD) emerged in 1971. Before TÜSIAD, business interests in Turkey were characterized by a deep schism between big industry and small-to-medium-sized Anatolian producers. In accordance with the Fordist regime of accumulation that dominated the logic of development at the global level, large-scale firms favored higher salaries for their employees (to expand its domestic consumer base), and were also interested in less state protection. Small producers, however, could not afford such policies. Both were forced to adhere to stipulations set by the Turkish Union of Chambers and Stock Exchange (TOBB), the state-sanctioned organization for private business in Turkey. According to Arat (1991, 136), "The TOBB could not provide a platform to express the demands of the big industrialists against those of the commercial interests dominated by the Union. Perhaps more importantly, the particular structure of the Chambers had lost its allure as a means of access to further economic and political gains." TÜSIAD was incorporated to better express the interests of industrial capital in Turkey; that is, the interests of the aforementioned family-based holdings that previously were charged with the task of Turkey's industrialization. When social and political street violence between 1977 and 1979 claimed more than five thousand lives, TÜSIAD led a public call for action by taking out a number of advertisements in seven major Turkish dailies (Arat 1991, 140–141).

Military Rule and a New Constitution

In the summer of 1980, low-level urban warfare overwhelmed Turkey's cities. After contending that the government failed to maintain social stability, the military seized state control on September 12, 1980. Noting TÜSIAD's role and observing the organization's alliance with the military regime that emerged after the coup, Boratav and Türel (1993, 214) argue that the 1980 coup and the social and economic policies that emerged thereafter "can be interpreted as a response of the ruling [i.e., capitalist] class." The architect of the stabilization and transformation regime was Turgut Özal, a high-ranking member of TÜSIAD who was appointed deputy prime minister of the economy just before the coup. The military regime under General Kenan Evren retained Özal to direct the Turkish economy through the crisis by seeing his pre-coup stabilization plan to fruition. Özal drafted this domestic-oriented liberalization strategy in relative secrecy, whereby "even key ministers had been unaware of the scope of the plan outside their own domain" (Kruger 1995, 351).

Istanbul's industrialists greeted Özal's restructuring plan with praise. Those represented by TÜSIAD, however, made it clear that if the military had any interest in seeing an economic stabilization plan succeed, it needed to return Turkey's political establishment back to civilian leadership as soon as conditions allowed.[6] The military agreed, and assured the entire country that its intent was to "defend the country as an indivisible whole against its internal as well as external enemies, and to see that the country will always be secure and its citizens happy and well-cared for" (General Kenan Evren, quoted in Heper 1985, 126). Before it could return the country to civilian rule, however, the military regime prioritized the drafting of a new constitution that would reaffirm the power of the Turkish state over Turkish society.

In the summer of 1982, the military government wrote a new constitution, which passed later that year with 91.4 percent of the military-appointed Parliament voting in its favor. On the labor front, the new constitution sought to appease the moderate elements of the Turkish left by making it the responsibility of government to raise the standard of living for workers, and to create suitable economic conditions for the prevention of unemployment. In the interests of political cleansing, the new constitution instituted a ten-year ban on all political parties and leaders who operated before the coup. It also bestowed additional powers on the office of the presidency vis-à-vis Parliament and the prime minster. In an effort to protect Parliament from internal squabbling and from ineffective coalitions, a 10 percent threshold was enacted that stipulated a minimum requirement of the electorate for a party to earn seats in government. In regard to civil organizing, the constitution offered a mixed message.

On the one hand, it re-articulated many previous restrictions on free speech and assembly.[7] Civil society groups (i.e., voluntary associations, public professional organizations, and trade unions) were all extended the continued right to organize, but only under state surveillance.[8] Moreover, such groups were not permitted to engage in politics. Strengthening a previous ban in the 1961 constitution, for instance, the 1982 law against the political engagement of voluntary associations stipulated that they "may not organize meetings or publish materials with the purpose of praising a political party, a corporate personality, a community, [or] a dead or living person whose aims or activities have been put under ban by law on account of their regimes, doctrines, or ideologies" (Özbudun 1991, 44). This clause thus defined "the political" in the Turkish context. No civil society group could openly endorse a particular political ideology, political personality, or political agenda. This stipulation is key to understanding the strategies used by the GM and other purportedly "nonpolitical" actors in Turkish politics after 1980.

On the other hand, the 1982 constitution also presented an amended Bill of Rights, which expanded the individual social, economic, and political liberties of Turkish citizens. Article V specified that all individuals were equal before the law and possess "inherent fundamental rights and freedoms [that] are inviolable and inalienable." Article XXVIII stipulated that individuals had a right to privacy and to freedom of thought, and that the news media were free and not liable to censorship without a court order, which could only be obtained "when national security or the 'indivisible integrity of the state are threatened." The expanded grip over voluntary organizations coupled with the expanded freedoms granted to the press helps explain why previously muted identity communities and associational interests turned to the media to express their agendas and to expand their projects for social mobility.

Liberalization and Muslim Politics

New avenues for expression in the post-1983 period favored religious communities whose members benefited from new social policies enacted after the coup, which played a direct role in the revival of Turkey's religious marketplace in the 1980s and 1990s. In an effort to stymie Turkey's left–right divide and to counteract the potential influence of Khomeini's Iran, following the 1980 coup Özal administered a policy originally drafted under General Evren that sought to consciously use religion as a means to unite the country amid intense ideological division. The result was "a new constitution based on a 'Turkish-Islamic synthesis' that was a combination of nationalism and Islam, and was intended to constrain the causes of political chaos" (Baskan 2004, 220). Turkey's bourgeoisie, the TSK regime, and Özal's Anavatan Partisi (Motherland Party, ANAP) single-party government that followed saw a conservative return to "moral values" and to Turkey's "Islamic roots" as something to be exploited in the interests of stability. Unanticipated by its architects, however, was the fragmented impact that Turkish national identity (in its rigid Kemalist form) had on the hearts and minds of voting Turkish citizens. While elements of Kemalism managed to penetrate the Turkish psyche very deeply (i.e., Turkish nationalism, economic populism, industrial modernization), the entirety of the Kemalist doctrine did not.[9] The policies of Turkish laiklik did not have a totalizing effect. As soon as the 1982 constitution lifted discursive and organizational barriers associated with religion, Islamic activists flooded Turkey's religious marketplace, forever redefining Turkish political culture.

Indeed, the GM's reliance on the processes of Turkey's liberalization is indicative of overlapping interests between its underwriters, who are represented predominantly by Turkey's conservative bourgeoisie (i.e., the various interests who have benefited from Turkey's shift to an export economy based in central Anatolia) and Turkey's traditional urban bourgeoisie who made their mark in industry following World War II. While they were slow to restructure in the 1980s, by the mid-1990s Turkey's largest corporations became globally competitive. In this sense they "needed a predictable economic and legal environment, instead of large favors often distributed on a highly arbitrary and clientelistic basis" (Öniş and Turem 2001, 444). Aware of their competitive potential, in the mid-1990s Turkey's bourgeoisie shifted toward collectively advocating for increased democratization, liberalization, and integration. Once Turkey liberalized its capital account in 1989, the state relinquished its control over capital flows. This, coupled with Turkey's quick adjustment in response to the first Gulf War, led to a substantial increase in foreign direct investment (FDI) in the early 1990s.[10] The most significant result of these developments was a rapidly increasing domestic consumer market, a "consumer revolution" that benefited old and new producers alike. After an initial dip following the first Gulf War, Turkey appeared to be headed toward unprecedented growth and prosperity. The architects of the neo-liberal world economy in the 1990s pointed to Turkey as a model for emerging markets:

> The domestic market of 60 million is currently undergoing a consumer revolution led by a 27% jump in automobile sales. . . . The resulting growth levels of retail sales are the fastest of any OECD country. With 38% of the population under the age of 15, and only 4.4% over the age of 65, the spending spree is expected to continue well into the next century. (Passow 1994, 5)

Politically, however, the early-1990s was also a period of revived tension.

A fundamental problem with Turkish integration following the 1980 coup was that the military entrenched itself even deeper into Turkey's governing regime. It did this while simultaneously expanding the freedoms of civil society organizations in business, media, and among voluntary organizations, which led to a contradictory political and economic environment. By the late 1980s, old business elites found themselves contending with a new export sector in Turkey's business class that was politically represented by an ascendant conservative political party. Moreover, both groups found themselves confronted by and increasingly powerful coalition between the military-dominated TSK, the State Security Court, the presidentially appointed National Education Council, and the National Media Councils. According to Keyder (2004, 65, 84), "The civilian governments that subsequently entered office [in the 1990s] . . . essentially concerned themselves with economic policy and with the management of the debt. Meanwhile, the State Courts served as unabashed organs of 'the deep state': their jurisdiction extended to everything political ranging from human rights to anything the state construed as separatist propaganda." Less reliant on state subsidies, Turkey's traditional economic elite found itself joining its socially conservative counterparts in calls for greater economic and political liberalization. In the late 1990s, a perfect storm was forming that would have a lasting impact on Turkey's political and economic development in the new millennium.

Having first mobilized a following in the early 1970s, Necmettin Erbakan's Milli Görüş Hareketi (National Outlook Movement, MGH) spent much of that decade expanding its platform to institute Şeriat (Islamic Law) as Turkey's source for civil law. In 1994, Turkey's coalition prime minster Tansu Çiller, the new leader of the center–right Doğru Yol Partisi (True Path Party, DYP), forged an agreement with the European Union on a Customs Union that went into effect on January 1, 1996. This led to problems when "the EU withheld the financial aid it had promised to mitigate the costs of the customs union deal, which deprived the state budget of tax income" (Passow 1994, 4). The result was a massive balance of payments deficit and an outflow of foreign capital. In mid-1994, Turkey experienced its first neo-liberal crisis. Stabilization schemes following the 1994 crisis achieved their targets and Turkey's GDP grew steadily between 1995 and 1998, only to crash again in 1999, rise again in 2000, and then fall to an all-time low in 2001. The social response to economic turbulence was a fracturing of political support for the DYP, whose leaders found themselves in competition with candidates from the DYP's Islam-identified counterpart, Necmettin Erbakan's reformed, MGH-affiliated Refah Partisi (Welfare Party, RP).

In the 1995 elections, the RP won 21.4 percent of the vote, which equated to 158 seats in Parliament. Due to corruption charges brought against Çiller, the DYP was quick to form a coalition with the RP, and Erbakan took over as prime minister. Mimicking the strategies of the DP in the 1950s, the RP advocated a populist approach to Turkish governance, and followed a policy of extensive grassroots organizing. It claimed to represent small producers, entrepreneurs, and exporters, and it paid specific attention to previously unacknowledged concerns such as environmental degradation and political corruption. It also promoted a notion of "justice" as a cross-class issue rooted in Muslim sensibility:

> Welfare's economic model was one of competitive capitalism with minimal state intervention, but also incorporated an ethical stance. . . . Welfare was concerned to protect small businesses from unfair competition and from tax and lending structures stacked in favor of big business. . . . What ultimately differentiated Welfare from other parties, however, was

its emergence as the visible tip of a populist iceberg. . . . The notion of a
just economic order appealed to the working class and to marginal people in squatter areas, as well as to small businessmen and entrepreneurs.
(White 2002, 124)

In mid-1997, after a series of military-sponsored press conferences and
a swing to the left in Parliament, the RP–DYP coalition collapsed and
Erbakan resigned. Critics of this event refer to it infamously as "The
February 28 Process" or "The Postmodern Coup." In early 1998, a Constitutional Court banned the RP from politics in a ruling, stating that
"the party's religious platform contradicted Turkey's secular constitution" (Kamrava 1998, 275). Erbakan was banned from politics for life.

The new government ushered in an IMF Staff-Monitored Loan to
tackle inflation. Negative tides, however, continued to rise when in
December 1997, the European Union decided to remove Turkey from its
candidate list, which forced the country to cut its ties with Europe (the
Customs Agreement, however, remained unaffected). As bad moved to
worse, "the Russian crisis in August 1998, the general elections in April
1999, and two devastating earthquakes in August and October 1999
deteriorated the fiscal balance of the public sector. The relative share of
primary surplus in the GDP decreased and the ratio of public debt to
GDP kept increasing" (Ertuğrul and Selçuk 2001, 24). Turkey ended the
twentieth century in crisis.

The "Conservative Democratic" Turn

Turkey began the twenty-first century in shambles. Within a year, the
economy suffered its worst contraction in history. As a result, there
was yet another political upheaval, which was catalyzed by a society-
wide lack of confidence. Early elections occurred in November 2002.
The one-year-old AKP, led by a formerly banned RP mayor of Istanbul,
Recep Tayyip Erdoğan, won a landslide victory, garnering 34.2 percent
of the popular vote and two-thirds of the seats (363 out of 550) in the
Turkish Grand National Assembly. Despite the fears of their critics, the
AKP asserted that it was committed to Turkey's global integration and
to EU membership; and, moreover, that it favored democracy and secularism. Its leaders insisted, however, that although they had let go of

their "Islamist past," they would never let go of their "conservative values." To highlight their new identity, the party included women in its
organizational hierarchy, expanded its platform to attract economically
liberal-minded voters who desired greater access to foreign markets,
and asserted its desire to weaken the authority of the TSK. In July 2007
the AKP won a second major victory, with 46.7 percent of the electorate voting in its favor. It returned to power with 341 out of 550 seats in
Parliament. This paved the way for the AKP's Abdullah Gül to become
Turkey's eleventh president two months later. This monumental event
democratically solidified AKP power in Turkey, which led to a third
major electoral victory in 2011, and to a commitment to draft a new
national constitution in its third term.

The AKP coalition between social conservatives and economic liberals indicates that contemporary political divides in Turkey are less
defined by "secularism" versus "Islamism" than by "defensive nationalism" versus "conservative globalism." "Defensive nationalism" refers to
"the defensive, inward-oriented nationalistic visions of the rival parties
with their authoritarian biases and fear-based politics . . . who, because
of an anti-progressive image . . . contribute to the AKP's electoral success" (Öniş 2009, 22). Conservative globalism refers to "an unusual
synthesis of liberal and conservative elements . . . a favorable attitude
towards engagement with global markets, democratization reforms,
and progress toward EU membership . . . [and] a defense of traditional
values and appeals to the conservative instincts of large segments of
voters, cutting across traditional class divisions in the process" (22). The
AKP's success, therefore, is attributed to its ability to symbolically link
its roots in Islam (which is reframed as roots in "moral values") with
neo-liberal aspirations (i.e., economic restructuring, privatization, and
EU integration). Similarly, the party links social populism and wealth
redistribution with tradition and moral obligation by supporting and
promoting the effectiveness of private Islamic foundations (*vakfı*) over
state-administered welfare institutions. This appeases neo-liberals
because it places the burden of social welfare in the private sphere, and
it appeases the poor because it illustrates that the party is concerned
with their plight. In this way, the success of the AKP is in many ways
comparable to the success of the DP in the 1950s—a socially conservative coalition built on a union of Turkish national identity, Islam, and

free enterprise. Yıldız Atasoy (2008, 50) explains the AKP's apparent transformation from "Islamist roots" to "conservative democracy" as a shift toward a synthesis between neo-liberal restructuring, European democratic reform, and Islamic cultural values:

> The AKP program argues that "combining world economic and European democratic normative standards with Turkish cultural values and moral precepts can produce an ethics that would apply in all aspects of the economy as a precondition for permanent and perpetual growth." Islamic moral principles seen as a strategy for asset building in human capital are combined with the transformation of the authoritarian Kemalist tradition to achieve greater social solidarity.

In January 2008, controversy erupted over the AKP's effort to amend Article X of the 1982 constitution by legally removing the state ban on wearing Muslim head scarves on university campuses. Parliament passed the measure on February 12, 2008, and President Gül signed it into law two weeks later. The main opposition, CHP, together with a majority of the country's university rectors, challenged the new law, and on June 4, 2008, the Constitutional Court annulled the measure, effectively reinstating the ban. Shortly before its third electoral victory, however, the AKP did manage to author an amendment package to Turkey's 1982 constitution on September 12, 2010 (coincidentally, the anniversary of the 1980 coup). The CHP and MHP opposition unsuccessfully challenged the referendum, primarily because of changes that it proposed to the structure of appointments to the TSK, the Constitutional Court, and the Supreme Board of Judges and Prosecutors (HSYK). The referendum passed with approximately 58 percent of the electorate voting in its favor, which marked the sixth consecutive nationwide political victory for the AKP since coming to power in 2002.

Devam Yol! (Onward!)

Led politically by the AKP, Turkey's ascendant "moral majority" constitutes a civil-society coalition within which the GM has emerged as the most central collective actor. Favors that GM institutions receive from AKP-appointed bureaucrats, support that its schools receive from AKP politicians, and tenders that its affiliated companies receive with the help of AKP policies indicate that although still uneven, the push for liberalization appears to favor Islamic actors at the expense of Turkey's traditional elite. What defines the current conjuncture in Turkey's political economy, therefore, is the revival of a long-term struggle between the Kemalist state and the social forces that seek to redistribute its collective power. The effort on the GM's part is to play an active role in normalizing the AKP's brand of "conservative democracy"—a reformed articulation of modern Turkish nationalism that embraces both markets and Islam, and that glorifies Turkey's Ottoman past in the hopes of constructing a twenty-first-century Turkish superpower.

The chapters that follow present Turkey's conservative democratic transformation through the lens of post-political market Islam as expressed through the person, institutions, and followers of M. Fethullah Gülen. In so doing, the presentation also highlights that although a civil, economic, and social success story, the GM confronts an increasing mass of contradictions that emerge when its self-described "nonpolitical" mobilization becomes co-opted by the demands of a free market economy. These same contradictions affect the AKP as it struggles to meet the demands of EU integration and, in the interests of not sabotaging its coalition, as it continues to walk a fine line between conservative social values, liberal economic reform, and institutionalized political power. In regard to the GM, these contradictions emerge when Islam is marketized in the interests of growth and accumulation, a process that has made Fethullah Gülen a product for mass consumption, and that has led to the trans-nationalization of GM-affiliated enterprises in education, media, manufacture, finance, trade, and influence peddling. In this context, the primary impediments to the GM's continued growth in Turkey (and around the world) consist of (1) the forces that constitute the remnants of Turkey's twentieth-century oligarchy who view the GM's collective mobilization as threating to their entrenched power, and (2) the GM's preference for ambiguity as a mobilizing strategy.

3

An Ambiguous Leader

I have never claimed to be a person in the vanguard, a leader
or a guide on any subject. I've never had a thesis of moderate and modern Islamism either. These are nothing but the
speculation and concoctions of people who know nothing
about these matters. I'm trying to explain Islam from today's
perspectives. If some people try and describe this according
to the mental patterns in their own minds, that's their problem, not mine.
—M. Fethullah Gülen

In the study of modern organizations, "strategic ambiguity" is often
cited as an effective means to allow for the expression of internally
divergent group interests, and to persuade outsiders that stated objectives correspond with observable outcomes. Contradicting common
beliefs, the theory of strategic ambiguity suggests that organizations—
be they for-profit, not-for-profit, or public—mobilize to achieve a variety of goals that may complement or contradict one another (Davenport
and Leitch 2005; Eisenberg 1984; Jarzabkowski, Sillince, and Shaw 2009;
Aragonés and Neeman 2000). In organizational logic, clarity of voice,
for instance, might be an assumed expectation but it is not an objective
feature of organizational ethos. In fact, "it is often preferable to omit
purposefully contextual clues and to allow for multiple interpretations
on the part of receivers. . . . Clarity is only a measure of communicative
competence if the individual has as his or her goals to be clear" (Eisenberg 1984, 231). Concerning communication, there are four overlapping
benefits of strategic ambiguity: the promotion of unified diversity, the
facilitation of organizational change, the ability to maintain plausible
deniability, and the preservation of privilege in organizational leadership (Eisenberg 1984).

In a piously identified conservative advocacy community like the GM, the desire to maintain "unified diversity" is essential because the alternative gives the impression of a cultlike group of followers who blindly obey the commands of an all-powerful leader. Indeed, the relative freedom of GM affiliates to participate at different levels of dedication, and to express their individuality as journalists, writers, teachers, engineers, doctors, and businesspeople, creates an organizational environment of "unified diversity" that facilitates a graduated system of affiliation. For instance, when GM institutions in Turkey and in the United States invoke the same symbolic categories (e.g., "dialogue," "tolerance," "universal values"), they do so in a way that leaves room for interpretation. Dialogue with whom, and tolerance of what? The answers are contextual; "ambiguity is used strategically to foster agreement on abstractions without limiting specific interpretations" (Eisenberg 1984, 233).

Second, concerning organizational change, the employment of ambiguously defined categories—what Eisenberg refers to as the "careful use of metaphor"—allows for a very loose understanding of "community" (cemaat) and "service" (hizmet) to be applied by different actors, in different ways, and for different reasons. Such autonomy facilitates a leaner, more flexible logic of organization. In the case of the GM, the community's identity is rooted on the fact that in the 1970s, Gülen encouraged his followers to build schools instead of mosques, and for affiliated businessmen to look on their faithful obligations as Muslims to give alms, as opportunities to provide an economic foundation for the community's expansion. GM institutions, therefore, emerged autonomously, connected via a loose network of social, financial, and ideational ties. This ambiguous organizational model allowed for school administrators, businesspeople, editors, and outreach coordinators to choose when they wanted to freely associate their institution's identity as being "part" of the GM, when they wanted to simply refer to their institutions as "Gülen-inspired," or when they wanted to deny any affiliation whatsoever. Depending on where a particular school was, and depending on who was inquiring about that school's connection, different loyalists provided different answers to the same questions.

When do I know if I am visiting a "Gülen-school," a "Gülen-inspired school," or simply a publicly funded charter school that just so happens to be under the management of Turkish individuals who so just happen to be inspired by the teachings of Fethullah Gülen? According to the theory of strategic ambiguity, by maintaining a certain level of nontransparency, actors in a collective can "alter operations which have become maladaptive over time" (Eisenberg 1984, 235). In Turkey's politically charged social context, such organizational flexibility becomes essential for the GM's transnational expansion, and in so doing, underscores the third function of strategic ambiguity—plausible deniability. The ability to plausibly deny the central role of Gülen's leadership in the mobilization of the GM overall, to deny institutional connectivity, social network connectivity, financial overlaps, economic opportunism, and politically motivated self-promotion, has been crucial to the GM's uninterrupted growth for three decades. Serving as the model for plausible deniability, Gülen himself typifies the GM's application of strategic ambiguity and thus highlights its fourth organizational function—the ability to preserve positions of privilege.

Indeed, all organizations position "highly credible people [to] have greater freedom in what they can say [so as] to maintain a positive impression. A source deemed credible who speaks ambiguously may be called a prophet, but a low-credible source speaking identically may be dubbed a fool" (Eisenberg 1984, 241). Fethullah Gülen provides a useful case by which to observe how the spiritually framed utterances of a self-educated preacher are transformed by an inner core of loyal followers into a blueprint for collective action, and into a foundation for social critique. As an organizational strategy, therefore, the strategic employment of ambiguous categories begins with Gülen himself, a charismatic leader whose influence has become near legend in Turkey, and whose impact has become institutionalized in education, finance, media, and trade.

"An Alien of Extraordinary Abilities"

In late March 1999, Fethullah Gülen moved to the United States, citing health reasons. A common Turkish conspiracy suggests that Gülen was tipped off about a yet-to-be-filed indictment against him for being the leader of a secret organization whose objective was to overthrow the secular republic. Regardless of one's opinion about the validity of this claim, in 2006 Gülen was acquitted of all charges against him. In 2008, Turkey's Supreme Court of Appeals (Court of Cassation) rejected an appeal to overturn his acquittal. Yet, despite his legal vindication, Gülen remained in the United States, where for the better part of the last decade he lived in a multihouse compound in the foothills of the Pocono Mountains.

After two years in Saylorsburg, Pennsylvania, the Golden Generation Students Association (now the Golden Generation Worship and Retreat Center) filed an I-360 application with the Vermont Service Center of the U.S. Center for Immigration Services (USCIS) for a change of residency status on Gülen's behalf. The original application requested a change from temporary visitor to "special immigrant religious worker" and was approved in August 2002. In signed testimony given to USCIS, Fethullah Gülen addressed his relationship to the transnational network of schools attributed to his leadership as follows:

USCIS: Has anybody on your behalf established schools in Turkey and elsewhere?

GÜLEN: Not on my behalf, but with promotion or encouragement maybe they have, because they know I appreciate education, and where they have opened schools I don't know.

USCIS: Do you have any role in the teachings in those schools?

GÜLEN: Absolutely not. I have nothing to do with it.

USCIS: Are you responsible for what is taught in those schools?

GÜLEN: No, not me. The government is responsible. It's happening under the supervision of the government.[1]

In an interview with a major Turkish newspaper, Fethullah Gülen explained that "volunteers" run the schools, and that the Turkish state was free to take them over:

The state can either back these activities carried out by voluntary organizations, and finance them, or they can totally take over them—by the army or civil servants . . . but they must do this. It would be wrong to ascribe different meanings to these schools and to show antipathy towards them just because some certain people are involved in them. (Gülen 2005a, in an interview with Mehmet Gündem)

In September 2006, a month after Gülen was acquitted of conspiracy in Turkey, the USCIS issued a notice to revoke Gülen's "special immigrant" status. Lawyers for the Golden Generation responded with a series of refutations, and on November 20, 2006, they filed for a permanent residency permit (i.e., a green card) on Gülen's behalf. Up until that time, Gülen remained in the United States as a temporary registered religious worker. In his permanent residency application, Gülen's lawyers redefined their client's legal identity as "an alien of extraordinary abilities in the field of education" (*Gülen v. Chertoff*, June 4, 2008). Lawyers for the Golden Generation also submitted an application for Gülen's legal right to travel outside the US (I-131, filed in October 2004) and for his right to seek employment (I-765, filed in August 2006).

By spring 2007, Gülen was still not permitted to travel, work, or permanently stay in the United States. Arguing that their client was a victim of intentional delay by the Department of Homeland Security (DHS), Gülen's legal team petitioned for a writ of mandamus (i.e., an appeal to legally force a lower body or government agency to fulfill its duties) with a federal judge on May 27, 2007. Their claim was that "the defendants failed or willfully refused to adjudicate [Gülen's] application(s) for several years" (*Gülen v. Chertoff*, May 27, 2008). The USCIS and the DHS responded by defending the slow handling of Gülen's applications as procedural, and eventually granted Gülen his rights to travel and to seek gainful employment. On November 19, 2007, however, Gülen was denied his green card on the basis that he *was not* an alien of extraordinary abilities. Gülen's lawyers immediately moved to overturn the USCIS decision. To be clear, despite Gülen's insistence that "Gülen-inspired schools" (GISs) had nothing to do with Fethullah Gülen, the American legal team representing Fethullah Gülen in the United States argued that the retired Turkish religious functionary deserved permanent residency because of his "extraordinary abilities *in the field of education.*" And although Gülen's lawyers cited his books as "educational" and his articles as "scholarly," the primary argument presented to validate his credentials as an educator was his leadership role in the worldwide network of what is now more than one thousand schools begun by his followers:

The record provides substantial evidence of Plaintiff's [Gülen's] national and international awards under 8 C.F.R. §204.5(h)(3)(i), evidence that

Plaintiff has authored more than 40 scholarly books and more than 100 scholarly articles under 8 C.F.R. §204.5(h)(3)(vi), evidence that Plaintiff's work was featured in the field of education at showcases under 8 C.F.R. §204.5(h)(3)(vii) and evidence that Plaintiff has served a leading and critical role in the Gülen Movement and the establishment of more than 600 educational institutions around the world under 8 C.F.R. §204.5(h)(3)(viii). (*Gülen v. Chertoff*, June 4, 2008)

Lawyers representing the USCIS reacted to Gülen's claims to be an educator by calling attention to the fact that he was neither a teacher nor a pedagogical scholar. Gülen's lawyers refuted this argument by submitting to the court letters of support from twenty-nine high-profile U.S. and Turkish academics, political operatives, community leaders, and religious leaders who all attested to Gülen's "extraordinary abilities." Among those who wrote letters were the widely published scholars on Islam and Muslim politics Dale Eickelman, John Esposito, and John Voll; the former high-ranking CIA officials George Fidas and Graham Fuller; the former ambassador to Turkey Morton Abromowitz; and the former Turkish prime minster Yildirim Akbulut. USCIS lawyers responded as follows:

In this case, the record contains facts which suggest that plaintiff has made contributions to the field of education by advocating the establishment of schools in Turkey. . . . The record also contains overwhelming evidence that the plaintiff is not an expert in the field of education, is not an educator, and is certainly not one of a small percentage of experts in the field of education who have risen to the very top of that field. Further, the record contains overwhelming evidence that plaintiff is primarily the leader of a large and influential religious and political movement with immense commercial holdings. . . . The difficulty for plaintiff is that the statute requires that he show that he has achieved sustained national or international acclaim in the *in the field of education* and that he has attained a level of expertise that places him at the very top *of the field of education*. His attainment of international acclaim in the field of religious tolerance and interfaith dialogue is irrelevant. . . . Religious tolerance and interfaith dialogue are not fields for which Congress has granted visa preferences. (*Gülen v. Chertoff*, June 8, 2008; emphasis in original)

On July 16, 2008, a federal judge ruled in Gülen's favor, which opened the door for his application for permanent residency to move forward (*Gülen v. Chertoff*, July 16, 2008). Despite the fact that Gülen repeatedly denied all association with the transnational network of schools begun by his followers, in November 2008 the USCIS granted Gülen his green card, proclaiming his new legal identity as "an alien of extraordinary abilities in the field of education."

So are GM schools products of Gülen's "leading and critical role in the Gülen Movement," or do the schools exist despite him? What factors explain Gülen's strategic use of ambiguity when explaining his leadership? These questions are addressed below by first providing an analysis of the charismatic leader Fethullah Gülen, followed by an analysis of the social structure, or in Weberian terms, "the charismatic aristocracy," that emerged under his tutelage.

Beginnings: Bediüzzaman Said Nursi (1877–1960)

When Gülen was sixteen years old (or nineteen, as the case may be; see below), he was exposed to the writings of "Bediüzzaman" (wonder of the age) Said Nursi, a learned religious activist in eastern Anatolia. Over the course of his lifetime, Nursi authored a large number of commentaries and answers to questions about piety, identity, and politics that his followers later compiled into a collection known as the *Risale-i Nur Külliyatı* (*RNK, Epistles of Light*).[2] Although a Kurd, Nursi was an active participant in the "Young Turk" struggle (1908) against the Ottoman Sultan Abdul Hamid II (1842–1918), and was an early supporter of the Turkish republican project. In addition to being a respected religious authority, Nursi was a volunteer soldier in the eastern front in World War I. Rationalizing the Ottoman effort as a moral jihad (struggle) against an invading power, Nursi fought the Russians and Armenians, "moving around the front lines on his horse, always to the fore of the fighting" (Vahide 2005, 113). Nursi was on active duty from 1914 until February 1916, when Russian forces captured him in the eastern Anatolian town of Bitlis. He was a Russian prisoner of war for two years before escaping in 1918. He explained to his students that it was during his long, cold, and lonely escape that he came to a higher realization:

That night in the mosque on the banks of the Volga made me decide to pass the rest of my life in caves. Enough now of mixing in social life with people. . . . I said that from now on I would choose solitude so as to become accustomed to it. (Vahide 2005, 129)

Despite this realization, it took another two years for Nursi's famous transition from the "old Said" to the "new Said" to be complete. In the interim, Nursi was received in Istanbul as a war hero. According to Vahide (2005, 132), "He received invitations from prominent pashas and dignitaries, or was visited by them. He was offered various positions of honors, and was awarded a war medal." Caught up in the excitement and confusion of a hero's welcome, Nursi put his transformation on hold.

Following the Ottoman defeat in the Great War, Istanbul was left vulnerable to foreign powers. A ceasefire was declared in October 1918. Beginning in 1919, French and Italian troops arrived on Anatolian shores, and in 1920 the British and French occupied Istanbul. After witnessing the situation firsthand, Nursi emerged as an unlikely supporter of Kemal's efforts to maintain the territorial integrity of the Anatolian heartland in Turkey's War of Independence (1920–1923). He lent his support to the idea of Turkish nationalism, albeit with a pious-minded critique. To this end, Nursi warned that *positive nationalism* emerged "from an inner need of social life and [was] the cause of mutual assistance and solidarity; it [was] a means for further strengthening Islamic brotherhood. This idea of positive nationalism must serve Islam, it must be its citadel and armor; it must not take the place of it." By contrast, Nursi's understanding of *negative nationalism*, the nationalism he viewed as characteristic of European republicanism, was "nourished by devouring others, persists through hostility to others, and is aware of what it is doing. . . . It [was] the cause of enmity and disturbance" (Nursi, translated from Turkish by Vahide 2005, 380).

After Turkey's War of Independence was decided, Nursi accepted an invitation to meet with members of Turkey's new Grand National Assembly (GNA). Upon his arrival, Nursi was "dismayed to find a lax and indifferent attitude toward Islam and their religious duties among many of the deputies in the assembly." In his own words, "I saw that an abominable current of atheism was treacherously trying to subvert, poison, and destroy their minds. 'Oh God!' I said. 'The monster is going to harm the pillars of belief'" (Vahide 2005, 169). Nursi called on the new government to uphold the mantle of Islam, and to account for the loss of the sultanate by assuring the people of the new Republic that their sovereign nation was a Muslim nation. Aware of his influence, Kemal tried to co-opt Nursi by offering him a state religious position as "general preacher of the eastern provinces." Nursi declined. When offered another post, he declined again. Instead, he directed his energies toward a decades-long plan to develop a new university in the eastern provincial city of Van, a crossroads town that sat the intersection of Turkish, Arab, and Persian cultures. Having previously been rejected by Sultan Abdul Hamid II in 1907, Nursi took advantage of an opportunity and resubmitted his request to the new Turkish GNA. He envisioned a modern university that would unite the Islamic and natural sciences, and that would provide the *umma* (community of believers in Islam) with an intellectual hub that would resurrect the grandeur of Al-Azhar during the height of the Abbasid Caliphate (750–950). Such an institution would not only create a model for national education, but it would also revive a sense of Turkish centrality in the Muslim world. Science and Islam would be taught side by side as complementary sources of human knowledge, and in Nursi's vision, students and scholars would descend on the region from the world over to take part in the exchange of ideas between faith and science, modernity and tradition.

There was no contradiction, as Nursi saw it, between the natural sciences and the unity of God (Arabic: *Tawhīd*). Epistemologically, Nursi viewed the natural world as evidence of creation, and science as the code by which humanity deciphered the secrets of God's universe. Nursi's was thus indicative of the Islamic modernist movement that swept through the region in the late nineteenth and early twentieth century. He posited that western Europe emerged to dominate the modern world system not because of cultural, racial, or political superiority, but because of its advancement in science, an endeavor that Nursi understood to have stalled in Muslim societies when the penetrating influences of positivism, materialism, and moral doubt corrupted Muslims the world over. Like his Arab counterparts, Nursi believed that Western achievements in science, industry, and war were vulnerable because their backers lacked moral purpose. He feared that a "modern

Turkey" that subscribed blindly to the assumptions of scientific positivism would suffer a collective fate of social and cultural anomie:

> The philosophy they call natural philosophy or science has plunged into
> the decorations of the letters of beings and into their relationships, and
> has become bewildered; it has confused the way of reality. While the let-
> ters of this mighty book should be looked at as bearing the meaning of
> another, that is, on account of God, they have not done this; they have
> looked at beings as signifying themselves. . . . In doing this they have
> insulted the universe. (Nursi, translated by Vahide 2005, 145)

The Van university project failed to pass the GNA, defeated finally in
November 1925 (Vahide 2005, 172). Two years previous, when Nursi left
Ankara en route for Van, he recalled his previous transformation, and
thereafter removed himself from public life. For the next twenty years,
Nursi devoted himself almost entirely to study.

It was during this period that he authored his oeuvre. This was also
the time when Nursi refused to comment on Turkish politics, or to
direct his followers to engage in political mobilization. In the *RNK*, he
responded to one of his students who inquired about his retreat as follows: "Service of the All-Wise Qur'an is superior to all politics so that
it does not allow one to lower oneself to world politics, which consists mostly of falsehood" (Nursi, translated by Vahide 2005, 68). Setting the tone for Fethullah Gülen, the "new Said" also contended that
"fanaticism, being violent and unreasoning devotion, is incompatible
with Islam. However deep it is, a Muslim's devotion depends on knowledge and reasoning. For the deeper and firmer a Muslim's belief in, and
devotion to Islam . . . the further from fanaticism a Muslim is by virtue
of Islam being the 'middle way' based on peace, balance, justice, and
moderation" (Nursi 1995, 263). Contrasting the life experiences of "old
Said" as a political activist and warrior, the "new Said" called his followers to "greater *cihad*," to the internal struggle with the soul (*nefs*).
Drawing on his spiritual roots in Naqşibandi Sufism, Nursi contended
that Muslims had strayed from their path and that it was necessary to
collectively return to the realization of Islamic truth by focusing on the
inner struggle with corrupting forces of materialism, positivism, and
moral decay.

Despite his retreat from politics, Nursi's rejection of the Kemalist project and his open admonishment of Mustafa Kemal eventually led the CHP regime to regard his teachings with contempt. For the rest of his life, Nursi was repeatedly placed under house arrest. The Diyanet banned the production and dissemination of the *RNK*, and shortly after his death and burial in 1960, Nursi's tomb was moved from the south-eastern city of Şanlınurfa to an undisclosed location to prevent his followers from making pilgrimage.

The Nur

Immediately following Nursi's death, a number of groups emerged to claim rights to his teachings. An organizational split occurred when one group sought to mass-produce the *RNK* (and thus to reform the text in accordance with the Turkish language reform). A smaller group disagreed on the basis that the *RNK* was a work of spiritual art, thus stressing the integrity of the text. This latter group, the Yazıcılar (Scribes), refused their Nur brethren's insistence to broadly distribute the *RNK*, and contended instead that Nursi's teachings required open discussion in the form of a *ders* (lecture) between the learned and the learning. To maintain the integrity of Nursi's prose, this smaller group advocated for the reproduction of *RNK* by hand in its original Ottoman script. The former disagreed. They believed that Nursi's teachings required a broad audience and that modern printing technologies provided an opportunity to broadly disseminate the message. In 1971 this group published the first edition of the journal *Yeni Asya* (New Asia), and has since been known as such.

Following Turkey's 1980 coup, another major division occurred pitting supporters and opponents of the post-coup political landscape against one another. Concurrent with the rise of Kurdish separatist politics in the 1980s in Turkey's southeast, another group splintered to focus on Nursi's Kurdish origins, and in doing so, advocated for a glorification of Nursi's efforts for Kurdish rights in Anatolia (Yavuz 2003a, 170–176). Today, there are three general divisions in the Nur Movement, and several more splits within each.[3] Despite their differences, however, the Nur are united in the belief that Bediüzzaman Said Nursi authored a blueprint for a Muslim engagement with the modern world.

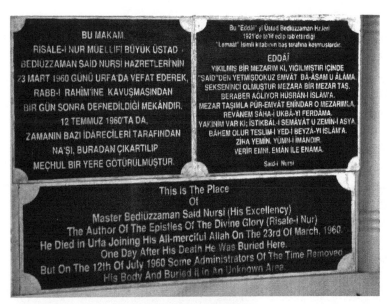

BU MAKAM,
RISALE-I NUR MUELLIFI BÜYÜK ÜSTAD
BEDIÜZZAMAN SAID NURSI HAZRETLERI'NIN
23 MART 1960 GÜNÜ URFA'DA VEFAT EDEREK,
RABB-I RAHÎM'INE KAVUŞMASINDAN
BIR GÜN SONRA DEFNEDILDIĞI MEKÂNDIR.
12 TEMMUZ 1960'TA DA,
ZAMANIN BAZI IDARECİLERI TARAFINDAN
NA'ŞI, BURADAN ÇIKARTILIP
MEÇHUL BIR YERE GÖTÜRÜLMÜŞTUR.

Bu "Eddâî" yi Üstad Bediüzzaman Hz.leri
1921'de te'lif edip tab ettirdiği
"Lemaat" isimli kitabının baş tarafına koymuşlardır.

EDDÂÎ
YIKILMIŞ BIR MEZARIM KI, YIGILMIŞTIR İÇİNDE
"SAİD"DEN YETMIŞDOKUZ EMVÂT BÂ-ÂSÂM U ÂLÂMA.
SEKSENINCİ OLMUŞTUR MEZARA BIR MEZAR TAŞ,
BERABER AĞLIYOR HÜSRÂN-I İSLÂM'A.
MEZAR TAŞIMLA PÜR-EMVÂT ENÎNDAR O MEZARIMLA,
REVÂNEM SÂHA-I UKBÂ-YI FERDÂMA.
YAKÎNIM VAR KI; İSTİKBÂL-I SEMÂVÂT U ZEMİN-I ASYA,
BÂHEM OLUR TESLİM-I YED-I BEYZÂ-YI İSLÂM'A.
ZÎHÂ YEMÎN, YÜMN-I İMÂNDIR,
VERÎR EMNİ, EMÂN İLE ENÂMA.

Said-i Nursi

This is The Place
Of
Master Bediüzzaman Said Nursi (His Excellency)
The Author Of The Epistles Of The Divine Glory (Risale-i Nur)
He Died in Urfa Joining His All-merciful Allah On The 23rd Of March, 1960.
One Day After His Death He Was Buried Here.
But On The 12th Of July 1960 Some Administrators Of The Time Removed
His Body And Buried It In An Unknown Area.

Photos taken at the original place of rest of Bediüzzaman Said Nursi in Şanlınurfa. (Author's original photographs, May 2007)

Followers of Said Nursi were also united in practice. Continuing a tradition that began during his lifetime, followers met regularly in small groups to discuss and study the *RNK*. In addition to providing a space for the dissemination of knowledge, over time the Nur tradition to meet at a *ders* developed into a rudimentary system of belonging to a *cemaat*. Referring to the location of the *ders* as a *dershane* (lesson house), this tradition "became one of the embryos of civil society in Turkey" (Yavuz 2003b, 8). Adapting the Naqşibandi tradition of direct oral transmission from sheikh to disciple, the Nur *ders* pluralized Anatolian Sufism by opening up the gates of reasoning and interpretation (*ijtihad*) through text. Moreover, because the *RNK* was written in Ottoman Turkish (not in Arabic or in Nursi's native Kurdish), it provided an alternative resource on which to construct a modern Turkish identity that accepted and promoted the centrality of Islam. When followers of Nursi assembled to recite the *RNK*, they actively participated in a shift from oral to textual Islam in Turkey (i.e., from an illiterate to a literate society), from a "folk" to a "modern" formation of community identity, and from Ottoman (universal) to Turkish (national) individual identity. The *ders* created a public space for an Islamic critique of secular Turkey, and at the same time, provided a social space where individuals could reproduce community by plugging into social networks that extended throughout the country:

> The informal dershane networks and their role in the constitution of the public require a new understanding of the public. Privately built trust and a new cognitive map for understanding the meaning of the good life have social consequences in terms of constituting a framework of public discussions. . . . In these dershanes, Islam becomes a source of solidarity and a chart of social responsibility in the constitution of Muslim self and community. (Yavuz 2003a, 169)

Followers of Said Nursi created a counter-public in Turkey that congregated neither around the square (modern), nor around the mosque (tradition). Nursi's counter-public, rather, congregated around the *dershane* (modern/tradition).

While I was conducting research with first- and second-generation students of Fethullah Gülen in Istanbul, a group of editors, writers, and executives took a field trip one day to visit Mustafa Sungol, a living student of Said Nursi and the leader of the Abdullah Yeğin Grubu branch of the larger Turkish Nur Movement (Field Notes, Spring 2007). This was a much-anticipated event for all those involved; I, however, was intentionally left in the dark. The meeting with Sungol took the form of a Nur *ders*, a guided reading of the *RNK*. Without my asking, a research participant who participated in the *ders* shared with me that the group was given specific instruction by their *hoca* (teacher, elder authority) not to share with me that a select number of them were going to pay their respects to the aged Nur leader. Having already told me about the meeting before he was told not to do so, however, this research participant considered that he had broken no rules, nor anyone's trust. He did tell me that he would appreciate it if I did not tell the others that I knew. I agreed. Notwithstanding, I realized that efforts such as these to downplay the continuity between the Nur movement and the GM exemplified the latter's more general tendency to employ ambiguity when discussing its organizational form and collective identity. By downplaying their ideological and institutional relationships with other Nur groups, GM actors are better able to separate their leader from a pre-existing collective mobilization, and thus better able to emphasize Gülen's unique qualities vis-à-vis his predecessor. So what factors distinguish Fethullah Gülen?

"Do you know how old Hocaefendi is?"

Alternation refers to the practice of altering (reimagining) the past for the purposes of the present. Drawing on Peter Berger, Estruch (1995, 21) explains that the concept of alternation "is especially useful to the extent that it permits us to become aware that the phenomenon of alternation in general, that it affects us all, and that it is not at all at variance with that we usually call 'sincerity,' because, among other things, we frequently describe as sincere 'the state of a mind of a man who habitually believes his own propaganda.'" Estruch cites alternation as a primary strategy used by followers of the Spanish Catholic organization Opus Dei (work of God) in its presentation of Opus's founder, Monsignor Jose Escriva Balaguer. As discussed earlier, Opus Dei and the GM are strikingly similar in a number of ways. First and foremost, however, is how followers in each organization ascribe infallibility to their leader, and how they rationalize infallibility by strategically alternating the past in the interests of preserving their leader's position of privilege.

For instance, at the beginning of each of his books, Gülen's editors write a brief biography of the author. There are also a number of internally produced interviews with him, as well as interviews with unaffiliated Turkish and international media, and an increasing number of professional and academic papers and books commissioned and produced by GM-affiliated presses. In addition to internally commissioned work, there are also a small number of unaffiliated academic studies on the growth and impact of the movement (Agai 2003; Balcı 2003; Hendrick 2009, 2011a, 2011b; Turam 2004a, 2004b, 2006; Yavuz 1999, 2003a). With the exception of the latter group, the typical presentation of Fethullah Gülen introduces him as a perfect individual who can (and should) be compared to such diverse and remarkable figures as Martin Luther King Jr., Mahatma Gandhi, Mother Teresa, Nelson Mandela, Immanuel Kant, and Jean-Paul Sartre (Can 1996; Carroll 2007; Ebaugh 2010; Ergene 2005, 2008; http://fgülen.com/; Hunt and Aslandoğan 2007; Sarıtoprak 2005; Ünal 2006; Ünal and Williams 2000; Yavuz and Esposito 2003). More often than not, Fethullah Gülen is presented as an awe-inspiring leader who never married, who is naturally gifted in a variety of fields, and who is filled with humility and love for all of humanity.

His supporters present Gülen as a "peace activist, intellectual, religious scholar, mentor, author, and poet, a great thinker, and spiritual guide who has devoted his life to seeking the solutions for society's ills and spiritual needs."[4] He is "original in thought and action . . . and is deeply averse to unbelief, injustice, and deviation. . . . [He is] profound . . . wise and rational. [He is] a living model of love, ardor, and feeling . . . extraordinarily balanced in his thoughts, acts, and treatment of matters."[5] If not completely ignored, the controversy and mystery that surround him are passed over as being of no consequence. To date, there exists no academically rigorous biography of Turkey's most influential religious personality. There are, however, a number of internally produced hagiographical accounts. In each, the strategically ambiguous process of alternation comes to the fore.

Gülen's birth date provides a useful illustration. In the Turkish edition of Enes Ergene's internally produced *Gülen Hareketinin Analizi*

Geleceğin Modern Çağa Tanıklığı (*Tradition Witnessing the Modern Age: An Analysis of the Gülen Movement*) (2005), Gülen is presented as being born in 1938 in the northeastern Anatolian city of Erzurum. In the 2008 English edition of Ergene's book, Gülen's birth date is updated to 1941. In Ali Ünal's internally produced *Geçmişten Geleceğe Köprü: Fethullah Gülen* (*A Bridge from the Past to the Future: Fethullah Gülen*) (2005), Gülen is again presented as being born in April 1941.

On the one hand, a three-year discrepancy in age is a trivial, albeit curious, factual inconsistency. On the other hand, when one takes into consideration the mass of ambiguity that surrounds the GM's public persona, this discrepancy in age becomes a signifier of consistent practice. When confronted about Gülen's age, Tuğrul hoca, one of Gülen's close students and personal biographers, "explained" as follows:

TUĞRUL HOCA: There are people who perceive this movement by exaggerating its religious sides. They are afraid that if this movement develops itself, there will be a regime change and it will result in a religious state. Do you know how old Hocaefendi is?

JH: Actually no, it changes. I have read that its 1938 . . . and 1941.

TUĞRUL HOCA: The correct date is 1938. In the eastern parts of Anatolia, people are used to registering their children's births later than usual. That's the reason. Now he's sixty-eight, sixty-nine. Let's call it seventy and not agitate people politically. By age seventy, he never founded a political party and never agitated people politically. When is he expected to change the regime? After he dies? Let's be reasonable. Anyone has the right to fear this movement, but he is seventy. (Field Interview, Winter 2007)

According to this interviewee, Gülen's age is reason enough that political charges against him are "unreasonable." The free authority enjoyed by Gülen's handlers to change the date of his birth illustrates the degree to which the GM alternates its history to meet the demands of the present. If Gülen's biographers presented his birth date as being in question, he would become less than perfect. There would need to be some account for why his parents waited three years to register him. Such an account would affect the official story of Gülen's life in general, and would lead to even more questions. A more accurate biography of

Fethullah Gülen would have to place it within the larger context of Turkey's regional development at the beginning of World War II, state policies regarding child birth and registration, Turkey's foreign relations in the context of an emerging Cold War, and so forth. Indeed, an academically rigorous biography of Fethullah Gülen would need to account for the *social construction* of Fethullah Gülen, which would necessitate a focus on the contradictions, ruptures, and imperfections that constitute all of human life.

The focused efforts to alternate Fethullah Gülen have succeeded. He was born in 1938 *and* in 1941. Equally, Fethullah Gülen has no affiliation with the GM; but at the same time, he "has served a leading and critical role in the Gülen Movement and the establishment of more than 600 educational institutions around the world." Indeed, Gülen's lawyers in the United States might have made this argument in court, but one year before, a senior confidant of Gülen's explained to me in an interview setting, "There is nothing official, I mean . . . 'Hocaefendi has one thousand schools' . . . Nonsense! Hocaefendi does not have any schools!" (Field Interview, Summer 2007). When a desired goal calls for it, therefore, Gülen becomes the reason behind the growth of a countrywide network of private educational institutions. When another goal necessitates it, however (e.g., when publicly funded charter schools in the United States are alleged to fund the expansion of a religious nationalist community in Turkey), Gülen is cited as having no connection whatsoever. Strategic ambiguity allows GM followers to claim that Gülen is at once the reason, motivator, and instigator behind the GM's transnational efforts, *and* that he leads no one and manages nothing.

Fethullah Gülen: Muslim Intellectual?

If Gülen is a public intellectual, how are observers expected to understand his identity as a recluse? Gramsci argued that intellectuals were not independent from social class, nor did they constitute a class in themselves. He developed his argument in opposition to Julien Benda, who contended that because of their separation from the factors and relations of production, intellectuals were in fact a social class unto themselves and acted according to their own interests (Kurzman and Owens 2002). By contrast, Gramsci (1971, 7) contended that all social groups produced their own strata of intellectuals, and that modern intellectuals only *appeared* to be separated from the social class to which they belonged. This is because, for Gramsci, intellectuals from a dominant social group, the bourgeoisie in industrial capitalist societies, are charged with the task of "organizing society" at all levels, in every sector, "right up to the state organism because of the need to create the conditions most favorable to the expansion of their own class" (6). The power of the intellectual is thus the power to design the social rationale for legitimate power. In order to develop a new hegemony, argued Gramsci, the working class needed to develop its own "organic intellectuals" who could define the categories of their struggle, and who could persuasively convince constituents to mobilize. More than convincing writers, "organic intellectuals" needed to entrench themselves in the intellectual sector to become what Gramsci called "permanent persuaders."

In the transition from Ottoman to republican Turkey, the "Young Turks" formed a new intellectual stratum that sought to engineer a new social consciousness in competition with the traditional intellectual authority of the Ottoman ulema. This new intelligentsia developed in the mid-nineteenth century when, during the Tanzimet era (1839–1876), a new educational system attracted an emerging elite whose eventual impact was overlooked by the ulema:

> The custodians of tradition [i.e., the Ottoman ulema] did not object when the school of medicine and other secular schools of higher learning were established; they ignored them as being outside their own realm and, perhaps, as ephemeral, worldly institutions expedient to the needs of secular life . . . but from the early years of the *Tanzimat*, the *medrese* lost ground inch by inch in the field of education. (Berkeş 1998, 187)

By passing off the impact of new system of secular-educated intellectuals, it was only a matter of time, a single generation, before a new intellectual stratum was able to mount a counter hegemonic struggle against the traditional ideology of the Ottoman state.

In the late nineteenth and early twentieth centuries, a similar process occurred when secularly educated "organic Muslim intellectuals" emerged to define the social and political situation of Muslims in terms that were accessible to a potentially revolutionary class of colonized people. This new intellectual fused the European language of leftist philosophy with categories from Islam to outline a project for "Islamic revolution." What manifested was a subjective practice of cultural "code switching" between European and Islamic varieties of modernism:

> Islamic parties thus interpreted the leading themes of the "European" political public with a vocabulary of their own, which gave the outside observer the impression that these parties were religious groups. (Schulze 2002, 10)

In the mid-twentieth century, organic Muslim intellectuals deployed a specifically "Islamic discourse" to outline the possibilities for an alternative social and political project. These new authoritative voices were defined by their challenges to the traditional ulema, their uses of alternative means to disseminate their ideas (e.g., print media, information communication technology), and their abilities to use their secular education to reframe modern social categories for Muslim consumption. Modern teachers replaced traditional *hocalar* (religious teachers), and modern classrooms replaced *medresseler* (Islamic schools). Van Bruinssen (2002, vii) thus defines "Muslim intellectuals" as highly educated, devout opinion makers who "engage with the social and political realities of contemporary society and with the philosophical and moral implications of modernity." To some extent, Fethullah Gülen indeed fits this mold; however, his role in Turkish society far exceeds that of public opinion maker or framer of symbolic authority.

In internally produced accounts, Fethullah Gülen is presented as having memorized the Qur'an by age five, and as leading prayer early in his teens. In the introductory article to the July 2005 edition of the *Muslim World* journal, which was dedicated entirely to Fethullah Gülen and the GM, Zeki Sarıtoprak and Sydney Griffith (2005, 331) present Gülen not only as a master of Islamic knowledge, but also as someone who is "extremely knowledgeable about modern Western thought":

> In addition the ideas of early religious figures such as al-Hasan al-Basri (d. 728) and Harith al-Muhasibi (d. 857), al-Ghazzali (d. 1111), and Jalal al-Din al-Rumi (d. 1276), Gülen avidly read the more recent works of

two Indian writers, Ahmad Faruqui Sirhindi (1564–1624) and Shah Wali Allah al-Dihlawi (1703–1762), as well as some Western classics such as Victor Hugo, William Shakespeare, and Honoré de Balzac.

Gülen's exposure to both "Western" and "Eastern" classics is treated by his admirers as an indicator of his worldly vision, and as the seed from which his mission to cultivate intercultural dialogue blossoms into a global project (Ergene 2005, 2008; Hunt and Aslandogan 2007; Kuru 2003; Ünal 2005; Ünal and Williams 2000).

This developed as a topic of conversation one winter night during my fieldwork at the Akademi. Cold temperatures resulted in a regular Tuesday night *sohbet* (reading group) at the Akademi's library instead of at someone's home, as was typically the case. On that night we read the introductory article in the *Muslim World* journal cited above. The first discussion began after the group's *ağabey* (elder brother) read the line that listed Hugo, Shakespeare, and de Balzac alongside Basri, Ghazzali, and Rumi. A man at the table asked a question:

> William Shakespeare? William Shakespeare?! Why is he there? He does not belong there. William Shakespeare, he was a writer, so what?! What does he have to do with anything?" (Field Conversation, Winter 2006)

An argument erupted. Some regarded the usefulness of putting Shakespeare alongside such notable Islamic scholars. One younger participant highlighted that the article previously introduced Gülen as coming from a "*medrese* culture," and that by listing these authors, Shakespeare included, the author simply meant to introduce Gülen as "not a normal imam."

The critic at the table would not budge, indicating that he was neither impressed, nor did he think anyone should care that Gülen read Shakespeare. The next day, this man approached me to gauge my thoughts about the argument I witnessed. He asked if I understood the *sohbet*, and I responded that I did, most of it, and that I recorded it for future reference. I told him that according to my understanding, he was making a point that Shakespeare was a writer, and that familiarity with his work did not warrant prestige or admiration. He responded, "Kind of, but not exactly." He then asked me for a sheet of paper and scratched the following:

H.E. [Hocaefendi]
Buhari, Sukravandi, Gazali, Mevlana [Rumi]
→ Aquinas, Spinoza, Newton
Hadis ["Hadith, "Sayings of the Prophet"]
Tefsir [Qur'anic interpretation]
Tasawwuf [Sufism]
→ Science, Research, Philosophy
W. Shakespeare
Honoré de Balzac
→ ???
(Field Conversation, Winter 2006)

This informant was a visitor at Akademi, and was not a longtime follower of Fethullah Gülen. In his opinion, Shakespeare and de Balzac,
however great they were as writers, were neither scientists, nor philoso-
phers. They, therefore, could not be compared to Ghazzali, Buhari, or
Mevlana:

> If you want to make a comparison, you have to compare two like things.
> . . . This . . . author [Sarıtoprak and Griffith] made a grave mistake
> including the fact that Gülen was familiar with Shakespeare and de Bal-
> zac. I read de Balzac when I was a boy, so what?! You cannot compare an
> elephant to a fly! You have to compare and elephant to an elephant . . . a
> tiger to a tiger, and a fly to a fly. (Field Conversation, Winter 2006)

Gülen was exposed to a number of "Western" writers in his adult life;
but he was not educated in Turkey's secular education system, and he
was thus not exposed to natural or physical science, mathematics, or
"Western" political philosophy in any formal way. Unlike Hasan al-
Banna and Sayid Qutb in Egypt, Sayyid Abdul al'a Maududi in Pakistan, Ali Shariati in Iran, Rashid Ghannouchi in Tunisia, or Turkey's
Ali Bulaç, Fethullah Gülen did not receive formal schooling, he did
not earn an advanced degree, he was not well traveled before he began
his ministry, and he grew up far removed from the power centers of
postwar Turkey. Despite his lack of a "secular experience," however, he
built a following by applying the traditional mores of Islamic authority to modern notions of nationalism, reason, science, human rights,

and democracy. That is, he emerged as a leader by engaging in a project reminiscent of what Gramsci termed "articulation."

Articulation refers to the mechanisms by which social classes adapt and reform aspects of bourgeois ideology to express their own class-consciousness. Stuart Hall (1996, 141–142) elaborates as follows:

> Articulation is both a way of understanding how ideological elements come . . . to cohere together within a discourse, and a way of asking how they do or do not become articulated at specific conjunctures to certain political subjects. . . . [It] asks how an ideology discovers its subject rather than how the subject thinks the necessary and inevitable thoughts which belong to it; it enables us to think how an ideology empowers people . . . without reducing those forms of intelligibility to their socio-economic situation or class location or social position.

As argued by Eickelman (1999, 261), "Islamic scholars pride themselves on continuity with past commentary and the integral and authentic transmission of the ideas of the past." In this way, Gülen goes beyond merely emulating his predecessor, Said Nursi; he applies Nursi's world-view toward opportunity-driven activism. It is not enough to focus on one's personal development (greater *cihad*); he must also focus on developing his community, his nation, and his identity. *Aksiyon* (action) is thus the most crucial of all endeavors. According to Gülen, to be an *aksiyon insanı* (man of action) is the highest honor. His call for pious activism is attractive both to Anatolian youth who long for meaning and social mobility in a historically restrictive Turkish society, and to unaffiliated scholars and journalists who appreciate Gülen's efforts to offer a "third/middle way" for modern Muslim engagement.

Although Gülen sometimes comments on specific social and public happenings, the majority of his writings deal with matters of faith and spiritual tutelage. He thus blends the role of "intellectual" with that of *alim* (traditional scholar), *hoca* (traditional teacher), and *imam* (prayer leader). This makes Gülen a focal point of reverence for other opinion makers, who look to him for validation, guidance, and direction. When recognizable writers on the editorial pages of the GM's *Zaman* newspaper, for instance, comment on Turkey's changing relations with Russia, Iran, and Armenia; when they analyze the latest tensions between the governing AKP and their opposition, Turkey–IMF relations, Kurdish separatism, or U.S. presidential politics, they do so in the shadow of their *hocaefendi*. In many ways, Gülen has become an intellectual for intellectuals, a light from which others reflect—a charismatic authority for authorities.

From Organic Intellectual to Charismatic Leader

Unlike intellectuals, elected officials, and other people of social influence, charismatic authority figures exist amid instability, and are legitimized by performing superhuman acts that are viewed by their followers as proof of their proximity with the transcendent, however defined. Although crisis and instability may not always lead to the rise of a charismatic authority figure, such conditions tend to produce individuals who purport to "fix" a situation by applying their unique insight and otherworldly skills in ways that are directly observable for everyone to bear witness. In the absence of crisis, charismatic authority figures tend to create the illusion of crisis, or embellish on a universally recognized problem by overstating their position as the key to the problem's cessation:

> Some charismatic leaders are able to induce perceptions of crisis through their own actions by exaggerating existing deficiencies or threats to the environment. Through their visionary and framing activities, these leaders may draw attention to critical situations which followers were only dimly aware of at the outset. (Shamir and Howell 1999, 261)

Citing such an analysis as "reductive," GM loyalists react unfavorably to those who link Gülen's appeal to subjective feelings of helplessness, anxiety, and frustration. In an effort to head off these claims, a longtime student and admirer of Fethullah Gülen explained that in his analysis, "the Gülen movement did not rise upon the values of a past movement or period of crisis. The movement has produced its own appearance, structure, social and moral values, and institutions" (Ergene 2008, 40). It is thus of central importance for the GM's collective identity that the world understands Hocaefendi's appeal to be original to itself, and that the GM be presented neither as a mobilization based on a reaction to state suppression, nor as a continuation (or latest form) of a

call to education

long-standing social or political project (i.e., the Nur Movement). In an effort to present his leader as being both charismatic and intellectual, therefore, Ergene (2008, 40) insists that the GM both "originates from itself," *and* that it is entirely dependent on the guidance, insight, and unwavering grace of Fethullah Gülen:

> The social and action-related dynamics of the Gülen movement have been shaped around Gülen's strong spiritual character, his articulate teachings, and his broad sphere of social influence. That is what we mean when we say that "the movement originates from itself."

Notwithstanding, in Gülen's view a lack of education among Muslims explains why "the happiness of humanity has been delayed." He defines the present crisis as dominated by *cehalet* (ignorance; Arabic: *jahaliyyah*), which he regards "as the biggest problem of not only our country but also of contemporary modern civilization" (Ergene 2008, 127). As such, Gülen views humanity as having strayed from the righteous path of Islamic morality by forgetting the primacy of Qur'anic revelation and Prophetic example:

> When ignorance and unfed hearts and souls increase, materialism and carnality gradually subvert the desire for truth and annul any nobility of purpose. . . . Wholly addicted to triviality and self-indulgence, they will deny any achievement to our ancestors and remain willfully ignorant of what real culture and civilization can make possible. (Gülen 2000, 194)

To lead the world from these "darkest of nights," Gülen contends that humanity requires a new "golden generation" (*altın nasıl*) of "ideal humans" who will strive to emulate the perfection of the Prophet Muhammad as they seek to replicate the model of his initial community of Muslims in seventh-century Medina (Gülen 1998c, 205). The crisis that warrants the coming of the "golden generation" is defined by an absence of *irşad* (moral guidance), which Gülen presents as a necessary foundation on which to develop tolerance of others:

> Among the many things we have lost, perhaps the first and most important is tolerance. From this world we understand embracing people

educated + communally oriented

regardless of difference of opinion, worldview, ideology, ethnicity, or belief. It also means putting up with matters we do not like by finding strength in a deep conscience, faith and a generous heart or by strength of our emotions. (Gülen 2006, 46)

Cultivating the "golden generation" will require the loyalty and dedication of numerous "volunteers" who exercise *hoşgörü* (literally "nice-seeing," compassion) in all their human encounters. Embedded within this vision is evidence of Gülen's eschatology, as in his view, GM "volunteers" will constitute the front lines in the end of times:

> What we need now is not ordinary people, but rather people devoted to divine reality . . . people who by putting into practice their thoughts, lead first their own nation, and then all people, to enlightenment and to help them find God . . . dedicated spirits . . . who wander like *Israfil* . . . on the verge of blowing the last trumpet in order to prepare dead spirits for the Day of Resurrection. . . . This can be regarded as our final attempt, our advancing to our true position, as well as being seen as an alternative message of revitalization addressed to humanity. As a matter of fact, nations that have been wrung with various crises have also been awaiting such a breeze of hope. How fortunate are the blessed cadre to be the fuse to such an event. And, again, how fortunate are the ones whose breasts are receptive to this breeze. (Gülen 2004b, 105–110)

Sociologically, therefore, Gülen both invents and embellishes on the crisis he purports to address, and he offers a visionary prescription for the future. Unlike Gramsci's intellectual, however, Gülen does not need to prove his authority rationally through verifiable facts and supporting evidence. To the contrary, as a charismatic leader Gülen must prove himself by performing "miracles," or by some other "supernatural" feat. Weber classically explains as follows:

> The charismatic hero derives his authority . . . by proving his power in practice. . . . Most of all, his divine mission must prove itself by *bringing well being* to his faithful followers; if they do not fare well, he obviously is not the god-sent master. (Weber 1978 [1922], 1114)

Indeed, Gülen legitimizes his authority by overseeing the GM's expansion, which is viewed by his most devout followers as proof of his grace. His prescription for *aksiyon*, therefore, is first and foremost focused on the expansion of the movement, which is framed as service (*hizmet*) for the betterment of humanity. And because Gülen ambiguously frames his community's aims as being for the betterment of humanity, followers view themselves as participating in an altruistic project for human salvation. A loyal *hoca* (teacher) in the GM hierarchy explained as follows:

> HOCA: Look, do you know what geometric probability is?
> JH: What? Geometric probability?
> HOCA: Within science, I will tell you.
> JH: By all means.
> [He grabbed a pen and jotted down on a small notepad so I could see.]
> HOCA: One and one equals two, OK. Two times two is four. Four times four is sixteen. Sixteen times sixteen is two hundred fifty-six. Two hundred fifty-six times two hundred fifty-six . . . "
> JH: Ahh, it will continue and continue and continue. I understand.
> HOCA: OK, would you reach ten million by the time you arrive at the one hundred set? This concept [the GM] has won geometrically. This is a mathematical progression.
> JH: Right, and so this is what you meant, when you said at the beginning of our interview that ten years out, in Turkey, people are going to have to sympathize with this movement; it is because it will be so big?
> HOCA: Absolutely! Well, not so big, so true! (Field Interview, Summer 2007)

The Rational Application of Irrational Charisma

According to Weber, all charismatic leaders require a "social structure" of deeply loyal followers to constitute a tight knit cohort around the leader himself, and in doing so, assume a promotional role in regard to legitimating the leader's profundity:

> Charismatic authority does not imply an amorphous condition; it indicates rather a definite social structure with a staff and an apparatus of services and material means that is adapted to the mission of the leader.

The personal staff constitutes a charismatic aristocracy composed of a select group of adherents who are united by discipleship and loyalty and chosen according to personal charismatic qualification. (Weber 1978 [1922], 1119)

Gülen's most devoted followers were inspired by his writings and his sermons delivered in the 1970s and 1980s. Today, most of these individuals have become successful authors, journalists, editors, and businessmen. They sit at the top of the many organizations that link the GM in Turkey and around the world. In a particular region or country, the heads of all GM organizations and affiliated enterprises meet regularly to discuss the activities and successes of their sectors. While not a micromanager, Gülen does direct (through "advice" and "guidance") a small and loyal group of seniors to set the priorities of the movement's expansion:

He says, "It would be good if it is done," he never says, "It must be done . . . " For instance, he says, "In our age, media and television are of the utmost importance." Or he says, for example . . . "Why don't you open a bank?" [But] he never says "you" [meaning a specific person]. . . . The person addressed may say there is no money [for him to embark on such a venture]. But a businessman can do it. . . . [But] he might not have the money [either]. [Nonetheless] . . . if he [Gülen] says something, they believe that it is very important, and we have to do it. (Field Interview, Spring 2007)

While I was conducting fieldwork with senior and mid-level members of the GM's charismatic aristocracy in Istanbul, many would leave for two-week to one-month trips to the United States. They would return to show me pictures they took with Gülen, before they would go on to discuss their visits to Houston, Chicago, New York, and other cities to meet with other senior members in the GM network. I asked one of these men about his admiration for his *hocaefendi*. He explained, "Gülen . . . possesses powers that an average educated person, an average person with average intelligence, could not possibly imagine. It is God-given. . . . If you find a more learned person in the world I would like to meet him" (Field Interview, Summer 2007). Such sentiments emerged with thematic regularity. When asked why he went to the United States to visit Gülen, for instance, a senior-level administrator at Akademi responded with a question of his own: "Don't you miss your parents?" (Field Interview, Spring 2007). Taken together, this cadre of loyal, highly educated lieutenants comprise the GM's stratum of "most faithful," and thus exemplify the "social structure" that Weber cites as typical of a charismatic movement.

At different levels of association, the task of the GM's "organic Muslim intellectuals" is to publish articles and books on Said Nursi, Ottoman and Turkish history, and religion and society, and to write popular opinions in newspaper columns and in magazines, to go on television to debate current events, and to promote current agendas. In doing so, they legitimize the discourse and influence of Fethullah Gülen, and thus the authority and influence of the larger charismatic movement. Indeed, sentiments of Gülen's perfection were iterated in interviews with a number of senior individuals in the upper tier of the GM's organizational hierarchy. This sample comprised individuals who were among Gülen's first generation of students in the early 1970s. Many of these men (and they were all men) were authors and senior editors at the GM's Akademi in Istanbul. Others were directors at one of the many GM cultural foundations around the world, while still others were journalists or administrators at GM media and educational institutions. As seniors in the GM enterprise, they exuded more love and admiration for their *hocaefendi* than any of the followers I interviewed. Each claimed that the success of the schools and affiliated businesses was proof of Gülen's superior, "God-given" abilities.

According to one senior figure, Gülen was able to succeed in Turkey in the 1970s where other community leaders failed because of his astute foresight:

> Hocaefendi, as an opinion leader, has charisma in the eyes of society. He is a thinking person. He examined all the political, ideological, and religious movements in order to see what was done. He calculated the pros and cons of those movements, and he concluded that everything resulted in fights and ideological separation. . . . Hocaefendi is a wise person and felt responsibility for the nation. He felt the necessity to stop all of the fighting and quarrelling because so much energy was wasted on ideological fights. He concluded the only way to solve this was through education. (Field Interview, Winter 2007)

Another member of the GM's inner circle explained that Gülen's ability to inspire human beings was unrivaled in the world, and that his abilities to bring out the best in others was his greatest talent:

> After graduating from theology school, I became a student of Hocaefendi. People don't know Hocaefendi's mastership in Islamic knowledge. There are many sides of Hocaefendi that are not known by people. I can clearly state that I understood a religious text in three days with Hocaefendi. . . . At theology school, I studied this same text for five years. [With Hocaefendi] . . . we finished reading ten volumes of these sources [primary *hadith*] in only one month. (Field Interview, Spring 2007)

Yet another senior figure in the GM's inner cemaat claimed that skepticism arises precisely because people do not understand Gülen's profundity:

> Many people are suspicious. Are they right? Of course they are right. Because I was right ten years before I got to learn "the real McCoy" [Fethullah Gülen]. But I tell you 6.5 billion people are not going to have a chance to meet Hocaefendi. And 6.5 billion people do not have six advanced degrees . . . and they do not have certain capabilities, they do not have faith, and a knowledge of Islam to be able to make an effort to at least realize the depth of Hocaefendi. . . . So there will always be suspicion. (Field Interview, Summer 2007)

Although very few members of the GM's inner cemaat would freely admit it, there was a small handful who acknowledged, perhaps unintentionally, that there were certain benefits to "volunteering," and that their original motivations to participate were neither spiritual nor in the interests of cultivating dialogue.

Rationalizing Charisma

Osman Bey explained that his coming to the movement began in the mid-1970s when, at the ages of eleven and twelve, he attended "religious summer courses" in a central Anatolian village. Growing up in the countryside, Osman informed me that it was a "tradition in Turkey . . .

in the summer children go to Qur'an courses" (Field Interview, Winter 2007). Osman went on to explain that although his plan was to prepare for the examination to enter secondary school, his *hoca* at the summer course persuaded his father to send him to an *imam-hatip* (religious) school. The year 1974 saw the official revival of the *imam-hatip* system in Turkey, and Osman began his secondary education in his institution's inaugural year of 1976. He stayed there two years, but lived in a mixed dormitory that housed students from a number of schools in the region.

Osman recalled the social tension that dominated Turkey in the 1970s, and explained that although he was an imam-hatip student, he was not focused on his spiritual development, and was not very interested in a religious education. He said that it was not until the eighth grade, when a new math teacher arrived, that he had a "spiritual awakening." Interestingly, what led Osman to this teacher's influence was not an enlightened conversation about faith or the Prophet, but an effort on the part of his teacher to help Osman with his living situation:

> Although he [the new math teacher] was not a religious personality, he was a believer and was a likeable person. Also, he was caring for the problems of the students. He observed that imam-hatip students didn't have a separate dormitory and initiated a project to build one by calling for the help of the businessmen. . . . He succeeded and a new dorm was opened. It was a brand-new building and nearly seventy to eighty people stayed there. Everything was new. Our beds, our school material, our food was better than the previous. He gained our respect by leading such a project. Then we started to like him. That teacher was in the Gülen Movement. *Later, the director of the dormitory happened to be from the Gülen Movement. He* was a university student and it was his second year. (Field Interview, Winter 2007; emphasis added)

In 1978, Osman moved into a new dormitory, with new beds, new books, and state-of-the-art construction. The head of the dormitory "happened to be from the Gülen Movement." When he established a relationship with his new teacher and his new *ağabey* ("older brother," authority at the dorm), he explained that "the leftist students" led a nationwide university boycott. Turkish universities in the 1970s were

centers for left-versus-right political activity, and the Turkish left dominated university faculties at the time. Many in the GM now assert that
the original enemy against which the GM constructed its identity was
the Turkish left, whose fusion of Kemalism and Marxism was believed
to pose a genuine threat to Turkey's social and cultural fabric.

When the university boycott commenced, Osman's *ağabey* redirected
his energies toward recruiting the students in his dormitory. He started
to actively seek Osman's participation in *sohbet* (the GM's renovation
of the Nur *ders*), and formally introduced him to the cassette-recorded
teachings of Fethullah Gülen. Osman's *ağabey* then suggested that they
should all take a fieldtrip to Izmir to listen to Gülen in person. Osman
explained that his trip to Izmir in 1979 was "a life-changing experience." What solidified his entrance into the movement, however, was
not only the moving narrative of Gülen's sermon, but the community
that he observed. While his biographers and official handlers insist that
the GM attracts participation, praise, and sympathy because of Gülen's
God-given genius, for Osman, this was only half the equation:

> The cemaat [GM] was 80 percent young, dynamic university students.
> There was a great dynamism. It was the first time we saw him. We both
> listened to the preaching in Izmir and we also visited the places where
> students stayed. We saw what kind of people they were. We were influ-
> enced by two things. The first was the person of Hocaefendi, and the
> other thing was the people we saw in the houses of the movement,
> because they were pretty good models. I mean we found their lives to
> be very spiritual. They were very friendly, very spiritual, *the houses were*
> *rather modern . . . they were unmarried people, but the houses were very*
> *modern and . . . we were surprised. . . .* Then we moved on to high school.
> We were imam-hatip students and the natural outcome of such an edu-
> cation was to become an imam. We didn't dream of going to university.
> We didn't predict that we would have such an opportunity. One day that
> same math teacher said that it was time to get ready for the university
> exams. We replied that we couldn't go to university. We told him that
> only very clever people and the people from the big cities went to univer-
> sity. . . . That our capacity was not enough to do it. He replied, "You are
> the ones who will go to the university." *He said that we would do in-house*
> *training soon and use extra programs in order to prepare for university.*

He brought us university entrance documents. . . . I then observed that motivation was a very important matter. . . . *To my surprise I was the top-grade student at our school. . . .* Then I graduated from [a university] in Ankara. (Field Interview, Winter 2007; emphasis added)

Modern housing, free tutoring, and a focused and engaged mentor all contributed to Osman's entrance into the GM. His affiliation led to an opportunity to study for Turkey's university entrance exam, and ultimately to his attendance at a premiere Turkish university. His affiliation with the GM led Osman to become a teacher and principal at a number of GM schools in Tajikistan, to his employment at a GM company in Istanbul, and ultimately to his promotion at the Akademi.

The recounting of Osman's experience exemplifies the process of GM recruitment in general. Teachers court young, bright, and impressionable students across Anatolia and coach them through a social and professional network that has limitless possibilities. Over time, recruits come to realize that if they internalize the project's aims, if they grow to truly love Hocaefendi, and if they reciprocate the resources they receive (free tutoring, money donation, etc.), they will have a professional future. However "irrational" the charismatic authority of Fethullah Gülen, therefore, recruitment, participation, and support in the GM functions as a hyper-rational, individualized process of reciprocity and social mobility.

The Weight of Material Interests

Expansion, self-righteousness, and notable success led to the GM's opportunistic rationalization, which seemingly validates Weber's warning that "every charisma is on the road from a turbulently emotional life that knows no economic rationality to a slow death of suffocation under the weight of material interests" (1978 [1922], 1119). Indeed, the further one moves away from the center, the more one observes how rational and market-driven GM individuals and GM organizations have become. Gülen's writings have become products for sale in a global marketplace; schools inspired by his utterance have become market leaders in math and science education. The GM's affiliated newspaper has become Turkey's highest in circulation, its bank has risen to the top of its class, and associated companies have expanded their export capacity the world over. Moreover, Gülen's prestige has morphed into a specific form of Islam, "Anatolian Islam," which is viewed by its producers as "more modern," and more conducive to tolerance and dialogue than its Arab and Persian counterparts. According to an editor at the Akademi, "Islam in Arab culture is harder, less tolerant than Islam in Turkey" (Field Interview, Winter 2006). This same interviewee told me that he was happy to have contributed to sixteen of Gülen's works being trans- lated into Arabic because "Hocaefendi can bring Arab people an Islam that unites the heart and the mind" (Field Interview, Winter 2006).

By introducing the GM's proclivity for ambiguity as a mobilizing strategy, its relationship to the larger Nur tradition in Anatolia, and the emergence of Fethullah Gülen as a charismatic leader, it is important to emphasize that in the context of Turkey's late twentieth-century devel- opment, the GM did not emerge as a nationalist liberation organization as did Hamas in Palestine or Hezbollah in Lebanon. Unlike the Jamaat i-Islamiyya in Pakistan, the FIS (Islamic Salvation Front) in Algeria, or even the MGH in Turkey, the GM did not morph into a political party. To the contrary, in accordance with its Nur predecessors, the GM's methods of engagement were politically passive. Moving beyond their predecessors, however, GM aristocrats found ways to rationalize their leader's teachings by carving niches for themselves in Turkey's market economy, and eventually rose to the top of their sectors in education, media, trade, and finance.

4

Community

Extensive power refers to the ability to organize large numbers of people over far-flung territories in order to engage
in minimally stable cooperation. Intensive power refers to
the ability to organize tightly and command a high level of
mobilization or commitment from the participants.
—Michael Mann

The GM's reliance on social, financial, service, and ideational networks
constitutes connectivity in a complicated system of partial, fragmen-
tary, ambiguous relationships. Relying on maximum efficiency through
the "flexible production" of these networks, the GM cultivates collective
identity through extensive social ties, shared practice, and communal
loyalty on the one hand; and through market competition on the other.
The result is a graduated network of affiliation anchored on a hierarchi-
cally organized core community (*cemaat*), an expansive loose network
of devoted friends (*arkadaşlar*), and a third level of broadly defined
"sympathizers" (*yandaşlar*). A fourth, more removed level of connectivity exists in the form of consumers who, knowingly or unknowingly,
purchase GM products for no other reason than they are the best available in a competitive marketplace.

Relations of Community

In his internally produced analysis of the GM (i.e., an analysis published by a GM affiliated firm and written by a loyal follower), Ergene
(2005, 2008) explains that the GM is a "community" of loyal and

"self-sacrificing" individuals who harbor no political aspirations, and who seek only to foster tolerance and dialogue in an increasingly inter-connected world: "In their effort to broaden the horizon of social rela-tions, the general ideal of the Gülen movement is to serve the indi-vidual, society, and humanity" (Ergene 2008, 17). According to Gülen (2000, 83–84), *hizmet insanları* (people of service) "are so faithful to the cause to which they have devoted themselves that, deeply in love with it, they willingly sacrifice their lives and whatever they love for its sake." Devoted and loyal followers of Fethullah Gülen thus refer to themselves as *hizmet insanları*, and to the larger GM as "Hizmet."

Fethullah Gülen defines his objective as a project to cultivate a "golden generation" (*altın nasıl*) under the guidance of "selfless volun-teers" who constitute a twenty-first-century "army of light" of *hizmet insanları*. In accordance with the postulates of Islamic revivalism more generally, Gülen equates the significance and necessity of the coming generation with the first generation of Muslims that emerged follow-ing Muhammad's ministry in seventh-century Arabia (*al-salaf*). Using the past as a metaphor, however, should not cloud the fact that Gülen's vision is about the future:

> The world of the future will be so enlightened by their light that the moon and the sun will dim in comparison. . . . The world will be saved by that "golden" generation who represents the Divine Mercy, from all the disasters, intellectual, spiritual, social and political, with which it has long been afflicted. . . . O long awaited generation! Rise, for the love of the Creator, to your sacred task, and replace the choking darkness around us with the light of your love, hope, and nobility! (Gülen 1998c, 105, 107)

Although the language he uses is sourced in Islam, Gülen's teach-ings share ontological parallels with modern religious revivalism more broadly. The world community is depicted as being lost under poor leadership, and wallowing in immorality, materialism, and self-indulgence:

> Humankind has never been so wretched as it is today. . . . The table of art and literature is vandalized by drunks; thought is capital wasted in the hands of people suffering from intellectual poverty; science is a

plaything for materialism; and the products of science are tools used in the name of unbelief. (Gülen 1998c, 106)

The realization of the GM's idealized aim is the responsibility of dedicated "volunteers" who teach math and science at GISs, and who educate the whole of society through GM-affiliated media. Equipped with an understanding that revelation and science are parallel articulations of the same truth, GM teachers, administrators, journalists, editors, authors, and organizers are presented as exemplifying enlightened "ideal humans," "men of action" who selflessly dedicate themselves to the betterment of humanity.

In his study of the impact of GM-affiliated businessmen in Central Asia, Şen (2001) argues that what Gülen and his charismatic aristocrats designate "service to humanity" actually denotes blind obedience in the interests of collective power. Rather than acting in accordance with their own free will, Şen contends that GM loyalists exemplify a successful articulation of Foucaultian bio-power, and thus constitute a deeply loyal, militantly disciplined organization whose actors achieve their goals in accordance with a very specific sense of purpose, and a self-regulating sense of determination. He concludes that successfully socialized recruits in the GM "have not only learned the inner language, symbolic universe, short- and long-term goals and ideals of the community, but have also internalized perception, evaluation, and interpretation schemes dictated by the community through systemic mental, spiritual, and bodily practices" (124). In other words, according to an insider account (Ergene), the GM refers to a social project focused solely on cultivating love, devotion, and service to humanity. According to a critical account (Şen), the GM refers to a self-disciplined, militantly devoted fellowship of conditioned followers. By both accounts, the GM is viewed as a specific community with a specific worldview that engages in specific methods to achieve specific goals.

When analyzing community affiliation as it relates to a "cause" or "purpose" (be it activist, religious, or otherwise), one of two theoretical models is invoked to explain individual affiliation. The first is a "communitarian model," which assumes that participation is zero-sum between an individual and a collective. The salient sociological point is that individuals exist *for the community*, not vice versa; "communities only cohere . . .

when their members practice traditional obligations . . . [when they] . . . share a sense of producing their lives together, depending on one another as the bearers of ongoing traditions that pre-exist and will outlast any individual members" (Lichterman 1996, 10). Both accounts of the GM presented above exemplify a communitarian point of view, in that both view participation at the expense of individuality. The individual "sacrifices" a piece or all of his or her "self" for the purposes of group objectives, which are viewed in the interests of a larger whole (nation, society, humanity, etc.). It is common for both observers *and* followers of the GM to incorporate a communitarian view to explain the GM's organization in Turkey, be it positively or negatively assessed (Caha and Aras 2000; Balcı 2003; Çetinkaya 2007; Ergene 2005, 2008; Hunt and Aslandoğan 2007; Krespin, 2007, 2009; Park 2008, Rubin 2008; Sarıtoprak 2005; Schwartz 2008; Şen 2001; Turam 2004a, 2004b, 2006; Ünal and Williams 2000; Yavuz 1999, 2000, 2003a; Yavuz and Esposito 2003).

Communitarian theorists are right to observe that humans find identity by participating in groups that mobilize for specific purposes. There is no such thing as a "pure self" separate from a collective; all of us define ourselves, at least in part, in opposition to others. It is also the case, however, that group identity is more often than not ambiguous, as are group objectives. Moreover, debates and inconsistencies exist *within* groups, despite public stances to the contrary. If we employ a critical view of community identity, we can better explain how group dynamics change, how individuals within groups act as agents of change, and how goals, institutions, and notions of belonging adapt to changing conditions. Indeed, if we employ a more nuanced perspective to the ways in which individuals and groups interact, we can help to debunk the "individual versus community, public gratification versus private virtue, personal transformation versus political change" debate (Lichterman 1996, 21). The task of political ethnographers is thus to study commitment as it exists on the ground, to ask "how activists define 'commitment,' and what assumptions they must share in order to practice commitment together" (Lichterman 1996, 22; see also Eliasoph 1998; Wood 2002).

In this political ethnography, we are attempting to determine the ways in which "*hizmet* the ideal" measures up against "*hizmet* in practice." That is, how do individuals internalize GM identity, aims, and strategies and how do contradictions help us understand the process of community and its reproduction? When we observe critically, we can see that the GM is neither the total institution that its critics claim it to be, nor is it the altruistic ideal that Gülen's aristocrats would have the world believe. There are levels of affiliation; and although personal accounts and observed actions illustrate that a "total community" exists for a relatively small core, instrumental rationality explains the majority of motivations that inform GM activism.

A View from the Inside

The editors, writers, executives, and visiting students at the Akademi are representative of the GM's core community of hizmet insanları. While the cemaat also includes a number of administrators at GM schools, executives at closely affiliated companies, and directors at cultural and dialogue centers in Europe and the United States, the Akademi produces most of the discourse that is read and transmitted throughout the GM's transnational network, and it was there I spent the majority of my time conducting fieldwork in Turkey.

At that time, the Akademi represented the GM's central ideational node. Although Gülen continuously wrote short essays in Pennsylvania, those writings were routinely sent via e-mail to GM brothers at the Akademi for editing, translation, and publication. Moreover, all of Gülen's previous publications in Turkish were translated and edited there, and this was also where about a dozen in-house writers and commentators (as well as dozens more commissioned authors) published hundreds of titles that were all dedicated to Islam, Sufism, Ottoman history, youth-focused religious and cultural education, and tourism/travel. Two of the GM's four primary periodicals, Yağmur ("Rain," a literary-themed periodical) and The Fountain (an English language science and faith periodical) were also published in-house. At the time (2006–2007), Sızıntı ("Trickle," the GM's first periodical publication) and another periodical, Yeni Ümit ("New Hope"), were both published by Akademi subsidiaries in Izmir. Since their initial publications, both Sızıntı (est. 1979) and The Fountain (est. 1993) have led off every issue with a short essay authored by Fethullah Gülen.

Seniors at the Akademi constituted a sample of Gülen's most loyal first-generation students. Most had offices on the second floor (of four), and most were internally referred to as the *hocalar* (intellectuals/teachers). Also on the second floor were a small number of classrooms where visiting students met for lecture and study. On the top floor were a large prayer room that doubled as a conference center, a small collection of offices, and a large conference room with a stunning view of the Bosphorus. During the daily call to prayer (three to four times during an 8:30 a.m. to 7:00 p.m. workday, depending on the season), employees congregated on the top floor for prayer. The management and executive staff offices, as well as the offices and departments of foreign editions, *The Fountain*, and *Yağmur*, were all on the third floor. At that time, most editors, translators, and managers at the Akademi were all former teachers at GISs in Central Asia, the Balkans, Russia, and Southeast Asia, or former journalists or staffers from GM-affiliated media.

The Akademi was part of a larger complex adjacent to a mosque, courtyard, school, and boarding center. Upon entering, employees and visitors first observed a display case featuring the Akademi's latest publications under twenty-eight affiliated labels. Next to the front door was a display case that showed off news clippings from GM-affiliated media sources that featured/promoted one or another Akademi-affiliated publication. As an institution, the Akademi had transformed since its construction in the mid-1980s from a religious congregation center to a business-oriented publishing house. In 2007, the corridors and offices on the main floor, as well as the basement cafeteria, were all surfaced with marble tile flooring. Cafeteria and canteen food was provided by a subsidiary of the larger holding company to which the Akademi was affiliated. On the main floor were the offices for Internet publications, graphics, and sales, as well as the canteen. Also on the main floor was the library, which was adorned not with tile, but with soft red carpet (the removal of one's shoes was required before entering). Similarly, the upper three floors were also all surfaced with soft red carpet, as they were, like the library, considered places where dust and filth from outside was to be kept to a minimum. On each of the above three floors, the walls were adorned with very large painted likenesses of turn-of-the-century photographs taken of Mecca and Medina. If not a place of worship, the Akademi was certainly constructed as a place where pious Muslims would feel at ease.[1]

GM and the Akademi publications experienced a boom in the late 1990s and early 2000s. In 2003, foreign editions were consolidated under one roof. English, Arabic, Spanish, and Russian texts were translated, edited, and published on-site. The protocol for foreign language publications was that they were first translated into English and then into a third language. When translation could not occur in-house (e.g., as with Korean, German, and French), the project was outsourced. During the time of my fieldwork, one non-Muslim native Spanish speaker and one Muslim native Russian speaker worked at the Akademi as recruited sympathizers (*yandaşlar*) on the holding company's payroll. All other editors were longtime, loyal followers of Fethullah Gülen who had all previously worked at one or more other GM institutions. Benefactors in the GM's affiliated business community were regular visitors, coming and going to speak with different hocalar, and to participate in sohbetler. Students from theology faculties from schools around the country also spent time in the Akademi's library. For the men who worked there, the Akademi was considered a place of privilege that accorded them with rank and social prestige within the cemaat.

Of the nearly one hundred employees at Akademi, nearly all were male. While in residence, I observed four female employees; three worked in children's publishing and one worked in the kitchen. The latter was actually employed by an affiliated catering company (Bereket Yemeği) and not by the publishing house. I interviewed one former female employee at the Akademi, an older woman named Tuğba who worked in children's publishing but who left her job due to a private conflict with another employee. She explained her experience working at the Akademi as an intellectually rewarding time that came to end for personal reasons. Concerning my observations about the uneven gender dynamic I observed at the Akademi, Tuğba commented as follows:

> I did not know whether it was a general problem, but I had this idea that [the bosses] could not manage to work with women. Well, it is not like "women should not be allowed to work." It is not logical, as many women work in every department of other [GM] institutions. . . . The situation is true only for Akademi, and I don't know why. (Field Interview, Summer 2007)

Although gender relations in the GM are essential to understanding the GM's internal power dynamics, it was not a specific topic of my research, so I restrict myself from commenting further. See Turam (2006) and Özdalga (2003) for further discussions of gender dynamics in the GM.

Applied Sufism

On one winter evening, a senior hoca gave a *ders* (lecture) on Sufism to younger editors and translators. The hoca focused his lesson entirely on one concept, *Marifet* (Knowledge of God; Arabic: *Ma'rifa*). Sixteen adults (excluding myself) and a small child attended the lesson, which took place in the library at the Akademi. At the table were fourteen men and their hoca. Separated by a fold-up partition were a young woman and her child, who were both visiting the Akademi to participate in the ders by listening from behind a curtain. Neither asked questions nor joined in the discussion. The lesson lasted seventy-two minutes, which included a ten-minute break for tea and *börek* (savory noodle pudding). It began with a group prayer at the front of the library, and was followed by an interactive seminar. Everyone had his own personal copy of Gülen's analysis of Sufism (*Kalbin Zümrüt Tepeleri*, "Emerald Hills of the Heart"), as this was one lecture in a series provided to employees at the Akademi.

The hoca opened by stating that *Marifet* was among the most central concepts in Islam, and was key to understanding what Gülen meant when he wrote about a hizmet insanı. The hoca explained that Sufi vocabulary helped to describe the full meaning of the human condition, and argued that a literal interpretation of revelation was "weak" in regard to applying oneself toward the betterment of humanity. During a break, the hoca engaged me directly to impress on me the difficulty involved in understanding Sufi concepts:

> In America, you study for three or four years and you get your doctorate. This is much harder. There, the terminology is obvious. Not so in Sufism. Sufism has a very rich terminology, and may be new and unfamiliar for a lot of people. This requires explanation. It cannot be understood easily or by oneself. You need to go deeper into the terminology. (Field Notes/ Direct Conversation, Fall 2006)

When the group convened again, the hoca pointed to Gülen's use of "modern analogy" to explain "the first rank of *Marifet.*" He quoted Gülen as follows:

> The tongue becomes, so to speak, a diskette of good words, and various lights form the light-giving truth of: "Unto Him good words ascend, and the righteous deed causes them to rise" (35:10) begin to be reflected on the screen of his or her conscience. (Read by the hoca to the group, from Gülen 2004b, 146)

In so doing, the hoca reiterated the GM objective to help Turkish Muslims cultivate wisdom of the heart alongside wisdom of the mind so as to unite scientific knowledge with spiritual knowledge.

In this ders, the hoca emphasized a reoccurring theme in Gülen's teachings. According to Gülen, Muslims (in Turkey and in the world) have forgotten the divine inspiration behind human knowledge. This led to a long period of estrangement and to a sociological state of ignorance (*cehalet*; Arabic: *jahaliyyah*) in regard to divine truth. Because Islam represents the human acknowledgement of Divine Oneness (*Tawhid*), to prefer profane knowledge (i.e., positivist science) over spiritual knowledge rejects Divine Truth, and thus rejects one's very humanity:

> Since "real" life is possible only through knowledge, those who neglect learning and teaching are considered "dead" even though they are still alive. . . . Science and knowledge should seek to uncover the nature of men and women and the mysteries of creation. (Gülen 1999, 42–43)

Building on the teachings of Said Nursi, the hoca explained that Gülen teaches *Marifet* as a "skill" and a "talent" that refers to one's "special ability" to realize his true self as reflecting humanity in total, which collectively reflects God in unison. In his writings, Gülen explains that the "ideal human" focuses on his heart (*kalp*; Arabic: *qalb*) to cultivate his innate ability for *Marifet* with an objective to eventually become an *'arif* (one who has knowledge of God):

> One who has acquired such *Ma'rifa* is immune to all evil and in enveloped by breezes blowing from the realms beyond. Corridors of light are

opened from his or her spirit toward the One known by the heart. . . . So long as they keep their eyes fixed on the doors of Truth, they are intoxicated by meeting him several times a day or even every hour, an are enraptured with a new manifestation at every moment. (Gülen 2004b, 146–148)

Gülen's focus on *Marifet*, in addition to three volumes dedicated to his understanding of Sufism, on the one hand, underscores the GM's ideational roots in Islamic mysticism. On the other hand, however, Gülen's focus on certain aspects of Sufi teachings (e.g., *Marifet*) at the expense of universal Sufi traditions (e.g., *dhikr*, vocal/instrumental/ meditative remembrance on God) and organizational strategies (e.g., orders, lodges), indicate that the GM is not a Sufi order in the classical sense of the term. Indeed, critics of the GM in Turkey often point to the GM's employment of Sufi vocabulary to insist that the GM is a Sufi order (*tarikat*), and that it is therefore an illegal institution (Sufi lodges were outlawed, with few exceptions, by the CHP regime in the 1920s). Equally, non-Turkish sympathizers (*yandaşlar*), who are typically non-Muslim as well, often refer to Gülen as a modern Sufi master (Michel 2005), as a "modern-day Rumi" (Eustis 2006; Michel 2007), or to his movement as some kind of "neo-Sufi" brotherhood (Gökçek 2005; Kim 2008; Michel 2005; Sarıtoprak 2003). None of these characterizations is accurate.

This is because the GM is not a *tarikat* nor is Gülen a Sufi. *Tarikatlar* are specific institutions that have specific histories rooted in the transmission of specific knowledge from masters to disciples. They also engage is specific practices dedicated to "remembering God" at every moment (*dhikr*), which function as physical and spiritual rituals used to embody a particular tradition of knowledge. Sufism connotes a spiritual tradition toward realizing (1) that every moment is a moment of theophany, a moment of God, and (2) that everyone has the ability within themselves to realize that moment. When Gülen employs Sufi categories to describe the goals and intentions of his community, this does not indicate that either he or his followers are representative of Anatolian Sufism. It does, however, indicate that Anatolian Sufism resonates with Turkish culture and that symbolic concepts can be applied to serve a variety of purposes. What should be observed and analyzed, therefore, are the strategies by which Gülen picks and chooses from a variety of Sufi-oriented categories to orient his community's objectives—objectives that he very clearly stipulates are *not spiritual*, not focused on "the other world":

> The field of our struggle for the inheritors of the Earth can be summarized as "action and thought." . . . Action is the most necessary component of our lives. . . . *Remaining aloof from action, not interfering in the things happening around us, not being part of the events around use and staying indifferent to them, is like letting ourselves melt away, like ice turning into water.* . . . Those who desire to remain true to themselves should really seek their essence with all their wishes, desires, hearts, conscience, behavior, deeds, and thoughts. . . . Existence and its maintenance demand from humans the action of our arms, limbs, heart, and head. (Gülen 2006, 59–60; emphasis added)

Sufism represents a form of spiritual alchemy, a "science for the cure of the ailments of the soul, for unifying the knots that entangle the soul and prevent it from becoming wed to the Spirit" (Nasr 1997, xxi). Gülen's emphasis on "action" in this world in accordance with "things happening around us" is a precisely *non-Sufi* prescription for human life. This is because it is *this world* that produces those "ailments that entangle the soul and prevent it from becoming wed to the Spirit." Unlike Sufis, hizmet insanları (GM loyalists) are concerned with this world, here and now.

Considering the "this-worldly focus" of the GM's Islamic ethic, it is inaccurate to refer to the GM as a Sufi order, or to Gülen himself as a Sufi sheikh. When I presented this dilemma to Mesut hoca, a resident author at the Akademi, he explained the GM's relationship to Sufism as follows:

> It can be said that there is a sort of rituality in Bediüzzaman [Said Nursi] and Fethullah Gülen but not mysticism. These are different things. Sufism and spirituality are different things. . . . There are many different elements and they are explained in Fethullah Hocaefendi's books. However, the existence of these elements does not render this movement Sufi. Fethullah Gülen has a side consisting more of spirituality. We can talk of

a mystical approach in the general understanding of Islam but it cannot be regarded as mysticism. We should differentiate between a mystical approach and being a mystic. (Field Interview, Spring 2007)

Savaş hoca, another resident author at the Akademi, explained the same distinction in more detail by hinting at the fact that Fethullah Gülen, and Said Nursi before him, attempts to "update" Islam in accordance with the dictates of modern life, and to instill an action-orientation to the essence of Muslim sensibility:

Spirituality is important in Islam. This began as an internally focused religious tradition in the past. It was against the outside world, against expanding. There was a refusal to expand. Then it changed in *tarikatlar*. In a *tarikat* [Sufi order], there is a Sheikh at the top and *murıds* [disciples] around him. He is the spiritual leader. He is the discipliner of the *murıds*. The Nur Movement is not a *tarikat* in the classical sense; Hocaefendi's movement is not a *tarikat*. But *tasavvuf* [Sufism] and spirituality are present to the same degree as in any *tarikat*. Spirituality is in the Qur'an itself, in Muhammad's life. It is only the technical organization of the *tarikat*. *Tasavvuf* is different. *Tarikat* is different. (Field Interview, Winter 2007)

The GM's employment of mystical, otherworldly categories to explain an otherwise-this-worldly orientation should be viewed as a form of applied Sufism. But unlike a Sufi sheikh, Gülen is not restricted to a specific lineage of scholarship or heritage of lived Islam. He is free to develop a composite of concepts and practices that speak to his own variation of the modern Muslim experience. Such an experience, according to Gülen, is not meant for aestheticism or contemplation; it is meant for action (*aksiyon*). Understood in this way, Fethullah Gülen comes into perspective as a charismatic leader who has cultivated a sense of spiritual obligation toward a this-worldly (i.e., secular) project. This is why leaders in the GM refer to themselves being part of a "movement." It is because their efforts are focused on fulfilling objectives in the social and material world of human society. For loyalists, "ideal humans" are not to focus solely on realizing God at every moment; they are to focus on realizing the goals of the movement at every moment, which, incidentally, are viewed as one and the same vis-à-vis the work of God:

Those who seek to enlighten others, seek happiness from them, and extend a helping hand have such a developed and enlightened spirit that they are like guardian angels. They struggle with the disasters befalling society, stand up to "storms," hurry to put out "fire," and are always on the alert for possible shocks. (Gülen 1999, 85)

Gülen does not seek to continue the tradition of Anatolian Naqşibandi, Mevleviye, or Rıfa'iya Sufism, nor does he ask his followers to focus their intellectual faculties on their efforts to annihilate the self (*fana*) into the Oneness of all things (*Tawhid*). His objective is to cultivate *action-oriented people of service* who dedicate their personal and professional lives toward the realization of a better future. This project is best fulfilled, in Gülen's teachings, by participating in the expansion of the Gülen Movement itself.

The Ambiguous Reality of a "Lofty Ideal"

Gülen frames his call to action as a call for "self-sacrifice." "Ideal humans" walk with the "consciousness of God" in an effort raise the "golden generation." Those who join them are purported to join a cadre of selfless "soldiers" who labor for all of humanity:

The person of thought and action moves actively while making plans; they are deeply concerned with bringing peace to the world, and representing the movement of raising once again the statues of our soul and meaning. . . . They are spiritual soldiers of Truth who, instead of conquering countries and winning victory after victory . . . train the general staff of the soul, the architects of thought, and the workers of new ideas; they always beam out thoughts about construction and lead their disciples to restore the ruins; they are the spiritual soldiers enthused with zeal and thankfulness who have been able to unite their will with the Infinite Will. (Gülen 2006, 67)

Those who seek to unite their personal will with God's "Infinite Will" view their secular education at school and their professional life at the office as seamlessly connected to their personal anthropology as subjects of God. Moreover, despite the fact that one might (and should) form social relationships outside his religious life, the majority of his existence should be perceived as fulfilling a religious objective. Weber meets Islam.

According to Gülen, the "unenlightened" denotes a spatially and psychologically removed individual who lacks a spiritual education, and who lets his secular education inform his social, private, and professional life. In Gülen's view, therefore, schools, businesses, cultural centers, and media initiated by his "army of light" represent a "movement" of social power that acts in the service (hizmet) of the Almighty for the sake of humanity. GISs, together with GM-affiliated media and business/trade institutions, function collectively as the "barracks" within which a "cavalry of light" creates a new world:

> The roses blooming all over the world today take on their hue from the enlightened faces and the comprehension in the spirits of these people, the social geography is being embroidered with their thinking and it is as if all of humanity is humming these ageless melodies. . . . As is required by the task itself, this cavalry of the light . . . is now competing, in the same way that rain clouds pour down on us bliss, joy, love, and hope, to turn those dry hearts that crave tolerance and love into the gardens of Paradise. . . . They take such great pains to succeed in worldly affairs that people who see these valiant ones take them to be people of the world unaware of the Hereafter. (Gülen 2004a, 106)

The GM's primary stated objective, therefore, is to educate for the good of the nation, society, and humanity. This is God's work. In many ways, this worldview offers an Islamic alternative to laic Kemalism without negating Turkish national identity. Thus, depending on one's political persuasion, the GM project might be viewed as either worthy or threatening, righteous or manipulative. To some, it might even come across as authoritarian:

> You have these things that kind of trigger your fears, and you know . . . things like "ideal humans" and "the golden generation" . . . you know, it sort of triggers visions of the Nazi youth and, you know, this kind of thing . . . for me. For me! So I just had this kind of [gasp] . . . what are they? . . . By being involved, and having contact, I sort of held my breath

and continued thinking, "Well, I haven't actually seen anything that supports that" . . . I mean, I read it and I think, [squeezed face, shrug and wince] . . . "Panic panic." But . . . I eventually realized that it was just my interpretation. (Field Interview, February 2007)[2]

Regardless of how they interpret GM aims or objectives, the majority of sympathetic *and* critical journalists, scholars, and politicians, *as well as many GM loyalists,* view the GM as a community marked by a clear "inside" and "outside," and as "ideal" (*mafkura*) organization with determined and righteous goals:

> If a movement has started to produce its own models, and people have started to admire it, following in its steps, and devoting themselves to this cause, making it their ideal, or if they have accepted it as *mafkura* (lofty ideal), in the words of Ziya Gölkalp, then the person who seems to be at the front of this movement would not even be aware of what is happening most of the time. People would do similar things here and there, even if they didn't know anything about each other, because they don't have any organic connection and because they have not been introduced to each other. But they are connected together by the bonds of a very serious thought and a lofty ideal. (Gülen 2005a, in an interview with Mehmet Gündem)

Upon closer scrutiny, the GM comes into focus neither as being clear with its objectives, nor uniform in its views. Indeed, rather than the "lofty ideal" that Gülen claims his movement to be, on the ground the GM comes into focus as a fluid and adapting organization of autonomous actors and institutions. Although managed in accordance with the same ethos, and although linked via extensive social and market ties, most GM institutions have the capacity (flexibility) to adapt to local contexts as conditions necessitate. Private GISs, for instance, might appeal to a Turkish expatriate community in the United States, Denmark, or Holland, or to a diverse upper class in Russia, Turkmenistan, Kenya, or Thailand. On the individual level, the GM *might* serve one's spiritual inclinations to better humanity, but it might also provide an avenue for social mobility, for a university education, for world travel, or for a sustainable income. To view the GM as a specific community of selflessly dedicated individuals takes both Gülen and his critics at their word. By contrast, paralleling Max Weber's notion of "elective affinity" concerning the ways in which European Protestantism linked with a European logic of capitalist accumulation, the motivations of GM followers must be understood as both spiritual and rational (Weber 2002 [1905]). That is to say, different people participate in the GM for different reasons. Why one stays or leaves may have less to do with the needs of the community than it does with the opportunistic drive of the individual. It is thus grossly simplistic to assume either that GM followers are blinded by a totalizing worldview (i.e., that they signify "cultlike" behavior), or that they act selflessly without any expectation of return. Despite the spiritual inclinations observable in his teachings, self-expression, instrumental rationality, and social mobility *also* play a role in one's subjective motivation to participate. Moreover, although Gülen's influence over his core community might be strong, his influence over the whole of the GM network is rather weak. It is this weakness, however, that provides the GM as a whole with its source of *extensive* collective power.

Social Capital and the Power of an Ambiguous Network

The GM mobilizes in accordance with an ambiguous prescription for action, which allows its followers to consistently redefine their identity to meet new challenges. For instance, according to Gülen it is essential for an ideal human to be clear about his aims and intentions:

> Founders and directors of all institutions, large and small, should often remind themselves of the purpose and reason for their existence, so their work does not stray from its objective, but remains fruitful. If they do not, the homes, hostels, schools, and other institutes, the purpose of whose foundation has been forgotten, work to their own loss on line against themselves—just like a person who forgets the purpose of his creation. (Gülen 1998a, 77)

Despite this, when school principals in foreign countries are asked about their affiliation with Fethullah Gülen, they are often quick to deny association. On no school's website will one find an introduction to Fethullah Gülen, his teachings, or his movement. When asked directly, at best one is likely to hear, "Many people here are inspired by the teachings of Mr. Gülen, but there is no organic connection" (Field Interview, Fall 2010). When the directors of "dialogue" institutions in the United States are asked about the political implications of their efforts to lobby specific members of the U.S. Congress about their support for the Armenian genocide legislation, they explain that when they do so, they are acting on their own behalf, and "not on behalf of the movement" (Field Notes, Summer 2008). When they are asked why they focus on cultivating the support of influential academics, political leaders, and religious leaders, a typical response includes the words "dialogue" and "peace."

Considering the GM's "nonpolitical" self-identification, it is not surprising that its actors refuse to acknowledge the political implications of their influence-peddling. Nonetheless, despite the curiously frequent editorials in GM-affiliated media by authors who preemptively defend GM activities as transparent, modest, and humble, it is clear that much of the community's internal culture is defined by a focused effort to downplay connectivity between people and institutions, and to monopolize public discourse about GM objectives.

When I asked a hoca at the Akademi about the connections that exist between schools, companies, media, and "dialogue institutes" around the world, he offered a verbatim answer that I heard throughout the GM network: "There is no organic connection between these institutions" (Field Interview, Fall 2006). The ubiquity of this phrase led me to understand that by stating this, GM loyalists were protecting themselves. On the one hand, total information about the structure and movement of people, resources, and intent is restricted to a very small number of directors and executives at varying institutions (i.e., the third function of strategic ambiguity). On the other hand, the majority of people in the GM share information horizontally "with the right hand unaware of the left at any particular time" (Field Interview, Fall 2006). What denials of affiliation communicate, therefore, is, "Who are you?" "Why are you asking these questions?" "For whom are you working?" Maintaining ambiguity is a strategy consciously employed to ward off perceived enemies, and to re-create identity as necessary.

Indeed, advocacy networks take advantage of social, financial, technological, and political connections to mobilize for social change. They constitute themselves both as "structures"—that is, as legally defined, organizationally bounded institutions linked by a common identity and shared purpose—*and* as "agents"—that is, actors in their own right that affect society in such a way that is greater than the sum of actors who constitute its parts (Keck and Sikkink 1998, 5). In order to perform as collective agents, advocacy networks need to reproduce a "structural connection" between institutions and individuals, which refers to the relationships cultivated between actors in a network that serve as start-up investments for the generation of social and cultural capital (Bourdieu 1990; Lin 1999; Passy 2003). Social capital, in this context, refers to "resources embedded in a social structure, which are accessed and/or mobilized in purposive actions" (Lin 1999, 35). Social capital is measured by the surplus available to individual actors in the network, the level of access to those resources, and the strategic use of those resources once accessed. When social, professional, informational, and financial networks collectively mobilize to express a single identity or to articulate collective intent, the possibility to affect social change grows exponentially:

> Networks . . . represent the dynamic aspect of the factors of power. They transmit resources, threats and opportunities, as well as public culture, and a set of norms that may differ from the private cultures held by individuals. They require rethinking of our static organizational ideas of movement, state, and other "entities." (Broadbent 2003, 205)

At which level an individual articulates with the GM's "lofty ideal" is determined by his willingness and desire to "plug in" to the larger GM network. But how do Gülen's teachings materialize into a structurally ambiguous, "nonorganic" composition of social, financial, and ideational networks to begin with? They do so by taking advantage of strong and weak social ties, instrumental outsourcing, and discursive flexibility.

For instance, the GM recruits and establishes belonging via two primary organizational strategies. The first, via schools and student dormitories/apartments (*ışık evleri*, "houses of light"), is institutional. The second, via *sohbetler* (conversation/reading circles), is ritualistic. Moreover, despite the popular inclination by both supporters and critics to insist on the GM's communitarian qualities, both of these strategies resonate differently in diverse settings. The closer an individual acts in accordance with the "lofty ideal," the more likely he is to identify as a hizmet insanı, and the more likely he is, in turn, to find employment with a GM-affiliated company, to travel the world within the GM's transnational network, and to eventually absorb the teachings of Fethullah Gülen. By contrast, the more an individual interprets or manipulates the "ideal" for instrumental reasons, the further away from the core cemaat that individual is likely to be, and the less likely he is to act in accordance with Gülen's notion of "ideal humanity."

Reproducing Community I: Inculcating the "Golden Generation"

The original GM institution in Izmir, the Akyazılı Foundation for Middle and Higher Education (Akyazılı Orta ve Yüksek Eğitim Vakfı, AOYEV), was founded in 1976. AOYEV now represents a central node in the GM's national education network. The use of "foundation" further illustrates the GM's use of ambiguous categories, as AOYEV coordinates the activities of several *for-profit* GM institutions. Its institutional members include the oldest and most prestigious of the GM's educational companies, Yamanlar College in Izmir, Fatih College in Istanbul, and Nilüfer College in Bursa, as well as FEM Dershanesi in Istanbul, Nil Dershanesi in Erzurum, and Korfez Dershanesi in Izmir, to name only a few. AOYEV also coordinates the management of approximately forty official GM dormitories (*yurtlar*) around the country. Although hundreds of other schools, *dershaneler*, and dormitories operate independently of one another, the AOYEV provides a useful piece of data to observe the dialectical tendency to organize, coordinate, and administer connectivity, even when decentralization continues to be the norm.

Although GM-affiliated dormitories under the AOYEV umbrella are officially registered with the Turkish Milli Eğitim Bakanlığı (Ministry of Education, MEB), and can house up to forty or fifty students, GM *ışık evleri* are student apartments lived in by five to seven university students and owned by semi-autonomous actors who constitute the GM's underwriting sector, and who form the bulk of the once-removed *arkadaşlar* (friends) level of GM affiliation. Funds for board come from a combination of modest fees collected from students themselves, and from sympathetic neighborhood *arkadaşlar* who are solicited by an *ağabey* (older brother), to donate *himmet* (religious donation). The money collected from students varies; some pay nothing, others pay as much as two hundred U.S. dollars a month (Field Interviews, Fall 2006, Winter–Summer 2007). In all cases, however, rent and board are either heavily or totally subsidized by GM neighborhood *arkadaşlar.*

Both *ışık evleri* and official dormitories are organized in accordance with an age- and experience-defined system of authority, which begins with an internal authority figure, a male *ağabey* ("older brother," informal = *abi*; female = *abla*) in each student apartment. The *ağabey*'s (or *abi*'s) job is to manage the affairs of students, to monitor study habits, to recommend reading material, to organize reading groups, to administer tutoring sessions for visiting high school students, and to function as liaisons between the house and the larger GM network. A house *abi* meets regularly with his neighborhood *abi*, who, in turn, meets regularly with a district *abi*, and so forth in a loosely configured hierarchy of authority that eventually reaches a central node such as AOYEV:

> There are regions. For instance, there are six houses in Taksim. These six houses have an *abi* over them. Each house has an *abi*, and there's another over these six. And every neighborhood has an *abi*. And there's an abi of Istanbul. It's the same in Ankara and for the others [cities]. There's a Mediterranean region *abi*, an Eastern region *abi*, and a Turkey *abi*. If someone continues his *namaz* [prayer] for a year, the *abi* of that house tells him to be an imam. If he continues for two to three years more, he is promoted. You always get promoted if you continue. There is a system like this. (Field Interview, Winter 2007)

According to Gülen's ideal, *ışık evleri* are at once student apartments, recruitment tools, and social conditioning facilities—incubators for the GM's "golden generation":

> The lighthouses are places where deficiencies of people that may have been caused by their human characteristics are closed up. They are sacred places where plans and projects are produced, the continuality of the metaphysical tension is provided and courageous and faithful

persons are raised. . . . Here these soldiers of spirituality and truth raised in lighthouses will pour the light God has given them for inspiration onto empty minds and help them flourish on the way to the conquest of the world in spirit and reality. These houses are one workbench, one school, where *saboluncu* [emulators of alien culture] generations who shape themselves without a way, without a method and according to different charm centers, are flourished and [where] the return back to the roots of spirit and meaning are provided. (Gülen 1998b, 12, quoted in Şen 2001, 111–112)

According to Gülen, houses of light are necessary to remove potential participants in "the happy future" from the evils of the present, "greed, infatuations, needs, and fantasies" (Gülen 1998c, 29). Only in a house of light can a young mind learn to filter out the corrupt influences of modern life, while continuing to focus his energies on worldly and spiritual studies.

Selim, an editor at the Akademi who was recruited into the GM while attending university before living for a number of years in Albania where he worked at several GISs, explained the function of the house of light as follows:

An *ışık evi*, what I understand . . . ahhhh . . . is . . . Well, let's say a group of university students come together, stay together . . . they have the same opinion, Hocaefendi's and Said Nursi's opinions . . . you call it an *ışık ev*. In such a place, for example, naturally, you don't watch everything on TV, like you know, obscene things . . . or maybe you don't have a television at all . . . you have, let's say ahhhhh . . . parallel opinions with your friends, you pray, nobody drinks . . . For example, when you compare it to a traditional, common house or apartment where students live . . . not our people . . . ahhhhh . . . outside Hizmet . . . well, they bring in their girlfriends, they watch pornographic movies, sometimes they have alcohol. Then you compare such things . . . in one of them you pray, and you know, you read such books of Said Nursi and Hocaefendi . . . you pray . . . there is some spiritual pride. I don't know where the word comes from, for instance, why *ışık ev* and not something else, but . . . I will say that, for example . . . when you compare the two, there is be a clear difference. (Field Interview, Winter 2007)

Both core followers and critics of the GM describe *ışık evleri* from a traditional communitarian perspective. They are framed as spaces where individuals are "protected" from the corrupt world "outside," or where they are "brainwashed" in accordance with the dictates of Fethullah Gülen.

In her study of the GM in Turkey and in Kazakhstan, however, Turam (2006, 79–83) provides a detailed account of a scandal that erupted in 1998 following the publication of *Hoca Efendi'nin Okulları* (*Hocaefendi's Schools*), a polemical publication that claimed GISs, and GM-affiliated dormitories and student apartments, were centers of brainwashing and insurrectionary mobilization. Turam illustrates how students become pawns in a larger contest between competing notions of "secularism" and "piety." Without becoming enmeshed in the debate herself, Turam explains that although "brainwashing" constitutes a loaded and tautological attack on the GM, there is no doubt that *ışık evleri* are where the GM recruits new youth, and where it initiates a process of welcoming them into the movement (Turam 2006, 63). My own research both confirms and expands on Turam's findings. While she is somewhat hesitant to explain it, Turam begins to emphasize that despite Gülen's "lofty ideal," "students from different backgrounds attend Gülen schools for different reasons." She continues: "Attractive for parents are high standards for safety, morality, cleanliness; the use of technology; the high quality of teaching; and the availability of guidance." Where Turam stops short is to explain why students (not their parents) are attracted to the schools. I argue that just as is the case with parents, for some students, attending GM schools abroad or living in GM *ışık evleri* at home might be viewed as a rational way to increase one's life chances in an increasingly competitive market society.

When explaining why he went to the prestigious GM-affiliated Fatih College for his high school education, for instance, an Akademi editor named Ferhat explained that although he wanted to attend school there, he had problems once he learned how much it would cost:

I told my father, "We should not be going there," you know, "This is too expensive." And I knew they could not afford it for my older brother. He had to attend a normal public school. So perhaps I thought he was going to be jealous of me. I told my father, "I should not be going there."

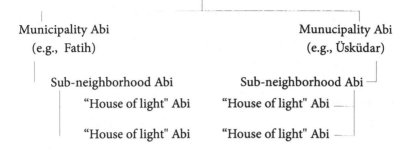

Hocaeffendi Fethullah Gülen in USA

Hoca in Istanbul
(i.e., authority at a central GM institution Akademi, GYV, etc.)

Municipality Abi   Munucipality Abi
(e.g., Fatih)   (e.g., Üsküdar)

Sub-neighborhood Abi   Sub-neighborhood Abi
"House of light" Abi   "House of light" Abi
"House of light" Abi   "House of light" Abi

The *Ağabey* network of authority.

But he insisted, and he was a very hardworking person anyway, and he paid for school. But I knew it was a kind of, ohm, ahhhh, you know . . . not religious I should say, but ahhhh, run by, or owned by pious people. But you, know, I was just eleven or twelve then. (Field Interview, Winter 2007)

Ferhat's family was not religious. His father rarely prayed or attended Friday prayer. His uncle "drank a lot," and his siblings were nominally Muslim but nonpracticing. Ferhat's mother, however, was a devout woman. She taught him how to pray, and one of his fondest memories as a child was waking in the middle of the night to find his mother praying by the filtered light of the bathroom. While not a practicing Muslim before entering high school, Ferhat recollects that he "had an affinity for pious people." Nonetheless, when Ferhat was deciding between high schools in the mid-1980s, he had no idea that Fatih College was connected to a larger religious community.

Ferhat explained that he wanted to attend Fatih College because he wanted to join his friend from secondary school, and because he knew he could because his ÖKS (High School Entrance Exam, see below) scores were high. Ferhat did not learn about Fatih College's connection to the GM until his sophomore year when he first heard Fethullah

Gülen on cassette, and when a friend showed him a video of one of Gülen's sermons. Later that year, Ferhat asked his parents if he could attend a live sermon, and they insistently forbade him from doing so:

> FERHAT: I asked my parents once; they would not allow me to go. Because they did not want us to know about it. But it was just very, you know . . . [pause] . . . Just before I was about to graduate, a year before that I heard that their was such a person who was behind Fatih College . . . and the network of schools . . . who inspired teachers, people to start such schools . . . ahhhh [pause] . . . and I think it was the first time when I watched a sermon on the video . . . yes, ahhhh, tenth grade, yes.
>
> JH: And so your parents were unaware that Fatih College was . . .
>
> FERHAT: [interrupting] Well I later realized . . . our relatives, my uncle, ahh, for instance . . . had criticized them a lot . . . had scolded my parents a lot because they were sending me to Fatih College . . . But I think that it was not until ninety-three, ninety-four . . . until Hocae-fendi appeared himself on TV, that people had suspicions about those schools, I assume. (Field Interview, Winter 2007)

Not only did Ferhat not go to Fatih College because of its relationship with the GM, his parents were deeply skeptical about that relation-ship before sending him. He was forbidden to listen to Gülen's audio-cassettes or to attend his live sermons. Ferhat is now a senior editor at the Akademi, and a well-respected ağabey in the GM hierarchy. It is interesting in this regard to note that originally it was *despite* Fethullah Gülen that Ferhat attended a GM institution. He went to Fatih because (1) he wanted to attend high school alongside his best friend, and (2) because he wanted to attend the best school he could. His admiration for Hocaefendi came later.

Ferhat was among the top students in his class at Fatih College and was among the entire city of Istanbul's top-scoring students on his senior year's university entrance exam. He attended Bogaziçi (Bospho-rus) University, thinking that he was going to "follow his dreams" by majoring in business administration. When it was time to study for the university entrance exam, however, Ferhat's teachers at Fatih College directed him and his friends to attend FEM Dershanesi, which was at that time a four-year-old GM-affiliated university entrance exam preparatory institution. It was at FEM where Ferhat met his mentor and ağabey, Sayid, who facilitated his entrance into the GM, and on whom he modeled his professional career:

FERHAT: Sayid came from the U.S. . . . . Sayid was like an idol for me, you
    know. [From him] we learned English properly. At grade eight and
    nine, he attended our class . . . and he was such a different person.
    Ahhhh, even my father always remembers him with great memories.
    He had this appeal, I cannot explain it. I mean, every one of our
    teachers were different. They were not typical street layman. They
    were all different. But Sayid, for me, was like an idol. I think I even
    tried to make my speech like him, I tried to walk like him . . . I tried
    to dress like him . . . and I later realized that many of my friends also
    tried to do the same in a way [laugh] . . . And he said, "Ahh, look.
    You know, so many schools are being opened, and they will need
    really qualified English teachers."

JH: In what year was that?

FERHAT: Ninety-three. January of ninety-three. And he said, "Lots and
    lots of publications will come out . . . we need to have really qualified translators. Ahhh, so, ahh, I recommend that you attend English
    languages, a foreign languages department at whatever university
    you want to go. Ahh, going into a business administration, management . . . you could do certain things for your own good. But, ohm,
    if you could be a really good teacher, or a good translator, then this
    could really could be a good service," he said. You know, that was a
    very hard moment for me. I know I cried a lot for this. And I, ahh,
    changed my mind, and I changed my department and I said that I
    am going to take the English exam. (Field Interview, Winter 2007)

On the "advice" of his ağabey, Ferhat majored in English and became a translator. In so doing, he found postgraduate employment before he ever began university. Why did Ferhat relinquish his dreams to follow his abi's advice? He did so, he explains, because the GM is about self-sacrifice, it is about hizmet to one's community and to one's nation. How forgoing one's dreams for the continued growth and influence of religiously identified advocacy community provides a "service" for anything beyond the interests of that community is a matter of personal opinion. But it is important to note that despite his "sacrifice," Ferhat found guaranteed employment, advanced rapidly through the hierarchy of the GM network, and is now recognized as an ağabey to dozens of administrative professionals, computer scientists, salespeople, and others, whose respect he has as a result of his position at the Akademi:

> From business administration . . . for me it was like giving up an entire idea . . . and entire personal individual life, career, for myself . . . and I said, "Alright." And even before the day I took the exam, the night before, I called him [Sayid], he was in the States. I asked him, "To which schools, to which departments should I apply?" And he said, "Well, as long as it has something to do with languages, linguistics, you can select any one." And I said, "Should I write this and that too?" and he said, "Alright." [laugh] . . . And al-Hamdillah . . . I managed to get into Bosphorus University. And this actually made my entire life more beautiful. I should confess that. I think it was a very important cornerstone in my life, having decided that. Perhaps that was the moment when I felt that I was kind of, that I was a member of a bigger group, a bigger . . . you know . . . I have my own family, and I will run my own business. But making that decision at the university entrance, I think I felt part of a bigger, ahhhh, service [hizmet]. (Field Interview, Winter 2007)

After opening GM schools in the United States, Ferhat's mentor, Sayid moved to the Australia where he is now a senior-level operative in the GM's public relations network, and an affiliate faculty member in the social sciences at a regional Australian university.

Both Ferhat and Sayid are representative of individuals in the GM's central cemaat. Ferhat's recollection of forgoing his dreams to study business at the request of his abi exemplifies the level of social conditioning that is both praised and feared in regard to living in a GM "house of light." It also represents the communitarian aspects of the cemaat, the inner space where loyalists are asked to sacrifice their individualism for the betterment of the group. Ferhat's personal success as a writer and editor, however, not to mention his position of hierarchy and prestige as a senior employee at the Akademi, should not go unnoticed.

That is, Ferhat received a great deal of reward for his "sacrifice," not the least of which was a highly subsidized lifestyle for him and his family. Indeed, Ferhat did not become active in the GM, nor did he come to admire Fethullah Gülen, until *after* his abi guaranteed him a professional position before he entered university.

Reproducing Community II: The Social Capital of Applied Sufism

In every city in Turkey, the GM network of authority manages vacancies at affiliated institutions. As Feza Bey at the Akademi explained, loyal followers at the cemaat level are recruited to work at different institutions according to their needs:

> Perhaps you know, at every city where there is the community, there is someone who deals with coordination. . . . If there is going to be someone hired for the paper, for instance, or for a dorm . . . we can say that it is similar to the head of Human Resources in that city. He coordinates how many people are going to be hired. *We can say that it is our human resources.* That is how it is. How many people graduated that year? Let's say twenty-five people. If you apply to work in Kayseri, how many vacant posts are there? There is *Zaman*, [other companies], and there are dormitories. He is the representative of Human Resources. He makes an interview . . . talk[s] with related people, inform[s] them that there is such an applicant, and ask[s] whether the applicant would be suitable for the job." (Field Interview, Summer 2007; emphasis added)

In a competitive economy in a developing country like Turkey, the rational choice to participate in the GM cemaat makes sense in terms of taking advantages of social networks, embedded resources, and professional opportunities. While there is no denying the devotion of core followers, thousands of individuals in Turkey and around the world take advantage of GM opportunities as a matter of rational choice.

Selçuk, the aforementioned young man who now works at an unaffiliated Turkish marketing firm, but who spent a year before high school and a year before university at a GM ışık evi to receive free tutoring for school entrance exams, recollected always being asked to participate in *sohbet*. Traditionally, *sohbet* refers to the conversation had between a Sufi guide and his disciple. Nasr (1997, 3) explains as follows:

> During the first four to five centuries of Islam, Sufi instruction was transmitted by an individual master around whom disciples would gather. Gradually the downward flow of time and further removal of the Muslim community from the source of the revelation necessitated a more tightly knit organization revolving once again are the master (called *shaykh*, *pir*, or *murshid*), and usually named after the master, but based on a definite set of rules or etiquette and behavior, litanies, forms of meditation, etc.

The term used to connote the oral transmission of knowledge from *shaykh* to disciple is *sohbet*. In the GM, *sohbetler* function as venues for transmitting the teachings of Said Nursi and Fethullah Gülen not orally, but through text. Further, I attended *sohbetler* where an abi read from academic journals, others where he read from newspapers, and others where he read from Nursi, Gülen, and from other GM-affiliated *hocalar* (teachers). The centrality of "traditional knowledge" in GM *sohbetleri* has given way to a tradition of community assimilation and intra-community communication.

Indeed, all closely affiliated GM companies employ "spiritual coordinators" whose job is to organize sohbetler within the company and in nearby neighborhoods. These people also tend to be those who collect money from employees and who organize fund-raising for larger donations (see below). Reading Nursi and Gülen, therefore, is by no means the only activity at a GM sohbet. Sohbetler are also used for fund-raising, organizational planning, and social networking. Expanding on the Nur practice to meet in regular reading groups (dershane), GM sohbetler reproduce an alternative public sphere that links individuals in Istanbul and London, Baku and Bangkok, New York and New Delhi, Buenos Aires and Timbuktu in a shared ritual of reading, socializing, money transfer, and communication exchange.

One of the primary mechanisms GM actors employ to distinguish themselves from the Nur, therefore, is to employ the Sufi category of sohbet in place of ders, which discursively bypasses Said Nursi by tracing the sohbet tradition back to the Prophet Muhammad:

Sohbet is a part of this culture because it has a central and forming place in the history of Islam, in Islamic societies, Islamic culture, and generally in Islamic civilization. And it is a cordial and direct way of communication and transfer. . . . There's a very important point here. Any person who studies Hocaefendi should pay careful attention to sohbet. The fact that sohbet comes from a tradition must be necessarily emphasized. . . . You cannot build something from the platform of sohbet in any other society, because this is a 1,500-year-old tradition. This must be absolutely emphasized. One must not start talking directly about the cemaat [Gülen movement] and the participants of sohbet. The central position of sohbet in the history of Islam and its importance in Islamic culture should be highlighted first. (Field Interview, February 2007)

Hocalar at the Akademi often asked their support staff to organize sohbetler for Akademi employees. Editors and foreign language translators, in turn, led sohbetler for employees in other affiliated companies, or for employees at the nearby Bank Asya, or for institutionally unaffiliated "friends" (arkadaşlar) that included GM benefactors from the business sector. I often attended sohbetler on-site at the Akademi and at people's homes. In both settings, sohbetler were segregated by gender: seven to ten men would congregate at a host's house while his wife (and sometimes his daughter) would remain in the kitchen to prepare dinner. She came out neither to serve nor to participate in the discussion. The sohbetler I attended were men's clubs, and for most of those with whom I related, it was a practice that began while living in an ışık evi during university.

Unlike the Nur ders, GM sohbetleri form not only face to face at ışık evleri and at personal residences and businesses, but also online in chat rooms, on Listservs, via instant messaging groups, and through podcasts. Moreover, participating in sohbet has benefits. Individuals can link up with a globally extensive social network that can provide opportunities, resources, and connections, all of which can serve a variety of purposes. Selçuk's early experience at the ışık evi and his participation in sohbetler, for instance, led to a "substantial discount" when he decided to attend a GM-affiliated exam prep course two years later, which echoed a reoccurring trend I observed through the GM network. Passively, and with great care, among an ağabey's tasks at an ışık evi was to recruit new GM activists by offering them tutoring services, and in so doing, to facilitate that student's initial participation in sohbet. After studying for a few months, and after participating in sohbet from time to time, a high school student would move on to take his university placement exam. When he scored well, teachers from his preparatory school would contact him to inquire about his living arrangements upon entering university. Freshmen students received an offer to stay in a dorm or smaller apartment, and upon moving in, they were asked whether or not they were interested in offering free tutoring to younger high school–aged students, and whether or not they would like to participate in a regular sohbet (Field Interviews, February–July 2007). If a student participated, then as he progressed through school, he was opened up the possibility of becoming an ağabey and to organize these activities for the group. Rather than a job, serving as an ağabey was framed as a sacrifice. Metin, an executive in GM media, explained as follows:

> JH: So you do not get paid . . . it is not a job?
> METIN: No, as I said, it is a responsibility and a sacrifice.
> JH: And what do you sacrifice exactly, your time?
> METIN: Of course. Your time, your energy . . . I mean. You should organize things. You should help if there is something wrong with any of your friends. And there are other functions in the house. Students are visiting, the neighbors, they send their children to have a kind of support for their education at high school . . . or even at the university. So you sometimes, you give . . . ahh . . . lectures . . . not lectures maybe, but some courses.
> JH: And did you organize sohbetler in the house?
> METIN: Of course. For students, and some people are working . . . for workers, or shopkeepers . . . they can visit you. You are supposed to talk to them, serve to them, help them. (Field Interview, Spring 2007)

Although describing Gülen's ideal, Metin's recollection of an abi's responsibilities to manage students at ışık evleri and to organize sohbetler is not necessarily typical of all GM affiliates. Yusuf, a GIS student from Baku, explained as follows:

There are some students who use the movement for their own benefit. They try to appear better to their eyes. They are not the way they seem to be. They claim to be good people. I do not know, maybe they have some plans for the future. After graduation, if you ask for a job, Hizmet [the GM] offers you one. (Field Interview, Spring 2007)

This trend of rational opportunism emerged with thematic regularity. Bilal, a former university student at the GM-affiliated Fatih University, told me about a phone call he received after he graduated from high school. A teacher at Fatih University informed his brothers in the network about Bilal's foreign language skills. With no experience and with barely an interview, Bilal was offered a job at the Akademi in translation. Despite attending Fatih University for four years, Bilal had always found Gülen's writings to be "boring" and "not for him." He had friends "in the community," but he never lived in a GM ışık evi and he rarely attended sohbet. Bilal went to Fatih University for reasons that had nothing to do with Fethullah Gülen, but he explained that when he was offered a job in translation, he "had to read in order to translate. And I loved my job. I wanted to have this job especially. I had many foreign friends . . . it was good practice for me." After two years, Bilal realized that despite his passion for language, his calling lied elsewhere: "Translation is not a kind of work that suits my personality. I have a hyperactive character; I prefer to socialize" (Field Interview, Summer 2007). He left the Akademi to work at an unaffiliated firm, and has since not participated in a GM sohbet.

Another interesting case I observed was Lale, a master's student at a prestigious private university in Istanbul, who explained that she accepted an offer to live a GM ışık evi because dorms were expensive and overcrowded. Lale then said that she had friends who left school because they went into debt, and she was scared of a similar fate, "so I took their offer and I moved to the house [ışık evi]." For three years, Lale lived in a subsidized rental that was close to campus and "worth the sacrifice" (Field Interview, Summer 2007). Lale described her two-year experience with the GM as "a really really prolonged visit." She said that living there was "good for [her], actually." She was never lonely, she liked that everyone shared everything, that everyone always went places together, and that people were always over, visiting, participating in reading groups, receiving tutoring, and so forth. Lale then contradicted herself saying that having people over all the time really bothered her:

> There was one time when I did not sleep for over a week, but it was my own psychology . . . When they talk about 'self-sacrifice,' this is what they mean . . . college students give free tutoring to *dershane* students, people go out of their way to help others when it inconveniences them. I was the only person who had a problem with everyone coming and going all the time. (Field Interview, Summer 2007)

Lale never tutored a younger student when she lived at the ışık evi, and in three years there, she participated in sohbet on only one occasion.

Although not totally dedicated, Yusef was socialized into the GM network as a "friend" (arkadaş). Bilal was self-described as a sympathizer (yandaş). Lale cut her ties almost completely when she decided to live with "non-Hizmet friends." By contrast, Ferhat and Metin were "ideal" students, and both have since become well-respected professionals in the GM network. Despite their differences, however, their varied career histories all illustrate that in a regulated and focused way, GM actors seek to condition the personal lives of individuals. They also illustrate that when it comes to participation, potential recruits are neither coerced nor "brainwashed." Rather, they are socialized in accordance Gülen's "lofty ideal," but are free to stay or leave, as they desire. But whatever they decide, the "service" (hizmet) provided to them cannot be overemphasized. In other words, an individual's choice to participate in the GM is an outcome neither of brainwashing, nor of Gülen's enlightened teachings; it is a rationally weighed choice on the part of young actors in a competitive market economy.

Graduated Affiliation

At the inner core of the GM is the cemaat, the level of community where Gülen's first- and second-generation aristocrats exemplify the "lofty ideal" of total devotion. At the second level of arkadaşlar (friends), individuals are recruited via a loosely regulated system of social and economic networking in education, media, trade, and civil/social dialogue. This large stratum of partially connected, partially dedicated individuals donate regularly to the movement, agree with its objectives, and look on their professional and personal lives as at least somewhat institutionally connected to the GM. At a third, more removed, level are the yandaşlar (sympathizers), individuals who may or may not donate to the movement, and who rarely participate in organized practices (sohbet, tutoring, etc.). At the same time, however, yandaşlar view GM activities in a positive light.

Organized by core members in the cemaat, GM efforts to recruit yandaşlar began in the 1990s, and expanded abroad soon thereafter. Outside Turkey, these efforts focus primarily in western Europe, the United States, and Australia, where GM actors target influential people in academia, politics, faith communities, and journalism to promote GM successes around the world. When its schools outperform, when its print news is well respected, and when its trade federation increases Turkey's integration with foreign markets, the GM attracts praise from yandaşlar who are called on to defend or to promote GM activities as necessary, worthy, and commendable.

Beyond yandaşlar, the largest and most fragile composition of GM affiliation is the unaffiliated/unaware consumer. She may enroll her child in a GM-affiliated charter school in the United States, but she may have never heard of Fethullah Gülen. She may be a student of the Turkish language at Stanford who uses Dilset Turkish textbooks, but she likely has no idea that Dilset is produced by a GM-affiliated firm. Or maybe she is an importer in Thailand whose employer recently signed a long-term deal with a GM-affiliated exporter from Turkey, but has no idea about that company's social ties to the GM-affiliated trade federation that facilitated the deal's fruition. The unaware consumer may know little of Fethullah Gülen, but he supports the GM just the same. Beginning in Turkey, the GM now constitutes a transnational network whose actors organize with tremendous flexibility, and whose institutions rely on an ambiguous organization of graduated affiliation. What affects one sector may have little effect on another; what social critiques one school, dialogue institution, newspaper, or

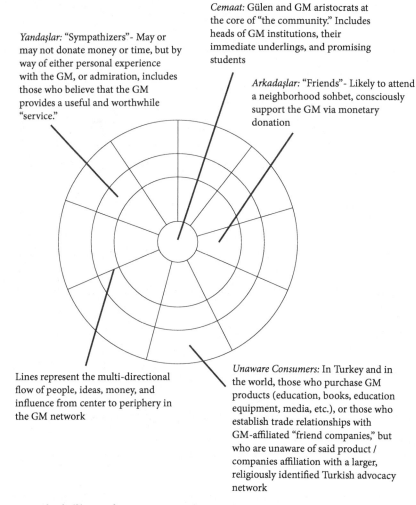

Yandaşlar: "Sympathizers"- May or may not donate money or time, but by way of either personal experience with the GM, or admiration, includes those who believe that the GM provides a useful and worthwhile "service."

Cemaat: Gülen and GM aristocrats at the core of "the community." Includes heads of GM institutions, their immediate underlings, and promising students

Arkadaşlar: "Friends"- Likely to attend a neighborhood sohbet, consciously support the GM via monetary donation

Lines represent the multi-directional flow of people, ideas, money, and influence from center to periphery in the GM network

Unaware Consumers: In Turkey and in the world, those who purchase GM products (education, books, education equipment, media, etc.), or those who establish trade relationships with GM-affiliated "friend companies," but who are unaware of said product / companies affiliation with a larger, religiously identified Turkish advocacy network

Network of affiliation from core to periphery in the GM.

construction firm may weather in Moscow, Amsterdam, or Houston will likely have little impact on the ability of other institutions to continue about their business. Beginning with education in Turkey, the GM network expands globally. But how did its organization begin? How did the charisma and community of Fethullah Gülen become institutionalized as the most influential collective actor in Turkey's expanding market society?

5

Education

If we are able to implant in the young firm belief, pure and
sound thoughts, a strong feeling of love of nation and country; if we enable them to come together around a sacred
cause to which they should be made to dedicate themselves;
if we bring them to prefer such values as honor and dignity
over passing pleasures; and if we inculcate in them the duty
of loyalty to the country and working for its good . . . then
the young will maintain their essential identity against mental and spiritual corruption.
—M. Fethullah Gülen

Although constituting a growing faith community in the 1970s, the
GM's institutional mobilization could not have expanded were it not
for deeply penetrating transformations that ensued in the aftermath of
the 1980–1983 junta. As noted previously, Turkey's turn toward liberalization and market competition in this period was a necessary pre-
condition for the GM's shift from a modestly sized faith community
to a transnationally active and powerful advocacy community. Indeed,
during this period, the state's monopoly over the hearts and minds of
Turkey's youth eroded, and new actors emerged to compete for youth
attention. The GM excelled in this competition by mastering the Turkish education system and the opportunities presented therein. GM followers built private for-profit schools that filled a market demand for
high-quality, low-student-to-teacher-ratio science and math education.
They built student dormitories and bought student-intended apartments to re-create the sense of community that first developed in the
late 1960s. Offering an alternative form of Turkish nationalism to Turkish and global consumers, education became the key sector in the GM's
transnational advocacy campaign.

Context: The Kemalist Youth Project

In 1924, Mustafa Kemal's CHP regime abolished the Ottoman Caliphate, and in accordance with the Unification of Education Law No. 430,
consolidated all educational institutions (except Istanbul University)
under the authority of the Ministry of Education (Güvenç 1998, 2:4).
Also in 1924, the U.S. scholar of pedagogy John Dewey was invited to
Turkey to consult on the implementation of a new, "modern" education
system. Dewey's opinion was that a country's education system created
the conditions for a cohesive social order, and that teachers were central in the project to develop a modern democratic society. In Dewey's
view, "The most urgent problem of Turkey was teachers and their situations" (Ata 2000, 124). Dewey validated Kemal's belief that Turkey
lacked an effective stratum of educators who could facilitate the emergence of a modern Turkish society. According to Şimşek and Yildirm
(2004, 155), Kemal believed that "the Turkish nation won the war on
the battleground but the job would not be complete unless the army of
teachers and educators would win another victory over ignorance and
the enslavement of minds." The early regime subsequently began one
of the most successful education reforms in modern history. By 1927,
"youth and education" became synonymous with "nation and prosperity" (Akinoğlu 2008; Güvenç 1998; Şimşek and Yildirim 2004; World
Bank 2005a, 2005b).

In 1927, Kemal delivered his famous Nutuk before the Turkish Grand
National Assembly. He ended his thirty-six-hour oration with a "message to Turkey's youth," within which he proclaimed his reasoning
behind the education reform and underlined why he thought education was central to the Turkish national project. This message was later
engraved next to Kemal's tomb, and Turkish school children since have
memorized his words in an effort to link their individual experience
with the larger narrative of the Turkish nation. Kemal read his message
as follows:

> Turkish youth! Your very first duty is to protect and defend eternally the
> Turkish independence and the Turkish Republic. The sole foundation of
> your being and future is this. This foundation is your most valuable trea-
> sure. Even in the future, you will have enemies, internal and external,

who will want to deprive you of this treasure. If one day you find yourself forced into the position to defending the independence and the republic, in order to take up duty at once, you should not think about the contingencies and the constraints of the situation in which you find yourself.

These contingencies and constraints may manifest themselves in very inconvenient ways. The enemies who will have designs against your independence and republic might be the representatives of a victory never seen before in the world. By force and intrigue, all the fortresses of the dear country may have been captured, all the shipyards penetrated, all the armies dispersed, and every corner of the country actually taken over.

Even sadder and graver than all these conditions, with the country, those who are in power might be inept or astray or even traitorous. Furthermore, those in power might unite their personal interests with the political aims of the invaders. The nation might be desolate and exhausted in destitution.

Harken, children of the future. So even under such conditions and situations your duty is: to rescue Turkish independence and the republic. The power you need is present in the noble blood in your veins. (Quoted in Parla and Davidson 2004, 205)

The protection of the Turkish state, of Turkish society in general, was placed on the shoulders of the "Turkish youth," to the "children of the future," to whom their national patriarch proclaimed to speak eternally.

Kemal's message focused less on those listening to his words, than it did on Turkey's future populations. It was their responsibility to uphold the sanctity and sovereignty of the Republic. Since the Nutuk's first utterance, Turkey's youth has been "devoted to preserving the result of his [Kemal's] energies." The effective result is that, to one degree or another, youth in Turkish society is "his youth . . . their upbringing in their formative years will be shaped and constituted following his lead. They shall forever be his offspring" (Parla and Davidson 2004, 207). The sociological impact of this technology of national identity is that regardless of one's social class, religious persuasion, or regional heritage, and regardless of one's acceptance of Kemalist notions of Turkish laiklik, youth populations are inculcated at a very young age with the notion that their nation's prosperity is their responsibility, and that their success in life will be the success of their nation. The "pedagogical state" in Turkey "links didactic methods with monologic themes to demarcate clear-cut definitions of citizenry and classificatory boundaries between state and society with which each child will identify during and after her formal schooling" (Kaplan 2006, 219). Education in Turkey is more than a right of national citizenship; it is a national duty and a sign of national loyalty.

Turkey's national focus on education, therefore, is both similar to and different from other newly industrializing countries. It is similar in that all modern states develop centralized education systems to meet the demands of educating a national citizenry. Moreover, all states infuse centralized education curriculums with an undertone of nationalist sentiment. It is different, however, because in Turkey, to be "educated" means that one is a participant in Kemal's youth project, which is a project for national protection and national development. In Kemalist Turkey, to be a citizen is to be a secular-minded patriot and a protector of Kemal's legacy. Indeed, although they do not represent a voting constituency, over the course of its twentieth century Turkey's youth became the most politically charged stratum of Turkish society, and thus the primary target for influence in Turkish political culture.

Teaching Nationalism

A Gramscian view of national education asserts that it is in school where subjects become citizens, because it is there where individuals appropriate the imaginary of the nation as constitutive of their identity:

> The individual consciousness of the overwhelming majority of children reflects social and cultural relations that are different from and antagonistic to those which are represented in the school curricula: thus the "certain" of an advanced culture becomes "true" in the framework of fossilized and anachronistic culture. (Gramsci 1971, 35)

Gramsci continues to explain that the teacher's role is to bridge the narrative of culture and society learned in the curriculum with the culture and society lived by the individual. Considering that these two experiences with culture and society meet in tension, children must unlearn their particular experience of family and community in order to become part of the universal, national experience.

In Turkey, Kaplan (2006) explains that equally important to Gramsci is the work of Foucault, whose notion of "discourse" is useful for understanding the ways in which "regimes of truth" create boundaries for the construction of human knowledge. "Discourse," in this sense, refers to the ensemble of ideas that constitute subjects through "practices" and "technologies" that have effects on the bodies and minds of conscious humans. When applied to the education of a national citizenry, a Foucaultian lens assists the cultural observer as he struggles to understand how a population internalizes "universal" truths, and how power effectively enters the consciousness of individuals by creating the categories of knowledge that are used to define the world and one's place within it. While citing both Gramsci and Foucault as crucial to understand the educational development of Turkish national subjects, Kaplan (2006, 19–24) also credits the work of Stuart Hall, who focuses on how the individual receiver of education negotiates a discourse and internalizes its "truth" subjectively, and often under protest. In regard to education, both Gramsci and Foucault assume that power and knowledge are infused into educational curricula (ideologically and discursively), and are transmitted in one direction with no agency on the part of the receiving student to interpret the information she receives. Hall points out that students are not blind receivers, and that ideologies and technologies of power are negotiated in the psyches of receiving subjects. Contrary to the national project, family, tribal, regional, and other communal orientations remain strong, and are not wholly supplanted by nationalist loyalties. Rather, they are fused with nationalism so that what emerges is a society of competing and often contradictory nationalist sentiments.

In order to understand the development of nation and identity in the Turkish context, it is necessary to fuse all three perspectives to account for universal unevenness of individual exposure to "a wide variety of sociological languages: the language of secular positivism [Kemalism], the language of Islamic eschatology, the language of the market, the language of the army, the language of newspapers, the language of adults, the language of children, and so forth" (Kaplan 2006, 23). Therefore, although every Turkish pupil will likely designate himself a citizen of the country, his notion of "citizenship" will be uneven at best, and identifiably schizophrenic at worst. In this regard, Atatürk's understanding of "Turkish youth" as the constant and future protectors of the Turkish republic actually refers to a diverse and competing population "replete with indeterminacy and contingency, given the uneasy relation between official canons of representation, performances of hierarchy, and different understandings of polity and society across generations" (Kaplan 2006, 24). Nonetheless, the same blanket notion of "youth," "citizen," and "nation" is incorporated and deployed by Fethullah Gülen, which highlights the political salience ascribed to Turkish youth, and the penetrating ubiquity of Kemalist categories among Turkey's competing worldviews:

> A nation's durability depends on the education of young generations, upon their being awakened to national spirit and consciousness and spiritually perfected. If nations cannot raise perfect generations to whom they can entrust their future, their future is dark indeed. (Gülen 1999, 35)

Contrary to this Turkish national imaginary, which is promoted as much by Turkey's secular nationalists as it is by its religious nationalists, the education of Turkey's youth *is not* a universal effort on the part of the entire society to produce the next best generation of Turks. Rather, education is the primary sector where competing interests in Turkish society vie for the participation and allegiance of Turkey's children in a contest of nationalisms.

Although it began to form a community of devoted followers and student recruits in the early 1970s, the GM did not emerge as nationally organized collective action until the early 1980s. Structural shifts in the education system, an increasingly competitive centralized examination requirement, and an newly open market for private sector interests collectively facilitated the GM's shift from a relatively small community of students to one of Turkey's most influential players in youth education, and ultimately to its emergence as Turkey's dominant Islamic advocacy network. Before explaining how the GM mobilized in education, the next section provides a brief overview of the education structure in Turkey to highlight the structural vacuum that was filled by GM institutions.

Education and Development

On the eve of the Lausanne Treaty, approximately 10 percent of Anatolia's men and less than 1 percent of its women were literate (Güvenç
1998 2:3). To address this, the late Ottoman state implemented reforms
in military-specific and in vocational schools, followed by a focused
effort to reform and standardize universal primary education.[1] Shortly
after the birth of the Republic, a new education system was standardized in line with the CHP's notion of institutional laiklik. In March
1924, all *medreses* and religious courts were closed, and all other religious institutions were consolidated under the authority of the Diyanet
(Güvenç 1998). The teaching and training of prayer leaders (*imamlar*)
and religious instructors (*hatipler*) came under the authority of the
newly created MEB in what were called imam-hatip okuları (imam-
hatip schools).

From a classically Kemalist perspective, Güvenç (1998) argues that
the "the Republican purpose behind these schools was to train enlightened and enlightening Muslim scholars." The use of "enlightened" and
"enlightening" underscores the importance of controlling the teachings
of Turkey's prayer leaders and religious teachers. Indeed, because the
Ottoman Empire was administered under the authority of a cosmopolitan imperial state, the early CHP regime struggled to construct a nation
where none had previously existed. Diverse religious and ethnic communities lived in politically restricted but corporately autonomous communities. Ottomanism failed as a nineteenth-century nationalist movement
because to be "Ottoman" carried little weight in the imagination of the
Empire's multi-ethnic, multi-confessional population. By contrast, Turkish was a legitimizing identity that could be collectively deployed in terms
of ethno-linguistic nationalism. In order to do so, however, the early
regime believed that Islam needed to be controlled so that an "Islamic"
alternative could not challenge the legitimacy of the Kemalist project.

İmam-hatip students thus functioned as pawns in the Kemalist effort
to consolidate faith under the authority of the state. Graduates from
imam-hatip schools were not originally permitted to attend university.
They had a role neither in Turkey's private economy nor in its professional class. İmam-hatip schools were vocational institutions that were
envisioned to train a specific group of workers for a specific civilian

bureaucracy. For everyone else, matters of faith were deemed matters for the private sphere. "Public religion" had no place in modern Turkey. Only a select few were permitted to engage Islam as a matter for discussion and inquiry, and they had to be licensed by the state.[2] Indeed, after removing the Qur'an from the classroom, the regime sought to devise a universal system that could satisfy the demands of an industrializing society. In 1927, public education was offered in Turkey's major cities as a public service. In the same year, the regime initiated the Turkish language reform, which sought to purge elements of Arabic and Persian from the Turkish language by shifting to a Roman alphabet, and by standardizing speech. The result, according to the linguist Geoffrey Lewis (1998), was a "catastrophic success." The new Turkish language was rationalized as a pure and historic sign system that predated Turkish interaction with Arab and Persian cultures. The early regime went so far as to promote the "sun theory," which sought to prove that Turkish was in fact the mother tongue of all world languages, the pure source from which human communication began. The regime sought to complete the language reform project as quickly as possible; however, as Lewis (1998) explains, modern Turkish was not normalized until the 1960s. Nonetheless, the message to Turkish society was clear: Roman would replace Arabic and Persian in print, and secular humanism would replace Islamic doctrine in thought.

In 1926, Turkey embarked on its second post-Ottoman education reform, stating that the country's primary goal was "to bring up good students who were sophisticated, who were giving importance to their national history and who adopted the Turkish reforms" (quoted in Akinolğu 2008, 197). This was matched by an effort in the countryside to institute two different educational projects, one to focus on the engineering of a rural noble class linked to the ethos of the cities (the "Village Institute Program"), and a second "vocational–technical" program designed to increase the number of semiskilled workers who could contribute to the country›s industrialization (Güvenç 1998). Although partially successful, these efforts met their limits in the late 1960s and early 1970s when Turkey's population exploded and when millions of Turkish citizens vacated Anatolia to find employment in the cities. In 1950 the urban-to-rural ratio in Turkey was 30/70, while in the 1990s the ratio reversed to 70/30 (Güvenç 1998). During this period, agriculture declined from 70 percent of the country's GDP in the 1950s to 16 percent in the early 2000s (State Institute of Statistics 2003, cited in Şimşek and Yildirim 2004, 160). So-called *gecekondu* ("night-built") communities expanded in the peripheries of Istanbul, Izmir, Ankara, and other population centers. The village and the city met in Turkey's rapidly changing public sphere, which ultimately led to a drastic increase in social tension, and to an upsurge of left-wing and right-wing conflict.

Since the inception of the Republic, Turkish education, like education systems elsewhere, has shifted in accordance with political and economic pressure at both national and global levels. In the case of the Middle East, uneven education, extensive age gaps between politicians and the general population, and an unstable labor market has produced state regimes that cannot meet the needs of their populations. Richards and Waterbury (1998, 130) explain that Islamic activist movements have exploited these environments by picking up the slack for inefficient state services:

> Islamic movements have always viewed the school system as a crucial battleground control of which may yield control over the hearts and minds of the students. In some ways, political Islamic groups seek political power not for its own sake but rather because it would provide them with control—so they believe—over the cultural and educational institutions and the mass media.

If this is correct, if political power is not sought for its own sake, then if another avenue is viewed as more effective, aspirations to seize state power should fade. Similar to twentieth-century Islamic activists elsewhere, the GM's goal is to reach the hearts and minds of potential recruits. Unlike other groups, however, the GM focuses less on the formation of alternative social services (welfare), and more on the formation of market alternatives (products for sale). The market for education provided an initial opportunity to expand.

Globalization and Privatization

Despite numerous periods of educational reform (1924, 1926, 1936, 1948, 1968, 1981, 1997, 2004, 2012), the underlying ethos of state-administered education has changed only slightly since the formation of the

Republic, from an overemphasis on national loyalty in the 1924–1981 period, to a "strong emphasis on international values, skills, and interactions" in 2004 (Akinoğlu 2008, 197). In 1997, compulsory education was raised from five to eight (five years of primary school [ilkokul] and three years of middle school [ortaokul]). Preschool before seventy-two months of age is still not mandatory.

In the late 1990s, Turkey's MEB sought to raise the country's eight-year compulsory program to European standards. Reform in line with EU norms was a by-product of the Turkey's efforts to meet the education requirements of the Copenhagen criteria. Meeting these goals, however, proved exceedingly difficult, as the lack of financial, technical, infrastructural, and intellectual resources restricted the state's capacity. According to the World Bank, Turkey's labor force lagged far behind European norms, whose average worker completed ten years of basic schooling compared to the Turkish worker's seven years. Turkey's overall competitiveness was thus viewed with skepticism as the country's ability to meet the requirements of the global economy was called into question:

> Turkish pupils do not acquire key skills for today's knowledge driven economy (e.g., problem solving, stating relationships between events, making complex inferences, creativity, and continuous learning), leaving them out of sync with the needs of the private sector. For instance, 55 percent of Turkey's 15-year-olds perform at the lowest level on the PISA assessment of mathematics-quantitative proficiency, where the average for OECD countries is less that 21 percent. Similar results are found in reading literacy. This is particularly worrisome considering [the fact] that employers in Turkey face a shortage of mid-tier, technician level workers. (World Bank 2005a, 2)

Between 1994 and 1998, the state added somewhere between 6,282 and 21,620 new classrooms each year (Şimşek and Yildirim 2004, 165). Students who longed for their right to an education, however, continued to overwhelm Turkey's public education system, which by 2004 was adding 1.4 million children to its classrooms per annum. Well aware of its problem with capacity, in the 1970s Turkey's MEB began to openly call for assistance from the private sector. But despite noticeable growth in private education, as of 2002, 97 percent of Turkey's student population (pre-primary through secondary) remained the responsibility of the Turkish state.

If private education accounts for only 3 percent of Turkey's total education system, how has the GM managed to develop such a large and loyal community of followers? The short answer: *competition*. According to the World Bank's 2005 education sector study, Turkey spent more than 7 percent of its GDP on education, compared to 5.2 percent in OECD countries (in 2002, only the United States and Denmark spent more than Turkey in percentage share of GDP). *Public* expenditure, however, was only 4.3 percent of GDP, which was far lower than its European counterparts. The difference was accounted for in how much private individuals spend on education—36 percent of regular spending. Much of this, however, was spent not on formal schooling, but on supplemental schooling designed to prepare students for secondary and university placement examinations. In a country where higher education cannot meet the demand of an aspiring youth population, supplemental education has become a billion-dollar industry.

During the time of this research, the entrance exam for high school was called the Ortaöğrentim Kurumları Giriş Sınavı (High School Entrance Examination, OKS).[3] The exam for university was called the Öğrenci Seçme Sınavı (ÖSS, University Selection Exam). The latter was regulated by the Öğrenci Seçme Yerleştirme Merkesi (ÖSYM, Student Selection and Placement Committee). The ÖSS was first administered in 1973 in response to rapid urbanization and the subsequent increase in student applications to university. The necessity to regulate the number of applicants, vis-à-vis the allocated number of seats, thus required some sort of competition. Similar to other newly industrialized states in the region, the result of such intense competition led to the development of a highly competitive tutoring market comprising students seeking to perform well on placement exams. Citing Egypt as an example, Richards and Waterbury (1998, 126) explain the class bias of this system as follows:

> Depending on the subject matter and the number of students in the tutorial, the fees can be very high, sometimes more than a low-income Egyptian [Turk, Algerian, etc.] may earn in a year. In this manner a parallel educational system grows up, based on fees, a system that favors the

rich and penalizes the poor . . . the well-to-do accede in disproportion-
ate numbers to those professional disciplines that will be most highly
regarded in terms of income and prestige.

In a comparative study on supplemental education in post-Soviet countries, Büdinenè and her collaborators (2006) explain how the shift to
a market economy has overloaded the capacity of state education systems to meet the needs of their populations. Büdinenè's study concurs
with Richards and Waterbury's assessment that competition for education leads to the development of a highly competitive market for private supplementary education, which exacerbates class polarization and
overall class tension. Bray and Kwok (2003), who note the following
percentages of youth populations receiving private tutoring around the
world, support these conclusions:

- Egypt: 64 percent of urban youth, and 53 percent of rural youth; estimated
  household expenditure = 1.6 percent GDP (1997)
- India: 39.2 percent of Delhi's primary school–aged youth population (1997)
- Japan: Over 90 percent of the youth population (1999)
- Kenya: 68.6 percent of the country's youth population (2001)
- Malta: 50.5 percent of the country's youth population (1999)
- Romania: 58 percent of urban youth, and 32 percent of rural youth (1994)
- South Korea: 73 percent (primary school), 56 percent (middle school), 32
  percent (high school) (1997)
- Taiwan: 5,536 tutoring centers and 1,891,096 students (1999).

Before 2005, when the ÖSYM enforced new rules for graduating seniors, it was common for Turkish high school students to forgo
their last year of secondary education to dedicate their time to ÖSS
preparation at supplemental learning institutions, known in Turkey
as dershanes (lesson houses). According to Tansel and Bircan (2003,
5), dershane prices, on average, cost students and their families nearly
US$1,300 (as of 2002). In the same year this estimate was calculated,
Turkey's average per capita purchasing parity was US$7,000.[4] Also in
the same year, 57 percent of young people surveyed indicated that they
did not attend a supplemental education course because of a lack of
economic capacity (World Bank 2005b, 6).

The dershane system in Turkey began in the 1960s to meet a demand for private instruction that was specifically focused on student exam preparation. The system boomed in 1980s. In 1984, there were 174 dershaneler in Turkey. In the same year, dershaneler were incorporated into Turkey's education system, which at once legitimized these institutions as primary actors, and brought them under MEB oversight. Economic growth, continued urbanization, and global economic integration led to a boom in the sector. By 2002, there were more than 2,100 dershaneler in the country (Tansel and Bircan 2006, 306). In the 2001–2002 academic year, Turkish families spent US$263 million on supplemental education (Tansel and Bircan 2003, 3). In 2005, 1.6 million potential Turkish students applied for university, and fewer than 400,000 attended (Aksit 2006). By 2005, the average cost for a university exam preparatory course had increased to US$4,711 (the country's purchasing power parity had increased to $12,000).[5]

This situation has produced an incredibly competitive atmosphere, not only among Turkey's aspiring university students, but also among companies competing for their patronage:

> There is also competition to attract students among the private tutoring centers. They advertise the examination results of former tutees. Some private tutoring courses offer lower fees to the students who perform above a certain level in an examination they administer. Those who achieve high are granted discounts in the center's fees. (Tansel and Bircan 2003, 5)

Rival dershane companies compete for the prestige of naming their clients (i.e., students) as among the top 1 percent on the ÖSS. Every spring following the publication of the exam's results, huge banners are erected throughout Turkey's major cities with images displaying a particular dershane company's students and their successes on the exam. And although several companies have risen to the top of the field and have established themselves as the market leaders in teaching the cram course in Turkey, the Istanbul-based FEM Dershanesi outshines them all with students dominating the top 1 percent in twenty-two of the past twenty-three years. Why does FEM prevail?

Refuge in the Market

The importance of Turkey's competitive education system cannot be overstated in regard to the GM's initial move to become an active player in the sector. By cornering this niche, tens of thousands of Turkish youth were exposed not only to mathematics, computers, and technical science, but also to social networks that linked them to groups advocating for faith-based social change. While a community of followers emerged in Izmir in the early 1970s, the GM earned public notoriety and garnered public suspicion in response to its emergence in the education sector immediately following the 1980–1983 military coup. Since 1991, the growth and trans-nationalization of the GM in private education and its specific focus on science and technology has attracted international attention, praise, and skepticism as foreign observers struggle with what to make of Fethullah Gülen and his unique network of followers.

While discussing the GM's initial move into the education sector, Mustafa Bey, a respected author and common figure in GM-produced media, explained that the vision of the schools emerged as a market rationalization of religious persecution:

> The first institution was a dormitory in Izmir. . . . During the coups [1980–1983], the military government took over the properties of all [religious] foundations [*vakfı*]. Hocaefendi [Fethullah Gülen] felt that this might happen as he was inspired by a verse in the Qur'an. . . . [He] stopped his ongoing constructions before the military took over . . . he thought that the military would take them. *This shows that Hocaefendi acted in accordance with the primary sources of religion. . . . In order to prevent its takeover, he changed the legal condition of the dorm and turned it into a school and registered it as private property. He gathered a board of directors consisting of businessmen. So that school wasn't taken by the military government because it was the property of a corporation.* This school became a model for future schools. Anybody who wanted to open a [Gülen] school started a company and owned a school in the name of that company. It then spread abroad. (Field Interview, Spring 2007; emphasis added)

The dormitory in Izmir that was later turned into a private school called Yamanlar ("The Very Good Ones"). Yamanlar was the model institution for the new dorm built for Osman and his classmates, and was a central node in the early formation of the GM's inner cemaat. The first "official" GM institutions were the Türkiye Öğretmenler Vakfı (Turkish Teachers Foundation) and the AOYEV; both emerged in Izmir in 1976 (Yavuz 2003a, 183). In 1979, the first edition of Sızıntı ("Trickle") was published. It was not until the incorporation of Yamanlar Koleji (Yamanlar College), however, that Gülen "acted with the primary sources of religion" to make his primary dormitory a private profit-making institution.[6] While the "chick was in the egg" before Yamanlar's founding, its emergence as a private high school represented the chick "hitting its shell to come out," and thus the *institutional* beginning of the GM in Turkey.[7] By 2007, Yamalar College managed ten campuses and was among Turkey's elite private educational companies. Like most GM schools to follow, Yamanlar emphasized science and math education and encouraged its students to take part in many national and international science and math competitions. In the first ten months of 2008, Yamanlar students took home forty-five national and international medals in math and science, including a gold medal at the Forty-Seventh Annual International Physics Olympics in Hanoi. In 2008, Yamanlar learned that collectively, its graduating middle school students earned more points on the ÖKS exam than did any other high school in Turkey. Two students scored a perfect 100.[8]

In Istanbul, GM followers applied the Yamanlar model to form another private institution. In a conservative Istanbul neighborhood called Fatih, followers of Fethullah Gülen incorporated a pre-existing private dormitory into a new private educational institution. In 1982, just after the opening of Yamanlar, Çag Öğretim İşletmeleri (Era/Age Educational Enterprises) opened Fatih Koleji. In its first year, Fatih sent over 85 percent of its senior class to prestigious universities in Turkey. By the late 1980s, Fatih College graduated some of Turkey's highest-performing students on the ÖSS. By 2007, Fatih College was known as one of the most reputable private education institutions in Turkey, managing six primary schools, three high schools, and five dormitories. Like their counterparts at Yamanlar, students at Fatih College in Istanbul (as well as students at numerous GM private high schools throughout Anatolia) spent the 1990s and 2000s continuously winning national and international science and math competitions, and continued to send the majority of its graduating classes to university. In 2007, students from the GM›s Fatih College in Istanbul, Yamanlar College in Izmir, and Samanyolu College in Ankara won an overwhelming majority of the medals presented at the Turkish Scientific and Technological Research Council›s (TÜBIAK) annual science competition ("Yamanlar, Fatih, and Samanyolu Make Their Mark in Science Olympics" 2007).

Why do students from these schools consistently outperform all others in national competitions and on national placement exams? When I asked Ferhat, a senior editor at the Akademi who scored in the top 1 percent on the ÖSS after attending Fatih College in the late 1980s, he answered that it was because of the dedication, work ethic, and encouragement of GM teachers. After visiting several GM schools and after talking with a number of current and former teachers, I had little doubt that many GM-affiliated teachers were impressively devoted to their craft. However, a number of other very prestigious private schools also produced top-ranking students and also employed teachers who earned noteworthy recognition. I soon realized that none, however, did so with such regularity. And although it was true that a rigorous internal examination assured that only high-performing test-takers entered private schools to begin with, I continued to find myself curious as to why GM schools enjoyed such a consistent level of success. In addition to the "selflessness" exhibited by GM "volunteers" in education, and beyond the pre-existing aptitude of many private school students in Turkey, I was unconvinced that these two reasons were solely responsible for the success of Turkey's GISs.

After months of research, I learned that Fatih College, Yamanlar College, and numerous other schools and companies in Turkey were connected via social networks to dozens of supplemental education institutions that offered students coming from Fatih, Yamanlar, or other GISs special services, discounts, and added attention because they were "in the community" (cemaatın içinde). Being "in the community" thus carried with it certain professional incentives. Religious devotion, respect and admiration for Said Nursi and Fethullah Gülen, and a conservative perspective on social matters were all attributes I discerned to be typical of a GM loyalist. Before an individual can express these inclinations, however, he had to be attracted to the community to begin with. He had to be recruited. But how?

In school, the GM found a way to appeal to the rational choice of individuals by offering added assistance when navigating Turkey's cutthroat education system. From executives to editors, from graduate students to businessmen, I consistently heard stories of recruitment or attempted recruitment via scholastic incentives. With few exceptions, and whether they chose to admit the correlation directly or to pass it off as being of no consequence, GM followers employed at affiliated schools, publishing houses, think tanks, trade and financial organizations, media outlets, and other places of private business recounted their initial exposure to the GM as being mediated by their desires to perform well on standardized exams, not because they sought to participate in a national revival of faith. The service of cram courses, in this regard, was perfected by the GM in the 1990s, and by the 2000s served as the primary mechanism by which new recruits were targeted and filtered for entrance into the community's mobility structure. Turkey's centralized, highly competitive system of higher education, therefore, was a key variable behind the GM's ability to reach a broad market of potential recruits.

Cornering a Niche

Selim Bey, a Russian language editor at the Akademi, explained that the ÖSS preparation period was an excruciating ordeal:

> It was a painful process . . . painful . . . I don't about other countries, but the situation in Turkey is . . . when you are at high school, all you care about the university entrance exam . . . it's the target that dominates everything. (Field Interview, January 2007)

Ali Bey, a man in his mid-thirties who now worked as an administrator at the GM-affiliated FEM Dershanesi, explained that his inclination when preparing for the ÖSS was to focus on English and to take a specialized version of the exam that was dedicated to testing English proficiency. When telling me why he chose FEM, Ali explained as follows:

> FEM had a reputation and actually . . . as a class [at Fatih College] we decided to go the same school . . . they made a special program just for

us. Because we got a really high level of education at Fatih College, at the high school . . . we wanted [our dershane] education to be of the same standard. Not at a lower standard. We didn't want to mingle with other students. We were just a bunch of students . . . like nine students. So we decided to go the same language school, and ask the dershane to open a special class for us. And they did so. (Field Interview, June 2007)

According to the MEB's 2007 list of dershane companies in Istanbul, one out of every seven was a branch of either FEM or its sister organization, "Sevgi Çiçeği" Anafen ("Beloved Flowers," Primary Science), which focused on tutoring adolescents and young teenagers. In 2007, these two companies controlled approximately 12 percent of the supplemental education market in Istanbul, and each had dozens of branches in numerous other cities around the country.[9] Established in 1984, by 2007 FEM Dershanesi was the most highly acclaimed supplemental education company in Istanbul with forty-seven branches. Other successful GM-affiliated supplemental education companies included Yeşilirmak Dershanesi in Bursa, Maltepe Dershanesi in Ankara, Nil Dershanesi in Erzurum, and Korfez Dershanesi in Izmir, to name only the most well-known. On the 2007 ÖSS exam, the majority of students in the top 1 percent in each of the above cities attended these respective preparation schools or attended GM-affiliated private high schools ("Highest Scores on the ÖSS Are Published" 2007).

Ferhat, a mid-level editor at the GM's Akademi, echoed both Ali and Selim when he told me that dershane courses were essential for anyone in Turkey who wanted to do well on the ÖSS. Like the others, he told me that he attended FEM because it was the best. FEM students achieved the success they achieved, according to Ferhat, because FEM teachers worked longer hours, and focused more on the home lives of students. While working part-time as a monitor at FEM when he was at university, Ferhat explained that he often would visit students' homes to observe their environments and study habits, and to talk to parents about how best to prepare students for the exam. Ferhat explained that at FEM, "self-sacrificing" teachers, monitors, and assistants offered students extra services, and that because of their dedication, other companies simply could not compete. I confirmed this claim in a number of interviews with a variety of individuals who had a history with the GM.

Selçuk, a young man who worked in marketing at a non-GM affiliated company, told me that although he did not consider himself "part" of the GM, he spent a year before high school and a year before university at a GM ışık evi to receive free tutoring for both the high school and university placement exams. Selçuk's affiliation with these houses got him what he referred to as a "substantial discount" when he attended FEM. Lale, a literature major at Bogaziçi University who attended the GM's Maltepe Dershanesi in Ankara, explained that she originally did not want to go because she knew of its affiliation, and "did not want anything to do with them." Based on her scores from a pre-test, however, Lale qualified for two tuition scholarships: one at Maltepe, and one at another institution. She took the latter, but after a month she switched to Maltepe. Lale explained that after watching unmotivated students sit around during breaks, extend those breaks, and treat the course more like a social space than a study hall, Lale made the switch despite her misgivings.

Lale said that the dershane, regardless of where one attends, was a "crazy place." She said that there were too many students and too many teachers divided up into too many forums. At Maltepe, Lale said that there were always extra courses, extra help, and one-on-one lessons with teachers: "They force you to study. . . . There are intense interactions with the students. At other dershaneler, people are not forced to study, it is up to them. At Maltepe, you are constantly watched and told to study" (Field Interview, Summer 2007). Lale then said that at Maltepe there was an added bonus to get extra tutoring from university students who lived at GM-affiliated ışık evleri. She took advantage of such resources and scored high enough on her exam to earn a seat at Turkey's prestigious Bogaziçi University.

Market Islam

During Turkey's development as a modern nation, its leaders employed a particular technology of discursive power that linked education to Turkish national identity, thus making the country's youth population a primary target for interest group competition. The primary arena where this contest played out was in the politically charged and impossibly competitive Turkish classroom. A central player in the current competition for hearts and minds is the networked community of Fethullah Gülen whose actors took advantage of market rationality to attract Turkey's youth by appealing to their opportunistic self-interest. In such a charged environment, however, the GM was careful to emphasize that its efforts were in the interests of "Turkey's youth," and by extension "the Turkish nation." The GM's Islamic sensibility and transnational activity should not cloud its national teleology. However transnational its mobilization, however many resources its actors drew on in the context of Turkey's integration into the world economy, the GM did not mobilize to become a "global" movement. To the contrary, the GM emerged as a network of religious nationalists whose actors drew on the universal categories of Islam, democracy, and capitalism to play a more effective role in the transformation of Turkey's national power structure.

Graduates from GM schools, both K–12 and dershaneler, are now among Turkey's leaders in science and math and are very well represented at the country's top universities, as well as in master's and doctorate programs throughout Europe and in the United States. The scholastic and professional success of graduates from GM schools has led to a popular theory that the GM seeks to infiltrate positions of power in the Turkish state and military bureaucracies, and ultimately to facilitate a slow transformation toward a Şeriat-governed society. While it is clear that GM indeed focuses its advocacy on accruing influence, however, its goal is not to establish an Islamic state. Such a development would be counter to its real aim, which is social power. Indeed, by becoming an active player in private education, and by cornering a niche in university placement preparation, the GM became a very real and appealing option for aspiring Turkish youth. Stories like Lale's and Selçuk's were constant in my research. In fourteen months of fieldwork in both Turkey and in the United States, the overwhelming majority of Turkish followers of Fethullah Gülen—be they teachers, journalists, or professionals at GM-affiliated institutions or businesses, or institutionally unaffiliated financial contributors to "the community"—attended either a GM private school or a GM-owned dershane while preparing for the ÖKS or the ÖSS exams. The younger the follower, the more likely this was the case.

In the 1990s, the GM model was applied outside Turkey in the Balkans and in Central Asia. In the later 1990s and early 2000s, the model

became transnational. Offering an alternative form of Turkish nationalism to Turkish and international consumers, education emerged as
a key strategy in the GM's transnational advocacy campaign, and ultimately functioned as the primary link between affiliated media, business, and public relations efforts in a complicated network of wealth,
prestige, praise, and conspiracy. In 1996, the GM expanded into banking. In 2005, it formed what is now Turkey's largest business-related
NGO, linking affiliated exporters in a coordinated effort to take advantage of market inroads created by GISs around the world. In the same
year, the GM's *Zaman gazetesi* became Turkey's most widely circulated
news publication. Naming only a few of the GM many successes, it is
important to emphasize that nothing would have been possible were
it not for the success of the schools that anchor the GM's national and
transnational enterprise.

6

Değirmenin suyu nereden geliyor?
(Where does the water for the mill come from?)

"Economic action" (*Wirtschaften*) is any peaceful exercise of
an actor's control over resources that is in its main impulse
oriented towards economic ends. "Rational economic
action" requires instrumental rationality in this orientation,
that is, deliberate planning.
—Max Weber

Economic communities based on trust networks such as those
observed in the GM are widespread in Turkey, and are not atypi-
cal of Muslim culture in general. Often these communities organize
under the cultural leadership of a spiritual mentor, which provides
producers, merchants, and exporters with valuable social connections as they struggle to compete with Turkey's traditional family-
based and vertically integrated holding companies (Buğra 1994; Öniş
and Turem 2001; Özbüdün and Keymen 2002; Özcan and Çokgezcen 2003, 2006). In their analysis of this phenomenon, Özcan and
Çokgezcen (2006, 147) stress the significance of cultural authority as
follows:

> The spread of Islamic companies and their promised moral economic
> revival took root in social institutions often under the guiding leadership
> of a paternal figure who had indisputable authority and recognition. The
> desire to be protected by a father figure manifests itself in different forms
> such as the respect shown to religious and spiritual leaders, teachers or
> those with political charisma.

Invested with cultural authority, Fethullah Gülen garnered the support of a tightly knit following in the late 1960s and early 1970s. When the Turkish state implemented a policy to cultivate a "Turkish–Islamic Synthesis" in the post-1983 period, GM actors managed to diffuse their identity throughout Turkish society. During the same period, structural shifts in Turkey's economy created opportunities for Anatolian producers to take advantage of liberalizing trade laws. Together, these shifts facilitated the transformation of what was once a small revivalist community into what is now Turkey's most influential Islamic advocacy network. Today, GM investment capital is collected via a rationalized system of religious donation that includes every institution at the cemaat and arkadaş levels of affiliation. GM actors collect, invest, and produce value via a network of mutually cooperative enterprises that subsidize startups by relying on "friendship networks" for needed resources. Once a school, company, or institution is self-sustaining, donation funds are no longer required, and market forces can take over. The result is a faith-inspired articulation of capitalist accumulation that has redefined the relationship between Islam, markets, and society in a new Turkey.

Islamic Economics

Islamic economics refers to the mobilization of Muslim merchants, investors, producers, workers, and peasants who organize their economic activities in accordance with Islam's symbolic authority. This sub-economy typically includes companies that donate regularly to Islamic foundations (*vakıf*), food producers who adhere to *halal* stipulations, restaurants that serve only *halal* food, corporations that provide time off (if not subsidies) for making *hajj*, and companies that allow (if not mandate) time for prayer during the workday. The Islamic sub-economy includes producers that supply markets with "Islamic fashion," "Islamic entertainment," and "Islamic arts"; hotels and resorts that serve the needs of the globally booming "Islamic tourism" industry; and financial institutions whose managers borrow, lend, and invest in accordance with the Islamic restriction on *riba* (an Arabic term that is most often translated as "usury" or "interest"; Turkish: *faiz*), and whose profits and losses are dispersed to all "participants" (i.e., investors and account holders) who contribute to the institution's demand deposit. Indeed, the assertion of Muslim identity in the market has become more prominent in the global era, as many Muslims view globalization to be synonymous with cultural imperialism, and thus as potentially threatening to an "Islamic" way of life:

> In a technologically advanced world, where career choices have to be made, where women pursue and interrupt careers outside the home, where investment choices require monitoring, and where markets offer abundant choice, economic decision-making absorbs considerable time. It follows that if economic choice is considered a secular activity, economic advances will make Muslim existence look increasingly secular. But if it is considered a religious activity, then economic development need not reduce Islam's perceived role in the lives of Muslims. (Kuran 2004, 85)

Echoing a trend occurring at the global level, Islamic banking, fashion, tourism, and consumption are booming in Turkey. Interestingly, however, the same processes that led to the expansion of "Islamic sub-economies" have also led some Muslim capitalists to move beyond the interests of cultural survival toward more general interests of bourgeois accumulation. The case of Turkey's Gülen Movement is exemplary in this regard. Beyond the Islamic sub-economy, GM affiliates have emerged as active players in a battle for the Muslim share of economic power, and many now compete at the highest level of Turkey's national economy.

The Politics of Development Revisited

Engineering Turkey's turbulent post-WWII development project was the task of the State Planning Organization (SPO), which, in turn, relied on a small number of family-based "holding companies" to facilitate Turkey's economic development. The family-based holding company model dominated the Turkish economy before the 1980 coup. Its primary characteristics were vertical integration and state subsidization. Buğra (1994, 50) explains the relationship during this period between the state and selected business families as follows:

[It was] more subtle than one that could be described in terms of sheer nepotism. It was a relationship in which the businessman, to be successful, had to convince political authorities of his desire and ability to serve the state through entrepreneurial activity. . . . The social status of the business class was largely defined by the nature of the national development project.

While there were only a handful of holdings selected to lead Turkish growth before WWII, after the war a dozen new holdings joined the ranks of state favoritism. By the 1970s, over 150 of Turkey's nearly 400 large private enterprises were represented by thirty holding companies (Buğra 1994, 56). For a foreign business to enter the Turkish market, it had to establish inroads through these domestic holdings, whose functionaries were versed in the complicated state bureaucracy, which led to very little foreign direct investment (FDI).[1]

As discussed previously, crisis in the 1960s led a number of Turkey's biggest holdings to consolidate under one umbrella, The Turkish Industrialists' and Businessmen's Association (TÜSIAD, est. 1971). Organizationally outflanking the efforts on the part of small Anatolian holdings, the interests represented by TÜSIAD were those of Turkey's favored capitalist class, and as such the organization viewed itself as more than a mere economic association:

TÜSIAD seeks to promote the development of a social structure that conforms to Atatürk's principles and reforms. It strives to strengthen the democratic foundations upon which civil society is based and supports a secular state based on the rule of *law*. . . . In accordance with the context of its activities [TÜSIAD] initiates public debate by communicating its position on a variety of issues. It conducts professional research projects, the findings of which are submitted directly to Parliament, the Government, the media, international organizations, and other states. (TÜSIAD Mission Statement 2007, available at http://www.tusiad.org/)

Buğra (1994, 247) explains the significance of TÜSIAD's favored share of the economy before the late 1990s as follows:

TÜSIAD is the organization of a small group of businessmen who believe in the necessity of social consensus generating approaches for the creation of a political and economic environment in which the business community would have solid, non-contested status.

Following the 1980 coup, policies of protection gave way to domestic liberalization. In the same period, electoral policies that once outlawed religious identity expression in state-managed public spaces (e.g., universities, government offices) came under stress. Over time, tensions between "Islamists" and "Kemalists" (secularists) were revived, which culminated in the events of February 28, 1997. Learning from the mistakes of their predecessors, Turkey's younger generation of Muslim-identified partisans stopped criticizing their rivals via the symbolic authority of Islam. Instead, they did so via the symbolic authority of international neo-liberalism, human rights, and democracy, which they framed to their constituents as compatible with social conservatism. The 2002 ascendance of the "Islamist roots" AKP to single-party rule was the effective result of this shift.

If the AKP represents the partisan victory of Turkish Islamic activism, what factors explain the growing influence of the GM in Turkish society? Although the two entities are indeed separate, overlaps between them, and their reliance on each other, cannot be ignored. Central to these overlaps are the financial connections that exist between Turkey's "new capitalists" who support both initiatives. These capitalists are primarily based in Anatolian cities such as Gaziantep, Denizli, Kayseri, and Adana, which, because of their rapid growth in Turkey's export sector, are compared to export enclave "tigers" in Asia, and are thus often dubbed "Anatolia's tigers." Exporters in these rapidly industrializing cities have created a comparative advantage in textiles, furniture, and light manufacture, and have come to dominate Turkey's post-1983 export economy. While most of the companies are exemplary small-to-medium enterprises (SMEs), a number are connected to larger corporations that now compete with companies represented by TÜSIAD. They have formed their own business associations, and have established their own favorable relations with the power centers of a transforming Turkish bureaucracy. GISs and GM media serve as social promoters for these organizations, whose leaders are subsequently invested in the success and continued expansion of GISs and GM-affiliated media. A symbiotic relationship has emerged, whereby Turkey's new bourgeoisie, its dominant political party, and its dominant civil/social influence rely on one another in a coalition to offset the power of Turkey's traditional oligarchy in an effort to increase "the Muslim share" in Turkey's political economy.

The Opportunity of Globalization

In 1989, the economist John Williamson coined the term "Washington Consensus." Signaling the dawn of a new era in capitalist accumulation, Williamson uttered in theory what states had been implementing in practice since the late 1970s: liberalization of national capital accounts, privatization of national industries, and implementation of austerity for social spending. In 1990, the world watched the fall of the Berlin Wall, and shortly thereafter, the emergence of newly independent states in the Balkans and in Central Asia. In August 1991, Saddam Hussein invaded Kuwait and the United States led a UN coalition force to protect its strategic influence in the region. These shifts in the global balance of power led to a reorganization of the Turkish role in global geo-politics, and all had noticeable effects on the Turkish economy.

In August 1990, Turkey became one of the first nations to implement the economic embargo imposed on Iraq under UN Resolution 661. This hurt Turkey's export sector to Arab markets due to hampered relations with Arab countries. Toksöz (2002, 141–164) explains that the effect of the first war in Iraq together with the fall of the Soviet Union cost Turkey US$30 billion:

> The Iron Curtain distanced Turkey from its western European markets. . . . The Gulf War cut the direct line of transport not only to lucrative projects in Iraq, but also to the richer Gulf. . . . The only place Turkey could turn . . . was crisis-stricken Russia and the land-locked and limited Central Asian Markets.

The policy to turn to Russia and Central Asia was rationalized as an effort to influence the development of the latter region under the discursive foreign policy guise of cultivating dormant Turkic affinity. Turkish elites promoted the nations comprising the resource-rich region of Central Asia as ethnic and cultural corollaries to Turkey, and a policy was developed to invest heavily in the region and to increase cultural exchange by focusing on youth and education. As a social and economic network, the GM capitalized on these policies. Affiliated businessmen invested in GISs and thereby created a model that was replicated in countries around the world. Beginning in 1992, GISs opened in Kyrgyzstan, Uzbekistan, Kazakhstan, Tajikistan, Azerbaijan, and Russia as well as in Ukraine, Moldova, Bulgaria, Poland, Albania, and Bosnia–Herzegovina. Affiliated businesses set up production and client networks in host states and supplied these new schools with start-up resources. Simultaneously, they established local contacts for investment and trade. GISs used English as the primary medium for science and math courses (taught by GM teachers who traveled from Turkey), whereas local history, physical education, and social studies were primarily taught in local languages. Turkish was always offered as a foreign language course, as were other languages depending on the host state and the surrounding region. By the late 1990s, there were twenty-nine GISs in Kazakhstan, twelve in Azerbaijan, twelve in Kyrgyzstan, thirteen in Turkmenistan, five in Tajikistan, six in the Tartar region of Russia, and five in Russia proper.[2]

Recently, the GM has come under pressure in Russia. In May 2007, Russian authorities legally banned the publication and distribution of Said Nursi's *RNK*, which, according to a court decision, "[aimed] to incite religious hatred, propagandize the exclusivity, superiority, and inferiority of citizens according to their attitude towards religion, as well as to substantiate and justify the necessity of such activity" (Fagan 2007). Although authorities officially stated that the crackdown against GISs was due to concerns over safety regulations and curriculum requirements, they became targets immediately following the *RNK* ban. In the summer of 2007, Russian authorities closed Russian school no. 664, "the Russian–Turkish College"; it was reopened in July 2008.[3]

Despite these obstacles, it is important to note that allegations against GISs abroad are rare. More often than not, GISs are recognized for their academic achievements and for the roles they play as interlocutors between Turkish and host-country business and political elites. Notwithstanding, in the United States a wave of criticism has emerged regarding GM-affiliated charter schools in a number of states. Discussed in more detail below, a unique characteristic of GISs in the

United States is that they emerged in accordance with public charter financing and thus without the support of affiliated GM start-up capital, which has produced an increasingly more delicate set of challenges for GM affiliates in the United States to navigate.

Rationalizing Alms

Yusef, an aforementioned student from Baku, told me that in Azerbaijan, GM schools are alone among the country's elite institutions:

> Before I started in this school, there were the advertisements for it. And it was very popular. It was prestigious to be a student of that school. It's like a comparison between Harvard, Princeton and an ordinary university in the USA. We can call those schools "our Harvard." Their quality of education was much better than the others. Unbelievable quality. Our teachers were very intelligent. So, my family wanted me to apply for that school. (Field Interview, Winter 2007)

Similarly, in Kazakhstan over 90 percent of the students educated at GISs since 1992 have gone to university. Around the world, GISs publicize such achievements to attract more students. Profits made by the schools are re-invested to open new facilities, to expand to new grade levels, to build new campuses, and so forth. If schools are successful, host states often offer support. In Nigeria, for instance, the Ministry of Education has allocated US$340 million for scholarships to the "Turkish schools" in that country, and around the world a pattern has emerged. Student success at GISs is heavily advertised and promoted in local media, and schools subsequently accrue legitimacy and prestige. The market success of GISs has led to a growing reputation of "elitism," as they attract only those students who can afford the high prices of a high-quality, imported education. In Central Asia, where GISs have become normalized as the region's primary elite institutions, tuition, board, and fees can run as high as US$12,000 per year, per student.[4] Tuition, board, and fees at GISs, however, vary with market conditions. At Thailand's Zaman International School, high school tuition is US$4,500 plus an additional $1,000 for board and $250 in fees. At Kenya's Turkish Light Academy, a high school student can expect to pay approximately US$1,323 per year for tuition, board, and transportation in addition to $200 in registration fees and refundable "caution money." At Nigeria's Turkish International College in Abuja, tuition and board total nearly US$6,000 per student, per year; and at the private Pioneer Academy of Science in Clinton, New Jersey, tuition and fees for high school without boarding runs approximately $8,750 per student, per year.[5]

Investment for GISs is generated in the form of religious donation (*himmet*) collected at the cemaat and arkadaş levels of GM affiliation in an organized fund-raising system. Original benefactors expect no immediate return from their himmet. They are told that himmet is a religious rite, and that trust networks will assure that it goes to a "faithful" cause (e.g., to pay for a student's scholarship, to provide start-up capital for a new school, to send a group of influential Americans on a two-week trip to Turkey, to sponsor an "academic" conference devoted to Fethullah Gülen). In this way, schools and other GM institutions provide businessmen with the service (hizmet) of satisfying their obligatory rites according to the Islamic tenet of giving.

At the Akademi, the operative who collected himmet from editors, writers, executives, and outsourced guests was named Orhan Bey. Approximately once a month, Orhan Bey would walk around the Akademi asking employees how much they would like to donate from their salary. I asked Levent Bey, a managing editor at the Akademi who spent much of the 1990s at a number of GISs in Southeast Asia, whether it would be accurate to liken the collection of himmet to the collection of taxes. He responded as follows:

> No, no. They are very different things. It is not as if I come to you to collect taxes, or "himmet." There is no such obligation. We collect money, for instance, when a school is going to be opened at some place. People who have money may donate; those who do not have money do not. Those who donate do so not out of obligation, but . . . because they want to. When you say tax, it means there is an obligation to give. When the state comes to collect taxes, when you do not pay your tax, you will be put into prison. So you cannot call it a tax. (Field Interview, Spring 2007)

Like Levent, GM operatives are often quick to deny that giving himmet to trust networks is obligatory. But like other social norms in the

GM—such as attending sohbet, tutoring younger students while living at a house of light, or obtaining a working knowledge of Gülen's and Nursi's teachings—giving himmet is a signifier of one's dedication to the community, and thus has social and economic returns. The regular levying of funds from GM loyalists and friends represents the realization of devotion expressed in material terms. And just to be clear: everyone in the cemaat and at the arkadaş level of affiliation donates himmet. And although core cemaat actors consistently contend that himmet is not obligatory, Aydın Bey, a close confidant of Fethullah Gülen, explained that when the GM requires funding, funding is received.

When collection time came around, Orhan would come into the office and sit in a chair without speaking for five to ten minutes. He would observe each individual, who in turn would immediately focus more closely on his work and end any conversations he was having with an office mate. When he was ready, Orhan would get up and visit each of the six desks in the room. He would ask individuals how much they would like to give this month to "assist a poor student." He would often remind the person to whom he was speaking about the amount they donated the previous month. His style was very passive, and he would often say very little. Rather, he would stand next to someone at their desk until they decided to hand him lira, or until they gave him a number that he would jot down on his notepad to deduct from that person's monthly salary (Field Notes, December 2006, January 2007, February 2007, May 2007). As discussed previously, every company in the GM cemaat has an employee like Orhan whose specific job requirements include organizing sohbet, collecting himmet, and overseeing the "spiritual coordination" of individuals in general by making sure that they showed up to work on time, that they managed their time efficiently, that they were aware of relevant company events, lectures, and so forth (Field Notes, Fall 2006, Spring 2007).

According to my observations, the method by which money was collected placed the responsibility of giving onto the giver. At the Akademi, Orhan asked how much someone wanted to give, and he waited patiently until he received an answer. Orhan's role was that of an excited collector; his job was not only to collect money, but also to remind the giver of the social service that himmet provided. Although they refused to call it a tax, the material reward of one's labor at the Akademi was recycled back to the community in the name of religious piety. Not to give would not necessarily bring penalty, but it would bring personal reflection, and potentially embarrassment. Not to give would indicate to others that one's personal hizmet did not represent his full effort, that he did not fully appreciate the rewards of affiliation. In this way, when Orhan walked into the room, individuals began to think about how much money they would give, about how much would be OK. And although jokes were often made to stall the exchange, eventually everyone gave.

The first time I gave himmet to Orhan was in the amount of 20YTL (approx. US$14.50). On this day, when Orhan approached everyone in the office, each started with light conversation, and some even joked around. After a minute or two, each proposed a number to Orhan, which he wrote on his notepad. After he collected a number from everyone, Orhan approached me and said, "İade ister misiniz, Joshua?" ("Would you like to give, Joshua?"). Although I observed the collection of himmet several times before, this was the first time Orhan approached me directly to inquire about a donation. Unprepared to respond, I looked at Orhan inquisitively before he iterated, "Miktar?" ("Amount?"). He said that if I wanted to help a school or a dorm, my money would go to where it was needed. I asked how much people usually give. He said whatever I wanted to give would be fine. I asked what would be a good number. He did not respond. We went on like this for a minute or so, until he said, "Yirmi lira olabilir mı?" ("How about twenty lira?"). I reached into my wallet and pulled out 20 TL. As I handed it to him, Orhan smiled and said, "Sadece verabilirsan, tamam mi?" ("Only if you can give, are you sure?"). I smiled back and told him that it was my pleasure. He put the money in his pocket, and told the room to "take it easy" (*kolay gelsin*).

The point to iterate is that those who gave himmet, including myself, did so not because they had to, but because *they wanted to*. Nakit Bey, a thirty-something editor at the Akademi, explained as follows:

> Let's say people donate 200 or 300 TL a month [approx. US$80–130]. He [Orhan] asked me whether I would like to donate, and how much I would donate. I didn't want to at first. Then I noticed other people donating. . . . But I got married recently, and I have debts. I have payments.

Then he mentioned how I received a scholarship myself, [and] that there were students in need of money. Then I decided to give. Sometimes, you need to be motivated to take action. (Field Interview, Spring 2007)

Nakit received money while he was in graduate school studying in the United States. He attended FEM when preparing for the university exam and then later lived at a GM ışık evi while attending university. His rent was subsidized, he tutored high school students, he attended sohbet, and eventually he became an ağabey. While in the United States, he volunteered at a number of GM-affiliated cultural centers in a number of different cities. Upon returning to Turkey, Nakit got a job at the Akademi and got married. When he did not think that donating to the cemaat was in his budget, Orhan reminded him of the "scholarship" he received while in school, and Nakit eventually agreed to give. When I interviewed him, Nakit explained that he regularly donates 200–300 TL a month.

For bigger projects, himmet was collected in a similar way, but with project-specific intent. Aydın Bey, one of Fethullah Gülen's closest advisers, informed me that the latest developments in the GM enterprise were to open accounting and law firms in the United States and Europe. This was viewed as a previously unforeseen venture that had become a priority in recent years. When I asked how these firms would be funded, Aydın Bey explained as follows:

AYDIN BEY: This is a concept at one meeting we had. You may see the first [law] office in twelve months, in Washington or in New York . . . for this project it will take some core capital. Funding, OK. So they will have to convince some people with money. Look, we are going to open a law office here. We need one million dollars to set up, and we need two million dollars to survive for two years. We need three million dollars with no promises. OK?

JH: And so, when you do that, you would call together a meeting of people you know, businessmen you know have that kind of money, and then you would try to convince them with a presentation?

AYDIN BEY: Absolutely! . . . I go to what they call sohbet. Reading groups, where we talk about religion and values. And you see a face come from another town, and they started a school. And they thought that they could finish with the budget they had, but it's not finished. Right at that meeting, I was the only one who could not give money, why? Because I had none. I had not a penny in my pocket. I don't carry money in my wallet. They went around once, and they counted the money. The ağabey said that he will take anything, but that they need this much. In one round, short. Second round, this much more. Third round, this much more. He then counted how much he needed, and then gave the rest back. Then they [the rest of the group] said, "No! You keep this, you keep the extra, too, because you made the wrong calculations and now you may need it." The guy started crying, "Go back with the money, back to Adana." This was my first experience. This happened fifteen years ago. (Field Interview, Summer 2007)

As previously discussed, sohbet act as social conditioning rituals, identity rituals, social networking sites, and alternative public forums for affiliates in the GM cemaat and among GM arkadaşlar. At higher levels, however, sohbet also function as pitch meetings where start-up/bailout capital is collected for GM projects. For three decades, the process of collecting himmet to open and run a school, to open and run a newspaper, to open and run a television station, or to open and run a hospital has produced the necessary funds for hundreds of successful institutions. Moreover, although initial capital is collected via donation, returns are all but assured:

AYDIN BEY: Now, you want to start a new venture, OK? And there is a core financing necessary. And a businessman who opened two schools. . . . Now these two schools don't need any money for material support. In fact, they make money!

JH: Right, by tuition, correct?

AYDIN BEY: Exactly, they charge eight to nine thousand dollars in tuition. By Turkish standards, that is unbelievable, OK? They don't lose money, I can assure you. At the beginning, they need a building, for a half-million dollars, and that money has to come from somewhere. Now this money is being paid back to these people by profits earned, slowly.

JH: From the school?

AYDIN BEY: Sure!

JH: So the profits are given back?

AYDIN BEY: Sure. At least the profits. This is . . . you scratch my back, I
scratch your back, and these people are, ahhhh . . . Muslims of strong
faith. They pay a great deal of attention to the hereafter, OK? They
know the meaning of Qur'anic *ayas*, verses, OK? And they invest in
the other side . . . you know. "Nothing belongs to me, everything God
gave me, if I lose it, I lost nothing. God took away what God gave
me." (Field Interview, Summer 2007)

Thus, while GM loyalists continuously assert that the money raised
for GISs is donated by everyone who is loyal, those who donate large
sums of capital look on their himmet as a twofold investment: one with
anticipated financial and preferential returns in this life, and one with
spiritual returns in the hereafter.

Concerning opening law firms, Aydın Bey explained that the growth
and expansion of GM enterprises has led to greater institutionalization,
which requires in-house knowledge of legal requirements, loopholes,
and obstacles. Harking back to Weber's warning that charismatic movements are destined to fall prey to modern institutionalization and to the
"weight of material interests," Aydın elaborated in detail as follows:

AYDIN BEY: One mistake I made, I never approached certain organizations for funding so I could put together ten to fifteen lawyers in
a group, to work for the community. I did whatever I could do by
myself, which was a mistake. . . . Let me tell you a story. . . . In 1997,
Hocaefendi came to stay for several months in the U.S. Two weeks
after he returned [unintelligible] . . . I came . . . We were left alone
with Hocaefendi and myself in one room, on the fifth floor. And
"Hocam" [my teacher], I said, "now . . . " I said, "Hizmet [the GM]
is opening up . . ." I said, "we are going to need professionals in
certain fields." Specifically, I mentioned two: lawyers number one,
and accountants number two . . . "Aydın Bey," [Gülen said], "what
are we going to do with lawyers? We don't do anything wrong."
Hocaefendi did not know the West. . . . It was because of my respect
that I stayed quiet.

JH: And then what happened?

AYDIN BEY: We tried to get green cards, tried to get visas . . . we had lease problems, and all of this. . . . We started to spend tens of thousands of dollars for lawyers doing business. And ten years later in a group, a sohbet, he [Gülen] touched my hand . . . he looked at me with a really sharp eye . . . and he said . . . "We need to bring up young people to work in the professional fields," he said. "Like law and *muhasabe* [accounting]." . . . You know how the West functions? The methods that worked in Central Asia are going to hang you in one week here. . . . And they [the cemaat] had to be punished several times because there is an expression: one *musibet* [bad experience] is worth more than one thousand *nasihat* [pieces of advice]. (Field Interview, Summer 2007)

Discussed in more detail later, as more GM affiliates moved to the United States for their master's and PhD educations, to "volunteer" at GM-affiliated cultural centers, and to teach math, science, and Turkish language classes at GM-affiliated charter schools, the more the GM as a whole needed to navigate U.S. labor/hiring laws, nonprofit law, immigration law, and small business law. And just as it was with other GM enterprises, why let other interests reap the economic reward of GM demands?

The GM Production Network

The companies formed to fill the demand for resources at GISs led to the development of Kaynak Holding, a group of fifteen companies that collectively manufacture a variety of products. An executive in the publishing sector explained by asking rhetorically, "Why let other people become rich from the needs of these institutions? This process started in order to fulfill the needs of the schools!" (Field Interview, Spring 2007). Although originally dependent on the continued expansion of GM education activities, Kaynak has since become Turkey's largest producer, distributor, and exporter of educational equipment and supplies in with subsidiary companies in publishing, ICT, retail, paper production, shipping, tourism, furniture, textiles, construction, and insurance:

Let's analyze a human being. A human has many needs. This holding [Kaynak] developed in that way. The first occupation of the holding was books, then audiocassettes, in Izmir. When the schools opened, there was need for technical equipment and stationery. When there was demand, people started to manufacture. . . . I was visiting the schools since I saw them as the primary customers of this holding, and then I noticed that some publishers already started to publish the needs of the schools. You see this is a market, an economic sector. (Field Interview, Spring 2007)

Contradicting much of the GM's public claims to contrary, Ferhat Bey at the Akademi explained, "That [was] not an accident. . . . First they aimed to establish schools, you know. After schools were opened in various parts of the country, and overseas, they started seeing that they had to meet their needs, I mean they had to meet their needs" (Field Interview, Winter 2007). Originally, the companies that constituted Kaynak Holding were independent. Cultural publishing started in Izmir alongside Kaynak's printing company. Zambak Publishing focused on academic publications (e.g., textbooks), and Sürat English Language Training on English language publication needs. As a corporation, Kaynak now exports its products to more than one hundred countries, and manages offices in fourteen cities around the world.[6]

Kaynak's publishing products are marketed and sold by an increasingly successful subsidiary retail company called NT Mağazları. With 113 locations throughout Turkey, as well as seventeen more that operate throughout Central Asia, Georgia, Russia, and the United States, NT is among Kaynak's most successful companies, has come to dominate Turkey's retail book sales, and is a primary player in the retail of supplemental educational resource materials, magazines, newspapers, small electronics, cameras, computers, and software. Complementing NT is Sürat Teknoloji, a Kaynak subsidiary IT firm that started by producing lab equipment for GISs, and that has since developed an impressively extensive portfolio. Highlighting the returns the GM enjoys from invested social capital among friends, Sürat is now an IBM partner company with clients that include the GM-affiliated Bank Asya and Kaynak Publishing, as well as unaffiliated large entities like Türkiye Finans, Istikbal Furniture, the City of Istanbul, USAID, and the United Nations. The City of Istanbul contracted Sürat Teknoloji to build, in conjunction with Cisco Systems, a citywide surveillance infrastructure known as "Mobile City Information and Security System" (MOBESE). Sürat Technology developed the MOBESE Command Control Center, and is responsible for system's support and maintenance. Kaynak worked with USAID in its "Rebuild Iraq Project," supplying educational furniture and equipment, and with UNESCO in Afghanistan, to whom it supplied similar resources (Hendrick 2009).

The GM's efforts to go global, therefore, have produced empirically observable rewards for the most central of the GM's for-profit institutions. Indeed, Kaynak is by no means the only beneficiary of this effort. For example, virtually 100 percent of the buildings constructed by Zambak Mimarlık (Zambak Architecture) are affiliated with the GM. These projects include twenty-one GM-affiliated dormitories, nearly forty GISs in Turkey, and another sixteen in countries outside Turkey, including Macedonia, Georgia, Azerbaijan, Albania, Belgium, Kosovo, Tanzania, Kenya, Bangladesh, Indonesia, and Afghanistan. Zambak has also designed cultural centers in Chicago and Pennsylvania, Turkey's "most luxurious hospital" in Istanbul (SEMA Hastenesi), and Zambak's grandest accomplishment, the state-of-the-art headquarters of the GM's *Zaman* newspaper in Istanbul.[7]

A longtime confidant of Fethullah Gülen explained that economic networks between clients and patrons in the GM's commodity chain provide the community with an accessible foundation on which to increase the competitiveness of arkadaş (friend) companies, and on which to expand the GM enterprise:

> You are a businessman, OK. Here are ten million people around the world, OK. If you are a businessman, you shall either sell something, or you offer a service. Out of ten million who will need your service, they will come to you first. Why? Because they know about your character! You are already two steps ahead of your competition with these people. (Field Interview, Summer 2007)

Osman Bey, the aforementioned managing editor at the Akademi who was also a former principal at a several GISs in Tajikistan during the 1990s, defined the practice of relying on social networks for business and development as "friendship marketing":

Friendship marketing [refers to] people's tendency to do business with the people they know. It is a strong tendency in Turkey, too. For instance, Oxford University Press wants to run business in Diyarbakir. They can't succeed [in] this with the director, Sir James Walter, in Diyarbakir, because his communication wouldn't be that successful, but when they assign Ahmet from Diyarbakir, he will know the people of the area and he will run the business better. This is friendship marketing. (Field Interview, Winter 2007)

Osman also explained that the tendency to seek guidance from a religious leader is a natural and efficient way assure that one knows who one's friends are, where to find them, and why those friends should be favored when doing business:

A while ago, I said people from Gülen Movement have needs. They need schools, books, hospitals and everything else. Someone has to fulfill these needs, and people want to do this business. Let's say the bank. How many banks went bankrupt in the last twenty years in Turkey? Many. A religious leader has to find a solution to these problems for the people. He must suggest a solution. He must give people hope and guide them. Then, he [Gülen] said that "only if some reliable businessmen come and found a noninterest bank, approvable by Islam." He only suggested this. After this, the listeners of these ideas—naturally they are his people—came together from Antep, Istanbul, and et cetera and decided to found a bank. They made an investment and opened the bank. There was advice and it was carried out. People are looking for reliable banks, since many banks are not trusted by the people. . . . When Ihlas Finans went bankrupt Asya Finans [Bank Asya] became the most reliable bank. People came there. Asya Finans is a multi-associated bank. Schools are a different entity, Kaynak is a different entity, Asya Finans is a different entity. For instance, the hospitals . . . there's SEMA Hospital, it's a different entity, too. Its management is separate. Do they make some contracts between them? Yes, they do, but it's a trade-based relationship. (Field Interview, Winter 2007)

On the one hand, therefore, GM-affiliated companies rely on other GM-affiliated companies to provide support in an Islamic sub-economy.

Kaynak pays its salaries using the GM's Bank Aysa (see below), and Bank Asya, in turn, hires Sürat Teknoloji to provide its IT services. GM schools contract with Kaynak Publishers for school equipment, textbooks, uniforms, etc. All of the above publish advertising in newspapers, magazines, and television stations that are managed by the various brands of the GM-affiliated Feza Media Group (see below), which helps them to reach a consumer base that is dominated by GM loyalists and arkadaşlar. In turn, GM-affiliated companies subscribe to the GM-affiliated *Zaman* newspaper, *Aksiyon* magazine, and other GM media products. What Osman Bey called "friendship marketing" assures that institutionally autonomous companies will, at the very least, have a minimum number of clients on which to expand.

On the other hand, although these institutions rely on "friends" for their initial clientele, once established, market forces take over. For instance, although in the 1980s Akademi-affiliated publishing relied on a preferred client within the GM network for its printing needs, Turkey's global integration eventually led Akademi publishers to China, where printing was offered at more competitive prices. Ferhat Bey at the Akademi explained the company's rationale for meeting printing needs:

> We have a printer in Izmir, but actually it depends on the quality necessary. And the costs. . . . Actually, we are beginning to use some Chinese printers. . . . It's crazy, it's crazy how those guys are really eating things up . . . really low costs and really high quality. (Field Interview, Fall 2006)

This was actually the first of many contradictions I observed between the presentation of the GM as a "selfless" faith community, and the GM as a for-profit network of products and services. During the same conversation, Ferhat explained, "Religion is the motivating force behind all of this"; and in nearly the same breath, he explained, "That's the thing you know . . . this is a business, I mean, we are not just publishing, we are making a business":

> JH: So this is a for-profit enterprise?
> FERHAT: Of course! . . . I mean some countries in Africa, and Pakistan
>   . . . the poverty is just so widespread, so unbelievable, that certain

arrangements must be made. I mean this book [picked up an English language *Fethullah Gülen: Advocate of Dialogue* from on his desk] ... This book is [looked on the back] $14.95 U.S. ... In countries like Pakistan some arrangements are made ... maybe to produce a lower-quality book at much cheaper costs so that people can afford to buy and read them. (Field Interview, Fall 2006)

Ferhat then indicated that the GM as a whole is in favor of a particular understanding of globalization, what he termed "cultural globalization." In Ferhat's view, economic integration was potentially destabilizing to Turkey's national well-being, but at the same time, he acknowledged opportunities in the context of what he called the "global village":

FERHAT: You know, we and the Russians, we don't have such a nice history together. ... Most of our history has been fighting wars. ... What these men [GM businessmen who donate money to GM schools] are doing, together with the Russians, is saying ... Look, that was in the past ... now we are neighbors ... Islam teaches to be nice to your neighbors ... to take care of your neighbors ... and the Russians think so, too. I mean, Russia, Armenia, Greece ... these are the hostile countries to the Turks, but they are also our neighbors ... in globalization we are all neighbors, and we should take care of our neighbors ... Islam teaches this ... and as far as I know so does Christianity, as far as I know ... and as far as I know so does Judaism. This is the kind of globalization were are OK with ...

JH: This kind of globalization?

FERHAT: Yeah, the globalization that makes us all neighbors. ... Not the globalization that is trying to take over everything. ... When McDonald's comes and these big guys, and they just wipe out local businesses. ... I mean, domestic businesses are just being wiped out. ... The world is now a global village, and villages need to be nice to their neighbors. In the global village you realize that your neighbors have different beliefs ... but you have to get along anyway. ... These schools [GISs] bring people of different nations together.

JH: When these businessmen go around the world to make a profit with schools and business, that is economic globalization, too, no?

FERHAT: Yeah, but I guess it was harder in the early days, when no one knew about the schools . . . when you are the minister of education in Thailand, for example . . . and you have this Turkish businessman in your office . . . you have never even heard of Turkey . . . and you ask . . . "Why do you want to build a school here?" But now, with the established quality of the schools, with all the students winning so many science olympiads, many places want the Turkish schools. It is good for Turkey to build schools around the world because Central Asia, Africa, Russia, these are big places and Turkey needs to be . . . In Russia, for instance, a Turkish school there was ranked twenty-fifth out of something like twenty thousand private schools . . . that is pretty amazing, no? (Field Interview, Fall 2006)

Explaining globalization both as potentially threatening and as potentially beneficial, and viewing the GM both as a religious community focused on *da'wa* (invitation to Islam, proselytization) and as a business community focused on profits, Ferhat exemplified the GM's Islamic ethic of capitalism. Indeed, although they rely on their identity community for start-up funds, GM enterprises as a whole constitute far more than a sub-economy of pious Turkish Muslims. Their aim, like the aim of all capitalist enterprises, is growth. Growth is exactly why a number of wealthier GM benefactors consolidated their financial resources to form what is now Turkey's largest "Islamic" financial institution, and why it centralized its affiliated and sympathetic arkadaş companies into what is now Turkey's largest business-oriented NGO.

The Muslim Share

The conscious link between cultural, economic, and social activism in the GM's core and extended network is apparent in the range of SMEs that now define Turkey's export sector (Demir, Açar, and Toprak 2004). In Southeast Asia, where several countries host a number of GISs, GM followers set up Pasifik Ülkeleri İle Sosyal ve İktisadi Dayanışma Derneği (Association for Social and Economic Cooperation in Pacific Asia, PASIAD). PASIAD is charged with three tasks: (1) manage GISs in the region; (2) develop relationships with state bureaucrats and with local opinion makers in media, faith communities, and academia; and

(3) cultivate trade links between local businesses and affiliated Turkish enterprises. PASIAD members, as well as members of other "associations of industrialists and businessmen" (SIADs) loyal to the GM, donate regularly in an organized fund-raising system, which generates initial capital for GISs in the form of himmet.[8] "Friendship marketing" provides an opportunity to begin a venture, but in order to grow, demand must extend beyond the community to the fourth tier in the GM's organizational logic: the unaware consumer.

The GM network of schools and affiliate businesses got so big, and covered so much territory, that in 2005, 124 separate SIADs representing more than ten thousand Turkish businessmen came together to form Turkey's newest and largest business-related NGO, Türkiye Işadamları Sanayiciler Konfederasyonu (Confederation of Businessmen and Industrialists in Turkey, TUSKON). TUSKON was founded under the leadership of Rızanur Meral, the SANKO Group executive who headed the GM's first business association, İş Hayatı Dayanışma Deneği (Business Life Cooperation Association, İSHAD). İSHAD first consolidated thirty smaller business associations in Turkey's Marmara region (which includes Istanbul) under the collective Marmara İş Hayatı Dernekleri Federesyonu (Marmara Business Life Association Federation, MARIFED). In 2005, MARIFED, led by İSHAD, brought together seven large federations to form TUSKON. İSHAD is given much of the credit for TUSKON's emergence, which, since 2005, has realigned Turkey's export potential to every corner of the world (Field Interview, Fall 2008).

Since 2005, TUSKON has organized a series of trade conferences with individual nations and with whole regions. The largest of these summits to date organized trade talks between private actors and state ministers between Turkey and Central Asia (September 2006), Turkey and Pacific Asia (April 2007, June 2008; both in conjunction with PASIAD), Turkey and Middle and Eastern European nations (September 2008, May 2009), Turkey and African nations (May 2006, 2007, 2008), and Turkey and "the World" (October 2011), a trade summit that included businesspeople from a number of Latin American countries that have little-to-no trade relations with Turkey. At each of these events, students from GISs in Istanbul provided interpretation services during multiple days of business-to-business transaction.

At the outset of the 2007 TUSKON Turkey–Africa trade summit, participants sought to double the previous year and sign US$500 million in contracts. After two days, US$2 billion was the final tally ("Brothers from Turkey, Africa Embrace on Trade Bridge" 2007). The TUSKON–PASIAD conference in April 2007 resulted in US$750 million, three times its initial target. The AKP's former economy minister, now foreign minister, Ali Babacan attended the 2007 TUSKON–PASIAD conference with Southeast Asian nations. AKP Prime Minister Recep Tayyip Erdoğan and Parliament Speaker Bülent Arinç both sent letters praising its achievement. During his seven-year tenure as the AKP's foreign trade minster between 2002 and 2009, Kürsad Tüzmen attended every TUSKON trade summit in Istanbul, opening and closing each event with a keynote speech. At the October 2011 "Turkey and the World" trade summit, over US$300 billion in trade deals came to fruition in just two days.

According to TUSKON's president, Rızanur Meral, TUSKON owes its successes to the hard work and dedication of what he called "Turkish schools" in countries around the world, whose founding entrepreneurs "play a crucial role in creating connections with businessmen of the region":

> Turkish businessmen are trying to be players in this globalizing world. . . .
> The Pacific region had fourteen countries, a 786-million-strong population, $7.3 trillion gross national product (GNP) and $1.4 trillion foreign trade volume. . . . [We aim at] increasing the trade volume with these countries, reducing the cost of Turkish imports from the region, increasing collaboration in the construction sector and benefiting from natural resources. ("Small Enterprises Star in TUSKON's Trade Bridge with Pacific" 2007)

Just as the leaders in TÜSIAD did before him, Meral spoke on behalf of all "Turkish businessmen." Unlike his older counterparts, however, he spoke to a global audience. In October 2011, just as TUSKON's "Turkey–World Trade Bridge" kicked off in Istanbul, the GM-affiliated *Today's Zaman* quoted Meral as follows:

> Many of these people are interested in jewelry; they provided revenue to Turkey by shopping in local malls. We have brought 556 national delegations with a total of 11,000 businesspeople to Turkey from 140 different

countries in the last fourteen months. TUSKON expects to receive an award from the Ministry of Tourism. ("TUSKON Summit Initiates $300 Billion in Trade in Two Days" 2011)

Although TÜSIAD's remains dominant in Turkey's capitalist class, the immediate success of TUSKON is indicative of a new sphere of elite influence in Turkey's civil society. This new powerbase draws from a transnationally networked religious community to expand its potential and to galvanize its resources. TUSKON's overwhelming success has catapulted the organization's influence in Turkey's business sector and has begun to attract criticism because of its ties to the GM. The strategy to handle such accusations is to incorporate the proven tactic of strategic ambiguity to downplay connectivity. A PASIAD board member explained as follows:

> CIHAN: The movement and these organizations are independent from one another. But the people who love the movement are of great importance in these unions.
> JH: Which one? TUSKON? PASIAD?
> CIHAN: All of them. PASIAD, and in TUSKON as well. (Field Interview, Spring 2007)

When asked to elaborate about TUSKON's institutional role in the GM's organizational logic, a TUSKON representative explained that it depends on whom you ask:

> Actually, if you ask me, officially, I mean, we don't say that we are part of the Gülen Movement. Why? Because, I mean we have our own board, we have our own interests, and these are the interests of the business people who are the members of TUSKON. So, I mean, there is not a kind of direct partnership, et cetera. But many of our members are Gülen Movement people. And they feel that we as an organization as well are a Gülen Movement institution. (Field Interview, Fall 2008)

Although maintaining ambiguity is routine for GM operatives who are asked to characterize their institutional affiliation, the networks that connect GISs abroad with GM businesses are well-known, even by the state dignitaries and foreign ministers who regularly meet with

TUSKON representatives, and who regularly attend TUSKON trade summits. At the 2006 Turkey–Africa summit, for instance, Chad's trade minister summarized his understanding of the GM link to Turkish trade as follows: "Westerners came to Africa to take from us but they brought nothing. The only thing we want now is real partnership. For Chad, the Turkish schools are the most important doors to the outside world. They also form the bridge between Turkey and us."[9]

Consolidating the GM's financial resources is the job of Bank Asya (BA) (formerly Asya Finans), an interest-free financial institution that began with start-up capital from sixteen businessmen loyal to Fethullah Gülen. In the fifty-five interviews I conducted, BA was among the more ambiguous institutions discussed. According to approximately half of my research sample composed of leaders in GM enterprise, there was no question that BA was "the GM's bank." Others, however, explained that in their view, there was no "organic connection" between the bank and the "the Movement." A senior executive at BA explained this discrepancy as follows:

> Hocaefendi said it would be beneficial for them [GM-affiliated businessmen], for their future enterprises, and he asked them to pray. So people came together and it started [Bank Asya] in this way.... But Hocaefendi does not have an account here. (Field Interview, July 2007)

Notwithstanding, when I asked an executive at Sürat Teknoloji why BA selected the firm for the bank's IT services, he explained as follows:

> Bank Asya sees us as being close to the Movement and thus works with us, but the quality of our work there brings in Türkiye Finans and other banks as customers. If the quality of your work is not good enough, no one will give you employment, I emphasize that people who set their heart to the Movement know this. If you look at Bank Asya, only the bosses have ties of love to the movement [gönül bağı]. But if I don't do good work for Bank Asya, they will not give me the additional work; or, if I do not provide good services for Kaynak Publishing, it won't give me more work either. ... We are a professional company working within the market. No one gives us jobs for our looks [kara kaş kara gözüne], or for our thoughts and feelings, nor do they avoid giving us jobs for these reasons, that is, because we have our own principles that we put forth. In fact, these principles are

mentioned in Hocaefendi's articles. He says "complete your work on time," "do your job in the right way," "be honest," "behave respectfully." There is a philosophy that Hocaefendi puts forth." (Field Interview, July 2007)

Just as it is with all GM companies, tenders are first offered to arkadaş. Once a company establishes trust among friends, it accrues enough expertise to expand its clientele to the unaware consumer. It eventually becomes an active player in the larger Turkish and global marketplaces. With modest start-up capital totaling less than US$1 million, by October 2011 BA's assets totaled more than $14 billion. In May 2006, BA went public with 20 percent of its assets offered in its initial public offering, despite a demand that was 50 percent higher. The same senior executive was very proud to explain, "This was a record in Turkey. It was mentioned in [the] *Financial Times* based in London" (Field Interview, July 2007). Although the newest of Turkey's four interest-free lenders, BA became the market leader, the fastest growing with 199 branches (as of October 2011), and the only participation bank that is majority Turkish-owned.[10] Among the fifty-one banking institutions operating in Turkey, in 2007 BA was ranked fourteenth in total assets and hoped to breach the top ten in the near future (Field Interview, July 2007).

BA's rapid rise in the banking sector is due in part to increased liberalization, and in part to new market opportunities created after the 2001 Turkish economic collapse. In this regard, BA is a source of pride and security for individuals in the GM, as followers trust that it will not succumb to corruption as other players in Turkey's "green capital" sector did in the run-up to the 2001 crisis:

[In 2001] A huge gap emerged in the market. It was explicit that the banks that would bridge this gap would come into prominence. Approximately forty thousand bankers lost their jobs. . . . This foundation's active growth has averaged 60 percent a year since then. This continued to 2006. 2007 looks like it will follow suit again. . . . Each year, it grows 60 percent; you can calculate how huge a growth this is. We are very proud of this fact. It is the consequence of the decisions made immediately after the crisis of 2001. . . . Today, we have approximately three thousand staff members. At least half, or more than the half of them, are personnel that were transferred from other banks. (Field Interview, July 2007)[11]

By 2007, BA was invested in projects throughout the Middle East, the Arab Gulf, North Africa, Russia, and Ukraine. Domestically, it increased its capacity to become involved in several major public works projects in Istanbul, including a new transcontinental bridge over the Bosphorus Straits, and a new metro transit system. Discussing these investments, the same informant explained as follows:

> The goal of Turkey is to be accepted to the EU. What is the difference in the infrastructures of European countries and Turkey? This is the point. . . . Highways, privatization biddings, et cetera. . . . Energy distribution biddings are near at hand. We have an active role in all of these biddings. (Field Interview, July 2007)

When it recently reported its 2008 profits, BA was among few of Turkey's net success stories weathering the 2008 global financial crisis. As reported by GM-affiliated media, BA profits grew by 12 percent in 2008, its equity increased by 64 percent, and its total assets by 30 percent. In February 2009, over 1.3 million Turkish citizens held a BA check card ("Bank Asya Sees Increase in 2008 Profits despite Crisis" 2009).

BA is the primary underwriter of all TUSKON trade summits, as well as all social and political conferences organized by the GM's Journalists and Writers Foundation and the GM's Turkish Language Olympics (see below), and is a major advertising contributor to the GM's *Zaman* newspaper. Downplayed by Fethullah Gülen, continuously skirted by my informants, and largely absent in the literature, however, is any detailed account of the correlation that exists between GISs and the *continued* success of affiliated exporters, Kaynak Holding, TUSKON, BA, and other institutions associated with the GM's economic development and production network. Just as the Kaynak subsidiary Turkish-language instruction textbook company Dilset receives a new client with every GIS opened, there are hundreds of companies in Turkey that enjoy continued growth in part because of market inroads paved by GISs abroad.

Conservative Democracy or Crony Capitalism?

Often seen on the pages of the GM-affiliated *Zaman* newspaper are advertisements and stories about the SANKO Group, GENPA Technology, and Çalık Holding. Directors at each of these corporations were original shareholders in BA. Since 1995, however, Çalık Holding has received a great deal of attention from journalists at *Zaman*, and since 2008, from journalists throughout Turkey. In addition to being the largest single shareholder of BA stock (through two subsidiaries), the Çalik Group is involved in textiles, commercial banking, power/electricity, and pipeline construction, with assets totaling $2.4 billion (Hayward 2007).[12] While its corporate origins date back to the 1960s, in the 1990s the Çalık Group expanded alongside GISs in Turkmenistan, where it also supported the production and distribution of a Turkmen version of the GM's *Zaman* newspaper (Mamedov 2005). For approximately fifteen years, CEO Ahmet Çalık was a government minister in Turkmenistan, and a personal adviser to the former Turkmen president and dictator Saparmurat Niyasov Turkmenbashı until the latter's death in 2006.

Turkmenbashı's "holy text," the *Ruhama*, is required reading for all Turkmen citizens. In the spring of 2009, *Shadow of the Holy Book* premiered at film festivals around the world, a documentary film that detailed the corrupt relationships formed between Turkmenistan's dictator and executives of transnational corporations who hope to establish inroads into the resource-rich nation. In the film, the director Arto Halonen explained that before Turkmenbashı's death in 2006, if a global company wanted to conduct business in Turkmenistan, that company was required to translate the leader's *Ruhama* into the native language of its executives. Interestingly, a senior-level aristocrat in the GM hierarchy, Muhammad Cetin, prepared the translation of *Ruhama* into Turkish in the 1990s while working as a teacher and administrator at a GIS in that country. Cetin's translation of *Ruhama* earned him an award for cultural service and a post in Turkmenistan's state ministry; most important, it opened the door for Turkish trade in that country.[13] Among the most successful recipients of the open door policies that emerged between Turkey and Turkmenistan was Çalık Holding.

The Çalık Group enjoys a great deal of favor in close proximity to the Turkmen regime. Çalık Holding operates Turkmenistan's largest textile factory, and Ahmet Çalık served as the country's minister of textiles and as a personal adviser to Turkmenbashı for fifteen years. In 1998, Çalık opened Çalık Enerji, a subsidiary that works in power systems, oil and gas pipeline construction, and telecommunications. In Turkmenistan,

Çalık Enerji operates a number of power plants and oil refineries, and controls all international telecommunications. After growing globally competitive there, the Turkish-owned Çalık Group went global with its endeavors and solidified its takeover of 76 percent of Albtelecom telecommunications in Albania in 2007. Such growth coheres with Çalık Enerji's stated mission "to be the biggest in the energy sector in Turkey and the close geography."[14] Indeed, Çalık Enerji became a major shareholder in the Trans-Anatolian Pipeline (TAPCO) project in Turkey, which broke ground on April 24, 2007. Since then, the Çalık Group became the first Turkish company to receive a contract for a Bosphorus bypass project, which, when finished, is projected to transport Russian crude from the Turkish Black Sea coastal city of Samsun 550 km across Anatolia to the Mediterranean port city of Ceyhan (Roberts 2004). The TAPCO project will make use of pre-existing passage ways created by the Baku–Tbilisi–Ceyhan pipeline, a 1,776-km pipeline that opened in May 2006, and that was lobbied for heavily by CEO Ahmet Çalık with overt support from the U.S. government (Fried 2007). Çalik Enerji was also recently awarded a no-bid contract with Israel to construct an underwater gas pipeline, a project that Turkey's secular-identified opposition party (CHP) alleged was the result of political cronyism in collusion with the AKP (Hendrick 2009).

The premise for these allegations was that Çalık's new general director is Berat Albayrak, who was also Prime Minister Erdoğan's son-in-law. The CHP alleged that the AKP minister of energy and the AKP foreign ministry lobbied on Çalık's behalf for the project's tender. Longtime Turkish media tycoon Aydın Doğan levied similar claims against Erdoğan and Çalık about Erdoğan's uncontested handover of an oil refinery project in Ceyhan. According to Doğan, the prime minster blocked a Doğan energy subsidiary from competing with Çalık for the tender ("Aydin Dogan Says He Won't Back Down in Media Row with Turkish PM" 2008). These allegations were exacerbated by the fact that in December 2007, Çalık won another uncontested tender, a US$1.1 billion takeover deal of ATV-Sabah, Turkey's second-largest media group behind the Doğan Group. This highly contested move was met with allegations of nepotism concerning the Albayrak–Erdoğan connection. It also met with allegations of cronyism in regard to an unprecedented US$750 million state-administered loan, and an apparent lobbying effort by Prime Minister Erdoğan to solicit Qatari support for the remainder of the deal. Although contested, the sale went through, and Ahmet Çalık solidified himself alongside his fellow BA majority shareholder Ali Akbulut (owner and CEO of the GM's Feza Media Group) in the larger effort to promote the identity and perspective of "conservative democracy" in mainstream Turkish news.

Whether someone praises or criticizes the Çalık Group's growing influence in the Turkish economy, or its preferred position in the Turkmen economy; and whether someone likens the success of GISs, Kaynak Corporation, TUSKON, or BA as indicators of a successful business model, or as intimidating indicators of a coming "Islamic takeover," are both matters of personal opinion and have little sociological significance. What *is* significant, however, is that the Çalık Group rose to prominence in Turkmenistan during the time of Cetin's tenure there as a GIS administrator, and both actors served as advisers to Turkmenbashı and as ministers in the Turkmen regime, which exemplifies the relationships that GM affiliates work to forge with host states around the world, and the network-wide rewards that can result from successful transnational ventures.

Conclusion

In the 1990s, the GM model was applied outside Turkey. By 1996, the GM had expanded into banking. Within ten years, the GM's Bank Asya rose to the top of Turkey's participation banking sector, and by 2005 GM-affiliated businessmen had formed TUKSON. In so doing, GM actors linked affiliated exporters with GISs around the world in a coordinated effort to take advantage of market opportunities. It is important to emphasize that none of these successes would have been possible without the success of GISs abroad, whose activities anchor the GM's transnational enterprise, and whose existence provide affiliated businesses with new opportunities to expand to foreign markets. By maintaining that its efforts are solely focused on education and bridging cultural divides, however, the GM has institutionalized an ambiguous system of wealth accumulation and economic power hoarding that has led to measurable successes, not only in the market, but in the generation of popular discourse and the subsequent manufacturing of consent in favor of Turkey's "conservative democratic" transformation.

7

Manufacturing Consent

Among their other functions, the media serve, and propagandize on behalf of, the powerful societal interests that
control and finance them. The representatives of these interests have important agendas and principles that they want to
advance, and they are well positioned to shape and constrain
media policy.
—Edward Herman and Noam Chomsky

In September 2008, a new round of turbulence began in Turkish public discourse, this time pitting Turkey's largest media mogul, Aydin
Doğan, against the ruling AKP government, and specifically against
Prime Minster Erdoğan.[1] The row began after Doğan-owned newspapers and television stations published and aired a series of reports
focusing on fraud, embezzlement, and money-laundering charges filed
in Germany against a Turkish-owned charity, Deniz Feneri Vakfı (Light
House Foundation, est. 2001). The director of Deniz-Feneri, Mehmet
Güham, together with his assistant Mehmet Taskan and the foundation's accountant Firdevsi Ermiş, stood accused of funneling charity
revenue collected from Turkish Muslims in Germany back to Turkey
to various corporate, media, and political recipients. Among the alleged
recipients of the nearly US$60 million (€42 million) were as follows:
(1) Deniz Feneri Vakfı, a charity foundation in Istanbul with the same
Turkish name as the accused foundation in Germany; (2) Beyaz Holding Corporation, an educational services and distributor founded in
1998 by Zaid Akman; (3) Zaid Akman, the AKP-appointed head of
Turkey's Radio and Television Supreme Council, and founder of Beyaz
Holding; (4) Zekeria Karaman, the owner of Kanal 7, the Turkish TV

station that aired the show *Sehir ve Ramazan* (*The City and Ramadan*) in 1997, which initiated the Deniz Feneri project; and (5) leaders in the AKP government, including actors connected to the Office of the Prime Minster.[2] A Frankfurt court found the three defendants guilty of fraud and embezzlement, which sparked a counterpart criminal proceeding in Turkey against Zaid Akman, and a number of people associated with the television Kanal 7 television network.

Doğan Yayın Holding is Turkey's largest media corporation and the owner of the widely read *Hürriyet, Milliyet, Radikal, Vatan,* and *Referans* newspapers, as well the owner of CNN Türk, Kanal D, Star TV, and Turkey's oldest English language daily, *Hürriyet Daily News* (formerly *Turkish Daily News*). According to Prime Minster Erdoğan, Doğan-owned media used the Deniz Feneri corruption case in Germany to level politically motivated attacks against the prime minster and the ruling AKP. In an unprecedented response to Doğan's initial coverage of the case as it unfolded in Germany in the fall of 2008, Erdoğan called on all Turkish citizens to boycott Doğan-owned media:

> In this country, the media has lost its credibility. So I say to you, members of the party, start a campaign against the media which publishes false news and do not take these papers to your homes. . . . Are you carrying false campaigns based on lies against us? That's okay. Now we [will] use our most natural rights and start a campaign against you and won't buy your papers. ("Turkish PM Calls Party to Boycott Critical Media" 2008)

Since its inception, the AKP has drawn attention to its acronym "A-K-P" in reference to its double meaning—to stand both for the party of "justice and development" ("Adalet ve Kalkınma") and the party for "purity" ("ak"). By calling attention to purity, the AKP sought to distinguish itself from the rampant corruption that was characteristic of Turkey's twentieth-century partisan political culture (Yavuz 2006). Erdoğan's call to boycott Doğan-owned media, however, was met with global criticism, not the least of which from European circles dealing with political and economic reforms in Turkey as a matter of the country's EU candidacy. For Doğan-owned media outlets, the Deniz Feneri scandal was a major story, and Erdoğan's call for a boycott was cause for outcry. As this manuscript goes to press in November 2012, CHP and MHP opposition leaders in the Turkish Parliament continue to voice their criticisms about the Turkish side of the Deniz Feneri case, and continue to cite AKP leaders as conspiring to disrupt the investigation and criminal proceedings in Turkey against Akman and his codefendants. AKP leaders, including Prime Minster Erdoğan, have called out their opponents as "pitiful" in response to what they contend to be baseless allegations of corruption and cover-up.[3]

In contrast to the high volume of coverage allocated to the Deniz Feneri fraud allegations, a story that receives more skeptical attention in Doğan-owned media are the day-by-day developments of what is known in Turkey as the Ergenekon investigation, which is alleged to focus on cleansing the Turkish power structure of the aforementioned "deep state," or *derin devlet*. As discussed previously, this alleged network of retired military leaders, media personalities, academics, and political party and associational leaders is accused of masterminding a number of high-profile murders and assassinations in Turkey's recent past, and of conspiring to topple the AKP-led government. As of August 2012, more than five hundred suspects were under arrest under the authority of seven indictments totaling more than eight thousand pages; many have sat is prison for months, some even years, without due process. For these and other reasons, Ergenekon is the subject of uneven reporting in Turkish media. Reports in Doğan media, for instance, tend to focus on mishaps and inconsistencies in the investigation, on the seemingly endless arrests, and on the subsequent fear that anyone might be next.[4] By contrast; Ergenekon receives the most attention, and is framed with a greater sense of urgency, by one specific news outfit—the GM-affiliated Feza Gazetecilik (Feza Media Corporation).

In the first year following the initial discovery of a weapons cache in Istanbul in June 2007 that sparked the AKP-led investigation into Ergenekon, Feza Media's English language daily, *Today's Zaman*, has published, on average, 1.6 stories a day dedicated to the story, excluding hundreds more opinion pieces and editorials.[5] Defending his paper's heavily weighted treatment of Ergenekon, the editor in chief at *Today's Zaman* commented as follows:

> Some of our foreign friends and readers, about whose good intentions we do not have the least doubt, say, perhaps for reasons attributable to

the influence of the circles attempting to defame the Ergenekon investigation, that they have difficulty understanding why we, as *Today's Zaman*, attach so much importance . . . and allocate so much space to the discussion of this investigation. . . . It seems that we have not properly fulfilled our duty, as we can conclude that we have failed to make sure that the significance of this matter is fully understood. However, the answer to this question is quite simple: Economic crises are temporary, but the troubles caused by shadowy Ergenekon-like networks will be permanent unless they are completely eradicated. Those who may lose their jobs today will face great difficulties in unemployment, but they will still have a chance to resume their happy lives after the crisis ends. (Keneş 2009)

Considering its more than daily coverage of the Egenekon proceedings why does the editor in chief of Turkey's most widely read English language daily feel that his paper has not properly underscored the significance of the Ergenekon case as his publication sees it?

To maintain their legitimacy as a part of a distinctly "nonpolitical" social project, GM media must accomplish two key goals. First, they must appeal to a Turkish public (and to an increasingly interested global public) in terms that bridge social conservatism with international neo-liberalism. In so doing, GM media must legitimize their support for AKP rule from a perspective that can be framed as "objective," and they achieve this by presenting the AKP as the clear and obvious choice for *all* democratically minded, human rights–oriented Turkish citizens. Second, because their worldview and their underwriters support the AKP as a conservative democratic coalition, GM media must frame their objectives in such a way that normalizes the ongoing shift from old to new power in Turkey. Indeed, the AKP's efforts in foreign policy to broaden Turkey's bilateral relations with regional neighbors, and with developing countries in Africa and Southeast Asia (aka "strategic depth") greatly favor GM-affiliated business interests whose leaders traverse the world in an effort to expand Turkey's trade relations. Not only is the GM-affiliated TUSKON Turkey's primary bridge between Turkish and host-country businesses, but teachers and administrators at the world's GISs act as cultural compradors, and its media (its English language media specifically) collectively act as Turkey's primary international voice. In this way, the AKP and the GM function as a mutually supportive, albeit tenuous, coalition whose actors work to continue Turkey's passive revolution.

Advocacy Networks, Muslim Politics, and the Media

According to Keck and Sikkink (1998, 23), the credibility of advocacy networks "depends in part on their ability to mobilize their own members and affect public opinion via the media." The incorporation of media strategies and technologies allows activist networks to reach a broad audience of affiliated, like-minded, complacent, and adversarial consumers alike. The fact that the support of public opinion is often won in terms of moral legitimacy confirms the fact that "networks cannot be undermined simply by characterizing them (the structures) as 'agents' of a particular actor or position [e.g., AKP/"conservative democracy" vs. traditional elite/CHP, Doğan Media, etc.]."

When possible, Islamic actors in Turkey and around the world seek to express themselves in all forms of media from journal publications to newspapers, from television to the Internet (Eickelman and Piscatori 1996; Eickelman and Anderson 2003; Cooke and Lawrence 2005; Kepel 2002; Lubeck 2000; Mandaville 2001, 2006; Roy 1994, 2004). Today, Islamic advocacy websites, journals, movies, podcasts, Listservs, print and virtual newspapers, and an increasing number of weblogs flood the Internet with the symbolic language of Muslim politics. In Turkey, Islamic activists have captured the market spirit of such technologies, and have produced a media and public relations network that aims to control the journalistic and academic treatment of Turkey's conservative democratic transformation. What has emerged is a sophisticated example of not only how Islamic activists have incorporated mainstream media into their projects, but also how they have constructed an organizationally competitive media infrastructure that accomplishes four tasks with great effectiveness: (1) promote the identity of their community, (2) promote the policies of the governing power that offers them strategic support, (3) stage effective attacks and counterattacks against perceived enemies, and (4) turn a substantial profit and redistribute resources. Thus, not only does the GM produce media for itself (i.e., media designed to construct and reaffirm an identity of community within the GM cemaat and among the GM's wide network of arkadaşlar), the GM also produces media for strategic economic and political gain. Indeed, by reframing its discourse in line with global neo-liberalism, the GM has become Turkey's leading voice on issues of human rights, democracy, EU integration, and constitutional reform. In so doing, its actors have developed an extensive and ever-growing mass media empire that attracts more international attention than any other public opinion-making source in contemporary Turkish society.

So political *

The Erosion of Monopoly

For most of the twentieth century, print and broadcast media in Turkey were monopolized by a mixture of state-owned enterprises, and by a small handful of family-based holding companies. Until the early 1990s, television broadcasting was controlled entirely by the state. In the early 1980s, the Turkish Television and Radio Corporation (TRT) broadcast one channel. By the late 1980s, it expanded to three. In 1992, Turkish television and radio broadcasting was deregulated, which legally permitted the private purchase of airtime. By the end of that year, there were six new private television stations competing with six state-owned stations (Sahin and Aksoy 1993, 31–32). The liberalization of Turkey's broadcast media led to a dramatic transformation. In the first year of their existence (1992), four of Turkey's privately broadcasted channels took away two-thirds of the TRT's audience (Sahin and Aksoy 1993, 32). When satellite television arrived in the late 1990s, the broadcast market expanded even further. According to Turkey's Office of the Prime Minister Directorate of General Press and Information, in 2008 there were 23 nationally broadcasted television stations, and 231 regional and local stations, approximately half of them only via satellite.

Concerning print media and news collection, Turkey publishes just shy of 2,500 newspapers, 55 of which are distributed nationally. News is collected by 23 agencies.[6] The primary firms producing mainstream broadcast media and print media are the state-owned TRT, the aforementioned Doğan Group, the Cukuruva Group, the Ihlas Group, the Çalık Group, and the Feza Group, as well as a number of smaller and independent firms. Doğan Media, along with papers and television stations controlled by the Cukuruva Group, and the independent but long-established *Cumhuriyet* newspaper, represent the "secular" or "statist" line in Turkish public discourse. *Cumhuriyet* is as old as the Turkish Republic and was actually first commissioned by none other than Mustafa Kemal himself. Today, however, *Cumhuriyet* is a curious publication. On the one hand, it is the preferred paper of the Turkish left, the labor-friendly, highly educated, European-looking, and staunchly secularist circles in Istanbul, Izmir, Antalya, and Ankara. On the other hand, *Cumhuriyet* also maintains a strictly conservative stance in terms of protecting "Atatürk's republic," and is thus noticeably obtuse when it comes to issues dealing with criticism of the Turkish Armed Forces, or when reporting about AKP-led successes in the macro effort to implement legal and economic reform.

If *Cumhuriyet* represents Turkey's primary left-wing, "pro-establishment" voice, media brands associated with the Doğan Media Group collectively represent the primary centrist, mainstream, "pro-establishment" voice. As the dominant force in Turkey's print media market, Doğan Media brands strive to appeal to the majority of Turkish society by catering to different political constituencies on the pages of a variety of dailies. The popular *Radikal*, for instance, caters to a readership that tends toward the center–left, whereas the group's flagship *Hürriyet* and its correlate *Milliyet* dailies appeal to Turkey's moderate center. A relatively new daily, *Referans*, appeals to a market-focused center–right, and the daily *Vatan* appeals to a readership that favors a more nationalist interpretation of Turkish current events. In addition to these dailies, Doğan also publishes Turkey's oldest, and until recently, most widely read English language daily, the *Hürriyet Daily News* (*HDN*, formerly *Turkish Daily News*). According to an Open Source Center (2008) study, *HDN*'s daily circulation in 2008 was a modest 2,802 papers, with an estimated 60 percent of this number comprising native English speakers in Turkey (e.g., dignitaries, businesspeople, tourists). In the same year, however, the paper's prestige waned significantly. Its format changed, as did its title. And although the paper's editors made no public comment as to why this was the case, according to GM-affiliated journalists the January 2007 emergence of the GM's *Today's Zaman* played a significant role (see below).

According to Kaya and Cornell (2008), the effort on the part of Özal's ANAP government in the 1980s was to push for media liberalization in an effort to facilitate the creation of private media outlets that would support ANAP policies. This process continued under different governments in the 1990s, but it was not until the emergence of the AKP in 2002 that party–media relations took on new meaning. This is because the rise of the AKP coincided with the further liberalization of Turkey's media sector, whereby private media conglomerates were permitted to expand their enterprises into other sectors:

> These business diversifications made it in the interests of the owners of the media holdings to be on good terms with the government—given the expectation that their media outlets' attitude toward the government could influence their chances in privatization tenders, not least in the backroom deals that appear to have characterized many of these. Indeed the AKP government has according to numerous reports made it practice to use soft state power—i.e., utilizing the power to accord or not accord various companies the licenses and tenders they seek. (Kaya and Cornell 2008, 2)

In addition to controlling 40 percent of Turkey's market in print journalism and selling a total of 4.1 million papers a day, in 2000 Doğan took over 51 percent of Turkey's state-owned oil company, Petrol Ofisi, the country's largest fuel distributor (Open Source Center 2008). Lending credence to Kaya and Cornell's analysis of the transformed nature of media–government relations under the AKP regime, in 2008, according to Doğan, Erdoğan and the AKP attempted to block a number of the Doğan Group's expansion projects, including the building of an oil refinery in the Mediterranean city of Ceyhan, and the construction of an annex to the Hilton hotel in Istanbul. The former project, Doğan alleged, was promised to Ahmet Çalık ("Aydin Dogan Says He Won't Back Down in Media Row with Turkish PM" 2008). The public war of words between Doğan and Erdoğan over the Deniz Feneri scandal, Erdoğan's call to boycott Doğan-owned media, and the fine of half a billion U.S. dollars levied against the Doğan Group adds even more evidence to support the fact that in the new Turkey, "the freedom of the press is increasingly called into question . . . as large parts of the media have come under the control of business interests, which in one way or another are connected to or indebted to the government" (Kaya and Cornell 2008, 3).

The second largest media conglomerate in Turkey is ATV-Sabah, which was seized by the Turkish government in April 2007 and sold to the Çalık Group for US$1.1 billion in December 2007. As discussed previously, the tender that led to Çalık's acquisition of ATV-Sabah was uncontested and led to allegations of cronyism and nepotism on the part of the AKP, which reached a global audience. Erdoğan's familial connections with Çalık, coupled with a historically unprecedented US$750 million in state-administered loans together with Qatari support, were also met with a great deal of suspicion by domestic and international critics. Nonetheless, the deal went through, and now, together with the smaller *Yeni Şafak, Vakit*, and *Bügün* newspapers, the AKP enjoys support from media that, while not collectively as big as their conglomerate rivals, are a competitive alternative for manufacturing consent in Turkish society.

In light of Kaya and Cornell's assessment, it is interesting to note that the entity leading the efforts to promote the perspective of the new Turkey is the media holding firm owned and operated by individuals loyal to Fethullah Gülen. With modest beginnings in 1986, and although still quite small in comparison to the Doğan and Cukuruva Groups, Feza Gazetecilik (Feza Media Group) owns and operates two nationally broadcasted television stations (Samanyolu TV, Mehtap TV), an English language satellite television (Ebru TV, based in New Jersey), a nationally broadcasted radio station (Burç FM), thirteen foreign edition newspapers, Turkey's most widely distributed political magazine (*Aksiyon*), a sizable and respected news collection agency (Cihan Haber Ajansı, CHA), and Turkey's most widely distributed English language publication (*Today's Zaman*). These successes, however, all pale in comparison to the success of Feza's flagship product, *Zaman*, whose average daily sales since 2007 have consistently outnumbered any newspaper in Turkey.[7] How do GM-affiliated media connect with GISs and GM-affiliated businesses to implement Gülen's project for conservative social change?

The Impact of Feza Gazetecilik

Although sincere in its efforts to advocate for pluralist reform in Turkish public discourse, and for democratic reform in Ankara, actors leading the GM's media effort are also involved in an interest-oriented propaganda project that is heavily invested in manufacturing consent in Turkish society. Their adversaries assert that the AKP and the GM work in collusion and "hide a secret agenda" that is against democracy, and that they merely use democratic means to meet an "Islamic end." A very well-known and influential opinion columnist and author at a major Turkish newspaper known for its staunch rejection of AKP governance explained this belief to me in no uncertain terms:

> Let me say this, it is very important. Fethullahcılar are Nurcu [i.e., followers of Fethullah Gülen; Said Nursi] and Nurcu people are the enemies of the freedoms of democracy, and they are the most dangerous enemies of America as well. (Field Interview, Summer 2007)

The first task of GM media is thus to present the AKP, the political representative body of Turkey's new bourgeoisie, and the GM itself, as collectively embodying the social mores of secular modernity *to a greater extent* than Turkey's traditional "Kemalist" elite. This means that despite the AKP's often-cited "Islamist roots," AKP leaders (with the help of GM media, and other supportive media) must present their party as "truly" secular, as "truly" liberal, and as Turkey's most effective leader in regard to reforming the country's power structure in accordance with global norms. It does this by publicly lambasting its adversaries not for being "un-Islamic," "infidel," or deserving of God's wrath, but for being "undemocratic," "authoritarian," or "fascist."[8]

According to Mustafa Bey, a senior hoca at the Akademi who was also an author and a former journalist at *Zaman* and CHA, the motivation behind *Zaman* was, in his words, to "correct fake news" in Turkish society:

> The newspaper was founded in 1986. Before then there were the attempts of other Muslim entrepreneurs but they couldn't survive. In that period, the schools, dorms, and dershanes continued to be developed. And there were supporters of these institutions and there were enemies. In Turkey, media was a monopoly. Journalists are raised by the paper *Cumhuriyet*. They are totally leftist, atheist people. *Cumhuriyet* [represents] a school [of thought] in Turkey. And journalists are always of that origin. So, there were aspirations to do something about this. . . . Then what

happened? The other papers could not write fake news, because now, our correspondents were everywhere and by then we had a newspaper and a television channel. You must think of *Zaman* as a tool to correct fake news. (Field Interview, Spring 2007)

Zaman was originally directed toward GM followers and toward a pious reading public. In the mid-1990s, however, at the request of Fethullah Gülen, a handful of young GM recruits attended journalism school in the United States. The intent was to raise the quality of *Zaman* journalism to what Mustafa Bey termed "global standards." Upon their return in 2001, *Zaman* underwent what Mustafa described as a "rebirth" (Field Interview, Spring 2007).

The group of men who now manage *Zaman* met while attending university in Istanbul. There, these young men lived in a GM ışık evi. Under the guidance of their ağabey, who himself was a recent graduate at the time, these young men formed the "*Zaman* Research Group." The group put together news reports and their ağabey got them published in *Zaman*. During my fieldwork in 2007, all of these men were senior executives in the GM's media enterprise and several were very well-known opinion makers who published regularly on the editorial pages of *Zaman*, *Today's Zaman*, and *Aksiyon*, and who made regular appearances the GM's Mehtap TV, Samanyolu TV, and Burç FM. The group's original ağabey had become one of *Zaman*'s most recognizable columnists, and was among many *Zaman*-affiliated journalists who at the time were working outside Turkey to promote and expand *Zaman* journalism in the United States (Field Interviews, Spring and Summer 2007).

According to a former member of the *Zaman* Research Group, *Zaman*'s renovation started in the mid-1990s, around the time the *Zaman* Research Group formed. Unlike the intent of "Islamist" media efforts around the world, however, the intent on the part of *Zaman*'s second-generation architects was less to increase the voice of piety in Turkish discourse, than it was to increase the competitiveness of the paper in the political economy of Turkish media:

[In the early 1990s] students of journalism came . . . who were, who had, who were coming from the Movement, from the Movement background.

Like [name removed], who is now a columnist . . . for instance, and
[name removed], who is now our editor in chief of our [place removed]
edition. So they were coming from the Movement's sources. So this process of gradual transformation came to that point. In 1994, *Aksiyon* was
organized. . . . What happened in 2001 was that all the different ideas
were systemized, you can say. But especially with the contribution, the
big contribution of [name removed]. He got an education in the States
. . . in journalism. But not just himself, there was a group of journalists
who studied there . . . who now lead the future of the newspaper. So they
were very much instrumental in my view in that change. (Field Interview, Spring 2007)

Zaman is the Feza Media Group's flagship brand. By 2008, *Zaman*
had emerged as Turkey's most successful individual newspaper as measured by its number of subscription-based sales. *Zaman's* high subscription and circulation numbers are often criticized by rival news
companies, which allege that loyalists buy up *Zaman* newspapers and
distribute them for free, and that the paper's high circulation gives a
false impression to observers because of *Zaman's* reliance on institutional subscriptions from GM arkadaş companies (e.g., Bank Asya,
Kaynak Holding, TUSKON) that purchase thousands of copies a day.
Notwithstanding, *Zaman's* business model produces subscription numbers that get attention. A Belgium external auditing firm produced a
2007 report that noted *Zaman* subscriptions as among the highest of
any newspaper in Europe (Palmer and Robinson 2007).

Collectively, Feza journalism has in many ways pushed Turkish
journalism to reach a higher level of excellence in terms of integrity,
format display, and accessibility. *Zaman* publishes thirteen foreign editions that are distributed in countries throughout Central Asia, Europe,
and the United States. A number of foreign journalists, academics, and
political observers now refer to Feza Media brands because they believe
them to be "more liberal in terms of its reporting," and "more transparent" in terms of presenting competing views (Field Notes, Spring
2007, Summer 2007, Fall 2008). In January 2007, Feza launched *Today's
Zaman*, which in its first month became Turkey's most widely distributed English language daily.[9] Given its publication in a country where
English was not widely spoken, and thus where the staffing, production,

Zaman headquarters. Located in the Yenibosna neighborhood in Istanbul, the *Zaman* building is also headquarters of *Today's Zaman* and *Aksiyon*. The state-of-the-art construction was completed in 2005. (Author's photo, taken on "Children's Day," March 23, 2007, in Istanbul)

printing, and distribution of an English language paper would likely yield a very small readership, I asked a number of senior editors and managers at *Zaman* what they expected to gain from the venture. I learned that executives spearheading the GM media initiative were acutely aware of the opportunities provided by Turkey's integration, and were even more aware of the potential to attract an international audience to cultivate support for domestic issues. Highlighting what Keck and Sikkink (1998) cite as the "boomerang effect" of transnational engagement, a central figure in the organization and management of *TZ* named Cem explained as follows:

> JH: How did the idea for an English paper come about?
> CEM: In fact, this idea was not a new one. Perhaps it was me who first put forth this idea of a newspaper in English. When I was the head of the [deleted] department in 1996, I went on a trip to Egypt. There,

we saw *El-Ahram*. Perhaps you know about *El-Ahram*? . . . It is the newspaper published in English in Egypt. I really liked it. We have a specific outlook to life and the world, but we express it through *Zaman* only to Turkish readers. English came to be a universal language. The world needs these ideas; you can regard this statement as my subjective opinion. In this universal language, this outlook should be expressed as much as possible. The material means and the possibilities of our substructure were not available to realize it. I proposed that we should make preparations and educate our staff in order to publish a newspaper in English. . . . Later on with the economic crisis [in 1999], the project remained in suspense and I resigned from the group in early 2000. When [name deleted] told me about this project, I said it is a project that should be realized and that I have been thinking about it for years; so I began working on it. . . . From the previous October onwards I began working on this project actively. After a period of preparation that lasted for three or four months, we established the staff and began publishing the paper in January [2007]. (Field Interview, Summer 2007)

Unlike its counterparts, *TZ* was not intended for a Turkish readership. It was intended for a global readership, for foreign press, dignitaries, and businesspeople in Turkey, and for anyone researching online about the Turkish current events, politics, arts, or culture. Before its first publication in January 2007, *TZ* executives developed organizational connections with the *Times* of London, the *Los Angeles Times*, and the *Washington Post*. Just as I observed in the various brands associated with Doğan Media, Feza Media divided its stated political stances in accordance with a diverse readership and in correlation to a variety of news brands. Indeed, to call *Zaman*, or Feza Media in general, an "Islamist" media organ would fail to recognize the group's ultimate mission, which is incidentally the same mission as its rivals in Turkey's media market: to earn a reputation as the most trusted name in news.

According to a longtime editorial voice in Turkish media who now works as a *Zaman* columnist, the balance struck between GM media for Turks and GM media for the world is one achieved with an acute awareness of its consumers:

Now it is interesting how they balance it. I guess they have to. But Samanyolu TV is much different. It is very conservative . . . you never see any
other viewpoints on its programs. But *Today's Zaman* is so very liberal.
And *Zaman*, too, is becoming so. Now they have their new television
station, Mehtab TV . . . and you will see lots of views on that. *Aksiyon*
used to be really conservative but it's beginning to open up a bit. . . . But
Samanyolu is still very rigid." (Field Interview, Spring 2007)

Indeed, despite its continuous claims to represent "democracy," "universal values," and "journalistic integrity," GM media started with a
goal of promoting and advancing the mission of Fethullah Gülen. And
thus, in addition to possessing an intrinsic quality for moral astute-
ness, marketing in the interests of a charismatic leader carries with it
both a high potential for success and a high potential to react to current
events in the interests of "the community." An original contributor to
CHA explained that the GM mission to expand its initiatives to "educate" the Turkish public through media was a rational outcome of new
opportunities:

A crowd of people consisting of students at the schools plus their families
. . . the people who listened to Hocaefendi's preachings in the mosques of
Izmir and Istanbul, in Sultanahmet, Suleymaniye, et cetera. People overcrowded the mosques and not everybody could listen to him. And there
was a need to inform people correctly. . . . So, a more general medium
was needed. Media fulfilled this. Instead of preaching in mosques, you
can use these tools. And you can address many more people from the
TV through several different kinds of productions. Thus it became a self-
sufficient institution. We did not have enough technical knowledge so
we got assistance from other people. I worked there personally. Let me
say something, not everybody in these institutions are Hizmet people
[i.e., followers of Fethullah Gülen]. There is variety in our institutions.
In the paper and in the TV, there are many people who are not from
Hizmet. . . . And there is the Cihan News Agency. It is a faster tool. It
plays the role of informing the paper and the TV correctly. It is not limited to Turkey; it is international. When I worked in CHA, Turkey had
the November 3 elections, and before the elections there was a broadcast
on BBC telling the world that an election was to be held in Turkey. And

on the screen there was a video clip from the seventies, a clip showing a bearded man with pincers in his hand who tried to pull out his wife's tooth. I am telling you this to explain the mission of CHA. There is disinformation in Turkey and in the world. . . . It is the primary objective of CHA to inform the world about Turkey correctly and fast. (Field Interview, Spring 2007)

Notwithstanding, although its efforts to reach a global audience are presented as complimentary to the GM's efforts to play a role in Turkey's democratization, it is also the case that GM actors use resources and skills cultivated in the network to increase the their advantage over competitors in a for-profit media market. Mustafa Bey at the Akademi explained as follows:

It is the same as publishing books. We publish in many languages. Maybe they seem very few but if it is a need, it will be. In order to introduce yourself to other people correctly, you have to address them in their language, not everyone can learn Turkish. People do not have that much time. You have to provide them with alternatives in their own language. If you do not, you are not able to build that bridge between you and them. Actually, I do not know what our friends intended with that new newspaper, I kept abreast of it from the media. [But] yesterday I was at a meeting in Antep, there was a friend from the paper [*Today's Zaman*] there. He told me something. There are mission chiefs in Turkey: consulates and ambassadors buy this paper, and they want to read it. The American consulate wants 150 copies every day. (Field Interview, Spring 2007)

By moving into the very small sector of English language journalism, the GM signified that its leaders were very well aware of the fact that there were only two competitors with whom to compete for foreign attention, *Hürriyet Daily News* and the notoriously low-quality *New Anatolian*. And considering the GM's global presence, *TZ* was guaranteed a significant advantage in international exposure. For instance, it is offered for free at all TUSKON trade bridge summits (see below); and in return, both *Zaman* and *TZ* publish regular stories and irregular addendum inserts devoted entirely to TUSKON activities. A number of representatives from different GM institutions explained the *Zaman's* relationship of affiliation in the GM community as follows:

> [According to a representative at TUSKON]: Look. For *Zaman*, we have a kind of institutional partnership. Why? Because *Today's Zaman* generally, with them, we made an agreement with them, and they publish a business, how do you say that? A section. Not a part of the newspaper, but a different kind of . . . addendum. Like "Style" for the *Washington Post*, or those kinds of things. And we distribute it to everyone. . . . I mean, the advertising, and all the coverage related to the event, and the news, et cetera. There is a kind of institutional partnership. Why? Because the other people are coming from abroad, and you have to partner with an English newspaper, and it is *Today's Zaman*. But other than that, who covers, if you ask who covers the event, it is everywhere. . . . Almost every newspaper covers [TUSKON]. But *Zaman* is covering it a little bit better, because of the close friendship, or close partnership, they consider us as a kind of, ehh, close, institutional friend, or how do you say that? (Field Interview, Fall 2008)

> [According to a representative at *Zaman*]: In the last three months in Turkey, we have been living through serious crisis, again during this time there has been two events that have been positive, and that can make us happy. And this group [Feza Media] realized these two events. In spite of the crisis, the TUSKON summit took place. Hundreds of people were brought from Africa, five hundred million dollars in contracts were targeted and hopes were exceeded when contracts totaling two billion dollars were signed. Again, other media did not notice that, they did not acknowledge this event yet again. Do you not think this should be heard? . . . From every county in Africa, hundreds of people, many ministers flooded to Istanbul and a civil initiative realized this, and it is in no way represented in [other] media. Think if *Zaman* did not exist! . . . From this, we can see the reason why this group and *Zaman* advanced in publication. We want to express ourselves. We do good deeds. When I say "we" I am not talking in the name of all, but I feel it to be the case in all these activities. We need a paper in English, a channel broadcasting in English and radio channels that can reach masses as well. And we have both the human and material power to realize these. So why would

we not? If [in Turkey] there were a similar environment as there is in the West and in the USA where news is reflected as news, events as events, and if media did not circulate false news in Turkey, maybe we would not need *Zaman*. (Field Interview, Summer 2007)

[According to a representative at the GM's Turkish Language Olympics]: If *Zaman* passes over to another structure, people would not pay attention to the name of the paper but to the unity of souls. So, there is not a concrete commercial or political circle that directs the paper. It is not seen, since it does not exist. But there is the unity of emotions. For instance, when you look at Turkey from America, you see one whole picture as [a country of] Turks, but when you look closer you see that there are others, if you look more closely, it is a different picture, and the closer you get it gets totally different. (Field Interview, Spring 2007)

Reframing News, Promoting Interests

Turkish reform in line with the requirements of the EU's Copenhagen criteria benefits traditionally conservative actors in Turkey's ascending Anatolian elite by creating opportunity spaces for increased economic gain. These opportunities provide communities with the legal space to mobilize their resources for export, to capitalize on traditionally neglected sectors in Turkey's service economy (e.g., education, health, medicine), and to take advantage of the structural shifts that facilitate the freer movement of resources, ideas, and people both inside Turkey's national borders and internationally. In addition to creating the conditions for increased competition in the Turkish economy, Turkish reform along European lines has also leveled the discursive playing field for the employment of language and categories that were traditionally reserved for "Westernized Turks." Journalists and opinion makers in the GM now realize that in order to "win" the discursive battle for public opinion, they must appeal to a global audience. By taking advantage of Turkey's bid to join the European Union, therefore, *Zaman* journalists and opinion columnists reframe "Islamic issues" like the ban on Muslim head scarves at universities in terms of "liberal" issues like the promise of individual "human rights." They reframe *da'wa* (invitation to Islam) in terms of Turkish nationalism ("the glorious Turkish nation"),

"Friendship marketing": Stacks of free copies of *Today's
Zaman* available at TUSKON's second Turkey–Africa trade
summit in Spring 2007. (Author's original photograph)

and they refocus their yearning to resurrect the Ottoman *millet* system of governance (i.e., when minority communities lived with relative corporate autonomy vis-à-vis the Ottoman state) in terms of global
"tolerance," "dialogue," and "pluralism." An example of these efforts
was observed in the advocacy campaign that began in the run-up to
the 2007 presidential nomination of the AKP's then foreign minister,
Abdullah Gül.

In the weeks before the presidential nomination, the Turkish Armed
Forces (TSK) and the opposition CHP expressed feared that the AKP's
nomination of Gül to become Turkey's eleventh president would lead to
a rollback of Turkish secularism and to an "Islamicization" of Turkey's

civil code. This crisis culminated on April 27, 2007, when at midnight the TSK issued a website memorandum that announced, in no uncertain terms, that the general staff was uneasy with what it perceived to be a threat to Atatürk's republic. The next day, the Turkish Constitutional Court capitalized on a loophole in the presidential nominating procedure and forced an early general poll to elect a new Parliament. This was the fifth time in Turkey's history that the military intervened in the political process. Just before the July elections, a senior *Zaman* columnist and founding brother in the GM network explained that it was not the AKP that was running for re-election, but "democracy" that was running for its life. In an editorial piece published in English and Turkish two days before election, this senior GM personality explained as follows:

> July 22 is a moment of decision. . . . Ask your conscience: Stability, peace and domestic integrity? Or tension, row, crisis and polarization? Ask your conscience: Democracy or status quo? Ask your conscience: Remain the inferior "other" or enjoy the protection of the fundamental rights under a civilian democracy? Ask your conscience: Ethnic nationalism or a brotherhood fostered through mutual tolerance and respect? (Gülerce 2007a)

Using the power of media to facilitate the AKP's re-election, this quote (in addition to weeks of similar reporting and editorial) highlighted the effective strategy of transnational advocacy networks to exercise "moral leverage" by reframing their goals in such a way as to invite international scrutiny on their adversaries. By exerting moral leverage and by demanding accountability under the rubric of "democracy," "peace," and "stability," this columnist, and *Zaman* in general, illustrated the ways in which a liberal discourse could be used to bring international attention to domestic political disputes:

> The disjuncture between the neutral discourse of equality implicit in liberalism and the unequal access to liberal institutions opens a space for symbolic action and the accountability politics of networks. In other words, liberalism carries with it not the seeds of its destruction, but the seeds of its expansion. . . . Network campaigns have been most successful

in countries that have internalized the discourse of liberalism to such a degree that there exists a disjuncture to plumb and expose. (Keck and Sikkink 1998, 205–206)

Despite its clear preference, endorsement, and support for AKP policies, AKP politicians, and the continuation of AKP power, according to the GM, it was not the AKP that won the July 2007 elections; it was "democracy" that prevailed:

> Generally, Fethullah Gülen does not say to people to support the AK party or not to support it. Everyone knows that the moderate, the best one is that one, and maybe 95 percent of this community [The Gülen Movement] votes for the same party. But nobody articulates this. Even in their home, because we are far from politics. I know, for example, I assume that 95 percent of our community voted for the AK party, maybe 99 percent. But nobody talked about this at their homes, or in their *sohbet* [groups]. Unfortunately, in the last elections, since there was a huge conflict . . . [the issue] was not supporting the party, but supporting "democracy" . . . so people talked a lot more than expected. And also, *Zaman* newspaper and Samanyolu Television, and some other friends blamed us for being more partisan now. But it is not partisanship. This is supporting democracy. (Field Interview, Summer 2008)

In addition to providing overt support for "democracy," however, GM media also act as public promotion outlets for the GM itself. *Zaman* regularly publishes stories about "Turkish schools" in Africa, about GM-sponsored "academic" conferences in Egypt, about the growth of Bank Asya, about the successes of TUSKON, and about the pageantry and spectacle of the GM-affiliated Turkish Language Olympics (TLO). When a student at a GM school wins a medal at a science competition, when TUSKON's president hosts a state minister from Bangladesh, or when the AKP foreign minster or prime minister visits a "Turkish school" in Kenya, Albania, or Mexico City, *Zaman*'s front page is filled with "news." But for whom is this "news" produced? In whose interests are columns defending Fethullah Gülen and the Gülen community written?[10]

The Limits of Liberalism

Nowhere in *Zaman* is it stated that it is the newspaper of Fethullah Gülen or of the Gülen community. Gülen never writes for the paper, and when asked, representatives throughout the upper echelons of the network insist that *Zaman* is not "organically" a GM institution. Just as *Zaman* reporters and columnists do in regard to their coalition with the AKP, they simultaneously deny support when giving it, and deny affiliation when affiliation is clear. Instead, they focus on alternative means to frame a story that seeks to avoid or to pre-empt criticism. The GM increases its legitimacy, therefore, by underlining the movement's national value for a skeptical Turkish audience. Skepticism was renewed in 2011 when *TZ* fired the columnist Andrew Finkel, a British expatriate based in Turkey, who since the early 1990s has been a mainstay on the pages of Turkey's newspapers. In the spring of 2011, four years after he was hired by *TZ* executives to lend legitimacy to the paper's claim to support healthy critique and liberal differences of opinion, Finkel was fired. In his final column for *TZ*, Finkel explained that from his perspective, political divisiveness was at such a high in the AKP's Turkey that the paper he once had great hopes for instead confirmed his longstanding belief that a democratic public sphere was still very much a myth in Turkey:

> The fight against anti-democratic forces in Turkey has resorted to self-defeating anti-democratic methods. This in turn has led to a polarization in Turkey. If your side loses power then the natural fear is that they will use your methods against you. (Finkel 2011)

The "methods" to which Finkel referred signified a growing atmosphere of censorship under the AKP, and to a media context that, in Finkel's view, directly threatened free speech and press freedoms. Indeed, as part of the ongoing Ergenekon investigation, Turkey has amassed a great deal of criticism from international observers who are deeply concerned about the targeting of journalists, who have been arrested en masse because of what critics refer to as their commonality in opposition/criticism of AKP rule.

The most recent examples Finkel cited were the cases of two Turkish journalists, Ahmet Şık and Nedim Sener, who were both arrested (along with a number of their colleagues) in March 2011 for allegedly "violating the confidentiality" of the ongoing Ergenekon investigation. Their arrest followed a police raid at the headquarters of OdaTV, a media outlet that was widely known for being publicly critical both of the AKP government and of the Turkish Armed Forces' role in Turkey's political landscape. What was particularly curious about Şık's arrest, however, was that immediately following, a story leaked that Şık had recently completed a manuscript titled "İmamın Ordusu" ("The Imam's Army"), within which Şık alleged that Gülen loyalists had taken advantage of their ranks in the Istanbul police force to take control of the Ergenekon investigation, which, in his view, had corrupted whatever legitimacy the probe once enjoyed. Worries deepened when in the weeks following Şık's arrest, a number of publishing houses believed to have copies of Şık's manuscript were raided, and when it was reported that copies of the text were destroyed by the Istanbul police. Mounting the GM's collective defense, all of Feza Media's brands denounced the allegations that there was a secret wing within the Istanbul police force loyal to the Gülen Movement, and mocked the idea as little more than conspiratorial fantasy. Despite attempts to delete it, however, Şık's manuscript found its way to the Internet, and soon after his arrest, "The Imam's Army" went viral.[11]

Despite the conspiracy theory that linked Şık's unpublished manuscript to his arrest, the official charges filed against him alleged that by publishing two previous books, *Guide to Understanding the Counter Guerrilla and Ergenekon* and *Who Is Who in Ergenekon?* Şık violated laws of confidentiality pertaining to the Ergenekon investigation. On November 21, 2011, Şık, Şener, and twelve other suspects linked to the OdaTV raid went on trial for allegedly taking part in a conspiracy to topple the AKP government. *TZ* reported as follows:

> Twelve out of fourteen suspects in the odatv.com investigation were arrested as part of the investigation. Yalçın Küçük, Soner Yalçın, Hanefi Avcı, Şener, Şık, Kaşif Kozinoğlu, Barış Terkoğlu, Barış Pehlivan, Müyesser Uğur, Doğan Yurdakul, Çoşkun Musluk, Sait Çakır, Mümtaz İdil and İklim Kaleli are accused of establishing an armed terrorist organization,

managing it, being a member of it, inciting hatred and animosity among the public, obtaining documents related to the security of the state, being in possession of documents that are confidential and violating the privacy rights of others. ("Şık, Şener Appear before Judge as Court Begins Hearing OdaTV Case" 2011)

In outrage, the president of Turkey's Freedom for Journalists Platform, Ferai Tınç, went on record to demand that Turkey's more than sixty journalists in prison be released and that the country's laws regarding press freedoms become a top priority for legislative reform.[12]

Transnational Religious Nationalism

In addition to media, GM actors are engaged in a transnational project to lobby powerful interests around the world. The result is a globally vast and fantastically complicated public relations campaign that extends from Turkey to Central Asia, from Thailand to India, from London to Houston. Discussed in more detail later, this public relations campaign works in coordination with GISs abroad and affiliated Turkish merchants and manufactures in a complicated network of market Islam and Turkish religious nationalism. The ten-year-old and counting TLO provides a useful access point through which to view this effort and its impact.

The TLO is an annual GM pageant of Turkish nationalism that further highlights the links, affinities, and connectivity between GM institutions and those institutions' affiliation with the AKP's foreign policy goals. The event, which now takes place every spring, is organized by a subsidiary of Kaynak Holding. In 2004, the event received official support from the AKP and has since become a major national occasion. In Spring 2007, 550 students from 102 countries were sponsored on a two-week visit to Turkey to compete in the fifth annual event. The TLO is now a major source of pride for the GM as a whole, and a story that gets a great deal of press in GM-affiliated media. Like investment in GISs and dormitories, GM benefactors cover student expenses, and despite being a competition, in 2007 all 550 students were awarded a stipend of US$1,000.[13] Although the TLO 2007 event received virtually no media coverage from Turkey's top news sources (*Hürriyet, Milliyet,*

Radikal, Cumhuriyet), the TLO received over a week of front-page coverage in *Zaman* and *TZ*, as well as extensive coverage in the AKP-leaning *Yeni Şafak* and the conservative *Bügün*. This lopsided media coverage is despite the fact that, according to a senior-level AKP deputy in the Turkish Ministry of Education, the GM has been more successful at teaching the world Turkish and promoting Turkish culture than has the state itself: "I watched it on TV. I was amazed! Because I send many teachers abroad to teach Turkish . . . and they were not successful like them" (Field Interview, Summer 2007).

Following the TLO final competition in Istanbul in 2007, an event that was broadcast exclusively on the GM-affiliated Samanyolu TV, I had lunch with an editor at the Akademi and a doctor who was visiting from the GM-affiliated SEMA Hospital. Neither could stop talking about the children they watched on television who sang Turkish songs and read Turkish poetry. While trying to understand their excitement, I inquired about their views about the event's keynote address given by the AKP deputy and then Parliament speaker Bülent Arınç, eight weeks before the July 22, 2007, national elections; about the virtual monopoly of media coverage by GM-affiliated media; about the meeting of all the students with Prime Minister Erdoğan; and about the obvious fortune that went into sponsoring the event and its publicity. My lunch partners were far more interested, however, in discussing the "self-sacrificing" teachers who graced the stage next to their Cambodian, Tartar, Kenyan, American, and Mexican students of the Turkish language. I learned a bit more about my observations when I interviewed an original organizer of the TLO. He explained that initially, the event was intended as a mechanism to measure the effectiveness of Zambak Publishing's "Dilset" Turkish-language instruction texts, a learning system that he helped to develop, which was used at GISs around the world:

> In the second year, the head of Parliament [Bülent Arınç] came to the program. *Where there are politics, there are media.* The head of the Parliament, Bülent Arınç, came and said, "This is really an important organization, because it seeks to make people love our language and to make it widespread. We should support this." Then, the head of the Parliament took the Olympics under his protection, saying that it was his organization, "I claim it," he said. Then it boomed! If the head of the Parliament

had not come to the organization, perhaps it might have died away."
(Field Interview, Spring 2007; emphasis added)

Bülent Arinç is a senior deputy in the AKP, and served as speaker of
Parliament from 2002 to 2007. Following the AKP July 2007 victory in
Turkey's national poll, Arinç was appointed to the post of deputy prime
minister, which as of November 2012 continues to be his role in the
upper tier of the AKP administration.

Praised by seniors in the AKP such as Arinç and others, the GM's
TLO has grown to become a bipartisan national event. After the success of the fifth annual TLO, an organizing committee comprising AKP
deputies in Parliament submitted a request to Speaker Arinç asking to
receive government sponsorship for the event in 2008. They succeeded,
which led to the institutionalization of a major GM public event into
the apparatus of the Turkish state. Much more than a pageant of nationalism, and much more than a spectacle for himmet-donating arkadaş
who purchase tickets to witness the "success" of their investment, the
TLO has become an occasion that highlights a number of contradictions in terms of the GM's projected identity as representing "moral values," "peace," "tolerance," and "dialogue." This is because when the GM
engages abroad, its stated identity comes into conflict with its actors'
rational opportunism, which leads to the former giving way to the
latter.

For example, at the fifth annual TLO in Istanbul, the event's hosts
and organizers found it appropriate to extend an honor to Saparmu-
rat Niyasov Turkmenbashı, Turkmenistan's recently deceased dictator,
at the event's closing ceremony. The deceased dictator was granted an
"Atatürk Prize" for his accomplishments in directing Turkmenistan's
national political and economic development since the independent
emergence of that country in 1991 ("Winners at Turkish Olympics Are
Champions of Peace" 2007). As discussed above, GM aristocrats and
GM arkadaş companies established a very close relationship with the
deceased dictator, which led to a great deal of success for GM-affiliated
firms in Turkmenistan. This is likely why TLO organizers did not find
any contradiction in honoring a man at an event that purported to promote world peace, but who, in the same year, Human Rights Watch
defined as having presided over "one of the most repressive countries

in the world" (Human Rights Watch 2007, 6). Indeed, *Zaman* published an obituary for Niyasov in 2006, wherein the paper referred to the deceased dictator as being "known for his support for fifteen Turkmen-Turkish schools and the international Turkmen-Turkish University founded by Turkish businessmen in Turkmenistan" (Yildiz 2006).

"Nonpolitical" Lobbying

Leading the GM's public relations initiatives is the sister organization to Feza Media, called the Gazeticiler ve Yazarlar Vakfi (Journalists and Writers Foundation, GYV; est. 1994). Part think tank, part publishing house, the GYV uses donations from Bank Asya and from affiliated GM business interests to produce a series of journals and books by or about Fethullah Gülen, "Turkish Islam," or "interfaith dialogue." Overlapping with both Kaynak Cultural Publishing and *Zaman*, the GYV has become one of the GM's most public institutions. The GYV traces its beginnings back to 1994 when, under the leadership of a number of *Zaman* journalists, the GYV organized into three "platforms" whose actors sought to bring rival sectors of Turkish society together into "dialogue forums." Similar to *Zaman*'s employment of "outsiders" like Andrew Finkel and other non-Turkish columnists, the GYV solicited the consultancy and opinions of outsiders at all of its dialogue events. This practice has led some to view both institutions as not wholly GM enterprises (Field Notes, Winter 2007). The cosmopolitan makeup of the GM's more public sites, however, should be viewed as a strategy used to cultivate external support and unaffiliated sympathy (*yandaş*), and to legitimize the GM's identity by becoming an authoritative voice in Turkish civil society.

The first GYV forum occurred in 1994 in the western Turkish mountain resort town of Abant. There, a number of journalists and academics met for two days to discuss fissures in Turkish society. Indirectly, the first Abant meeting led to an increased level of legitimacy for the GM as a whole, and for Fethullah Gülen in particular. According to Süleyman Bey—a GM aristocrat, longtime organizer at the GYV, former *Zaman* journalist, and a regular contributor to a number of other Feza Media publications and news productions—the first Abant meeting was a "coming out" event for the GM. Its primary objective was to

bring together people of influence to discuss their problems and to recognize their similarities. The net effect of the Abant meeting was that it
positioned a major GM enterprise to become one of Turkey's primary
policy-directed think tanks:

> The central idea of our foundation was to gather together people who
> came from different worldviews. . . . That was the idea. . . . They said, "If I
> come together with so and so, a fight might arise." Our response was that
> you would not fight, but discuss. They all said that it could be possible
> but it is going to be hard. Thus, six or seven months later, I am not sure
> of the exact date, we gave various people awards in the name of tolerance
> and democracy and living together. We invited and brought together
> everyone. They were very pleased. They might have criticized each other
> from afar, but they shook hands there, they talked. Then, they said the
> idea was great and they wanted to continue, so we continued from the
> end of 1995 onwards. (Field Interview, Spring 2007)

The GYV now regularly gives awards to influential politicians, academics, and journalists. Similar to "peace awards" given at the TLO, these
awards overwhelmingly target civilian and political leaders with whose
sympathy the GM might be able to increase its legitimacy as a nonpartisan collective actor. The issuance of awards is now standard practice
and has become routinized. They are presented first at a primary event
(e.g., an Abant Platform), and are then widely publicized on the pages
of GM-affiliated media.

In what started with one meeting in 1994, the Abant platform and the
larger GYV now host regular conferences in Istanbul and abroad that
focus on topics including "Islam and Secularism in Turkey," "Alevi Identity," "Turkish–French Relations," "Turkey and the EU," and "The Kurdish
Issue." A GYV conference took place in Arbil, Iraq, in mid-February 2009;
it was titled "Searching for Peace and a Future Together," and focused on
"the Kurdish issue" in both countries. The event was widely publicized in
Zaman and *TZ*, and was framed as a major public diplomacy event for
Turkish–Iraqi relations. Among the participants were a number of GM-
affiliated and non-affiliated journalists, as well as the new principal of
the GM's recently inaugurated Işık University, the eleventh GIS campus
opened and managed by the GM-affiliated Fezalar Eğitim Kurumları

(Fezalar Education Foundation), which as of November 2012 managed thirty-six GISs in northern Iraq (see http://www.fezalar.org/index.php).

Despite the presence of a number of AKP officials, and despite the GYV's widely known affiliation with the GM, organizers of the Arbil conference refused to acknowledge either the political implications of a high-profile international conference in the midst of a still-war-torn Iraq, or the GM's relationship with the meeting. Employing strategically ambiguous language, Mümtazer Türköne, a Turkish academic who writes regularly for Feza Media publications, explained that in his view, the GYV in Iraq was not to be viewed as a political platform for the furthering of AKP policies under the cloak of a civil society event. In his words, "We [the GYV] are a nongovernmental organization and do not have the capacity to represent the government." Another journalist and organizer of the GYV event in Arbil, Altan Tan, also strategically dismissed the GYV's ties to the larger GM when he told journalists, "Connections with the Fethullah Gülen movement are irrelevant here" ("Platform Travels to N. Iraq" 2009). By denouncing political connections to the AKP and organizational connections to the GM, GYV participants could sincerely claim that their event had no political impact and that connections to Fethullah Gülen were "irrelevant." This was despite the fact that the event was publicized in GM media for over a week, was recorded, stored, and disseminated throughout the GM's hundreds of social networks on the Internet, and was funded by himmet donations from affiliated arkadaş in the GM's business network.

Recalling the GM preference for being strategically ambiguous, it is important to note that by recognizing the Arbil conference, or any conference hosted, sponsored, and organized by GM actors, as "political" would contradict the GM's strategy to insist on its "nonpolitical" nature. Süleyman Bey attempted to explain the "nonpolitical" implications of the GM's activities as follows:

> This movement is not a political movement. For it to be so, a political party should be supporting it or it should establish a party. Others have done this, we do not have such a thing. . . . But, as we relate it to everyone, as my friends relate Hizmet, we could explain it to [the CHP] or [to] the AKP. . . . There can be friendly relations with each of them. As it is the case in Turkey, in America as well we can meet with both Republicans

and Democrats; it is to express ourselves. It is not a political gesture. . . .
It is only to express, this act of expressing does not render us a political
movement. When I meet with Joshua, I do not become someone like
him and vice versa but we just meet and share. . . . I do not think that
our friends lobby on behalf of the Turkish government or Turkish state.
There is no need for it anyway as Turkey has an official lobbying company working under agreement. The Turkish embassy does it. I guess the
sympathizers of Fethullah Gülen in America might have worked for the
Armenian bill not to pass [in Congress], as it would damage the Turkish–American relations. That would not be good and they might have
worked with this in mind. [But] I do not believe they work as a lobbying
institution in the general sense. (Field Interview, Spring 2007)

GM actors around the world have adapted the GYV's "nonpolitical" tactics for a global audience. Similar institutes now exist in cites throughout the United States, western Europe, Australia, India, and elsewhere.
Together they regularly visit local and national political leaders, host
community, academic, and media personalities, conduct outreach initiatives in their local communities, organize Turkish cultural events,
sponsor trips for influential people to visit Turkey, and sponsor conferences that promote the ideas and impact of Fethullah Gülen. Although
self-identified as nonpolitical, these institutions enjoy nominal support
in the United States, for instance, from congressional representatives
and senators on both sides of the aisle, from dozens more local mayors
and police commissioners, and still dozens more influential scholars of
religion, social sciences, and Middle Eastern studies. Although mobilized as a civil society network independent of the Turkish state, and
although presented as a nonpartisan effort to increase "dialogue," it is
simply disingenuous to refer to the GM's efforts to cultivate influence
and to influence public policy as having no political intent.

Conclusion

In the 1980s, Robert Biancchi (1984, 106) argued that Turkey's political
and economic development in the late twentieth century was defined
by a revived contest between the country's political and economic center, and its rapidly urbanizing, upwardly mobile periphery:

> Center–periphery tensions are increasingly manifested in a series of confrontations and compromises between the modernizing state pursuing ambitious goals of economic development and the representative association of newly emergent social and economic groups that favor conflicting distributions of the benefits and sacrifices of modernization.

With his eye on Turkey's managerial state, Bianchi viewed the Turkish elite as becoming less homogeneous, and its representative associations more plentiful and more independent. In his view, this tendency led actors in Turkey's civilian bureaucracy, its major political parties, and the military to confront these transformations by co-optation, "to organize and manipulate representative associations as relatively non-coercive mechanisms for preserving the dominance of a strengthened political center over an increasingly differentiated periphery" (Bianchi 1984, 106). A central question is whether the Turkish experience in the late twentieth century and into the twenty-first century will tend toward deepening democratic pluralism, or whether Turkey's historical tendency to repress the majority in the interests of a corporatist elite will prevail. More than twenty-five years have passed since Bianchi posed this question. His prediction was that actors leading the alliances between state bureaucracies, political parties, big media, and big capital would attempt to manage their erosion, and to make room for more players in a controlled environment defined in terms of an "organized democracy." The unforeseen rise of the AKP, however, together with the civil–social support offered by the GM and other sympathetic representatives, has produced a paradox. This is because the GM and its arkadaş among the "pro-AKP media" are in danger of repeating the same mistakes of their "pro-establishment" adversaries by conflating their own vision of what is best for the Turkish nation with their vision of what is best for the interests they represent. These interests are politically represented by the AKP and civil-socially tied to the GM. And although they receive much-deserved credit for their efforts to pluralize free expression in Turkey, it is essential to underscore that GM-owned newspapers, magazines, television stations, and radio stations are all also beholden to their underwriters. Indeed, just as it is with all actors involved in manufacturing consent in modern society, they are immersed in a journalistic environment of half-freedom, corruption, and financial influence. Andrew Finkel (2000, 166) summed up this paradox in one expression, *burası Türkiye*:

> The common colloquialism "this is Turkey" ("*burası Türkiye*") used to explain the failure of basic standards is the cry of a society in which priorities are too complex to unravel and private interests too deeply entrenched.

In the case of the GM, *burası Türkiye* is applied outside Turkey as well, including in the United States, where the application of strategic ambiguity in the interests of expansion, although initially successful, has produced a rather difficult situation. Indeed, the GM's preference for strategically ambiguous communication, coupled with increasingly more blatant self-promotion has led to a backlash in the United States, where the community's efforts in charter school education and GYV-modeled public relations appear to be reaching their limits.

8

Strategic Ambiguity and Its Discontents
(i.e., the Gülen Movement in the United States)

On the road from the City of Skepticism, I had to pass
through the Valley of Ambiguity.
—Adam Smith

Schools, interfaith institutions, media institutions, trade organizations, and businesses associated with the GM in Turkey are connected in a complicated network whose actors share overlapping social and economic ties, and whose leaders share a deep and passionate devotion for "Hocaefendi" Fethullah Gülen.[1] As detailed in previous chapters, connectivity in the GM network is characterized by an ambiguous system of strong and weak social ties and client–patron relationships that extend throughout the world economy. After nearly two decades of relatively uninterrupted domestic and international expansion, however, in the late 1990s the GM fell victim to a state-led backlash against religious identity communities in Turkey. It was then when Gülen cited health reasons and fled to the United States, where his followers have since replicated their education and economic network. As this manuscript goes to press in November 2012, there is no place outside Turkey where the GM cemaat and arkadaş manage more institutions, or go to greater lengths to simultaneously promote their leader than in the United States. The United States is thus an informative case environment to observe both the successes and the discontents of the GM's strategically ambiguous "post-political" mobilization.

Strategic Ambiguity Revisited

Since their emergence in Turkey in the 1970s and continuing for more than thirty years, GM-affiliated actors have sought to control the presentation of their collective mobilization and to adapt to local contexts as necessary. By maintaining ambiguity about when affiliations are made clear and when they are denied, for instance, the GM can more effectively reinvent itself for local consumption. This "flexible" model of collective behavior parallels structural changes in the world economy that facilitate the freer flow of goods, services, finances, and people in a "compressed" and "borderless" world system (Castells 1997; Harvey 2000). But although the GM's organizational model has, on the one hand, led to noteworthy success in Turkey and around the world, the GM's lack of transparency has, on the other hand, led many critics to revive concerns that some of its most vocal enemies have espoused for years—that its aims are hidden, and that its leader has suspect intentions. For this reason, a primary component of the GM's collective mobilization is to legitimize Fethullah Gülen as a politically benign faith leader, and as a modest and frugal author and scholar. In so doing, GM loyalists continuously defend or pre-empt attacks against Fethullah Gülen, and routinely promote the successes of GISs in Turkey and around the world.

Tied to its media initiatives, in this regard, is a larger effort to market Fethullah Gülen, and by association "Turkish Islam," to a global audience. This project is coordinated by hundreds of individuals and dozens of institutions around the world who host conferences and workshops, court and lobby influential opinion makers, promote the value and legitimacy of GM activities in education and business, and advance the strategic transformation of "old Turkey" (framed as corrupt, oligarchic, Ergenekon-led) to "new Turkey" (framed as democratic, just, AKP-led). Focused primarily in Turkey, Europe, the United States, and Australia, these efforts have proved successful. The GM enjoys both sympathy as well as solicited and unsolicited promotion from many notable scholars in religious studies and the liberal arts, as well as from scores of influential European and American community leaders, high-ranking American and European politicians, and appointed officials. Together, the GM's media and public relations campaign illustrates not only that a new civil/social power base is on the ascent in Turkey, but also that its actors are consciously aware of the domestic gains that are possible through international effort.

Interfaith Dialogue (aka GM Public Relations)

In the United States, Europe, Australia, and elsewhere, GM loyalists spend a great deal of effort promoting Fethullah Gülen, Turkish Islam, and "the new Turkey" to eager foreign audiences. Modeling themselves after the GM's Journalists and Writers Foundation (GYV) in Istanbul, these institutions engage in a variety of activities to achieve this end. Far more than cultural foundations, representatives from these institutions regularly visit and play host to elected and appointed people of power in city, county, and state governments, as well as to people of influence in academia, media, and faith communities. Collectively, GM activists in the United States spend hundreds of thousands of dollars a year on events that range from "interfaith dinners," to citywide Turkish cultural festivals, to speaking forums, to lavish overseas tours of Turkey's conservative democratic transformation. The intent behind these activities is to introduce social leaders to the applied teachings of Fethullah Gülen and to the shift in power underway in the new Turkey. Choosing not to present these activities as mere influence peddling, GM activists who "volunteer" for these organizations frame their objectives as "nonpolitical," preferring instead to ambiguously define themselves as simply serving the interests of "dialogue."

When I exercised my skepticism regarding the "nonpolitical" impact of the GM's outreach tactics, I asked many loyalists *and* critics about their views regarding the practice to specifically target people of influence for "dialogue." Responses ranged from that of a loyalist who insisted that the GM's aim was "to show people how members of different religions can live together in peace," to that of a critic who contended that such activities were akin to "Turkish imperialism!" (Field Interviews, Summer 2008, Spring 2007). What I eventually realized was that despite their claims to the contrary, when given the chance to control their collective presentation, many GM activists admitted that their efforts had intended and penetrating political effects:

All these activities show that a very powerful Turkish lobby is being established in the U.S. . . . which will open a new page in Turkish–U.S. relations. (Gülerce 2007a)[2]

The lobbying firms that have been paid loads of money in Washington by Turkey actually worsen the image of Turkey at the Congress, rather than helping. Instead, civil grassroots' visits [i.e., GM visits] to the Congressional members, especially in their districts, made the biggest differences. (Kemal Oksuz, president of the GM's Turquoise Council of Americans and Eurasians in Houston, quoted in Tanır 2010)

Turkish constituencies maintain their close relationships with their Congressional members and host them when it is possible for dinners and award ceremonies. . . . With persistence, but while respectfully elaborating their cause, those Turkish grassroots (i.e., GM activists) in the U.S. become more convincing . . . than the Armenians. (Mahmut Yeter, executive director of the GM's Mid-Atlantic Turkic American Association, quoted in Tanır 2010)

In the U.S. case, GM affiliates create a viable and effective alternative to the more traditional "Turkish lobby," which is presented to foreign audiences as historically representative of Turkey's "Kemalist establishment." Indeed, although activists insist that the GM's primary objective is to foster dialogue between faiths, another characteristic of the GM's impact emerges as well: the GM is second only to the AKP in promoting the interests of Turkish "conservative democracy" to foreign audiences.

Now in competition with the long-established, defense-focused American–Turkish Council (ATC), the policy- and business-focused Association of Turkish American Associations (ATAA), and the arts- and culture-focused American Friends of Turkey (AFT), are the GM-affiliated Turkish–American Business Improvement and Development Councils (TABID), as well as the collection of GM-affiliated institutions that constitute the recently mobilized Assembly of Turkic American Federations (ATAF).[3] As the most recent GM venture, ATAF brings together six regional federations, which each bring together individual GM-affiliated "dialogue" institutions, under one umbrella. The GM's Pacifica Institute (formerly Global Cultural Connections), for instance, operates under the umbrella of the recently formed West America Turkic Council (WATC). The latter includes the GM-affiliated Foundation for Intercultural Dialogue (FID) and the Sema Foundation in Arizona, the Mosaic Foundation in Colorado, the Rose Garden Foundation in Oregon, the Acacia Foundation in Washington State, and the Multicultural Arch Foundation in Utah.[4] Collectively, these institutions constitute the western U.S. region under the larger ATAF compass. When asked about these organizations, GM "volunteers" explain that their efforts focus on nothing more than the cultivation of "tolerance" and "dialogue" between peoples of different faiths and different cultures. Invoking Gramsci, I argue that, in addition to dialogue, what U.S. politicians, academicians, journalists, and faith leaders are also bearing witness to the ways an ongoing "war of position" for domestic hegemony in Turkey touches down in the United States (Hendrick 2009). Together these institutions constitute a long-term, calculated, and specific project with two primary goals: (1) to redefine the Turkish narrative for U.S. audiences in government, academia, and the media; and (2) to cultivate client and patron relationships between market actors in the United States and GM-affiliated Turkish business.

The first GM culture and outreach institution in the United States was founded in 1999 in Washington DC. Widely known as the biggest and most well connected of all GM-affiliated institutions in the United States, the Rumi Forum began with start-up resources collected as himmet from arkadaş GM businessmen. A senior GM hoca operating in the United States discussed the importance of the Rumi Forum and its strategic beginnings in DC as follows:

> Washington DC is the most important place in the United States, you know. The world is governed and ruled by Washington DC. You can say that the think tanks are here, and all important institutions are here, the Senate. . . . So yes, the Rumi Forum is the most important dialogue center in the community [GM]. (Field Interview, Summer 2008)

Although framed as nonpolitical, according to this hoca in the GM's U.S. cemaat, it was very important for the GM's overall U.S. organization to first target DC, and to consider DC the most important node in the GM's U.S. network.

With modest beginnings, the Rumi Forum has since become a recognized Turkish lobbying organization inside the Beltway. It regularly hosts luncheon speakers to discuss issues ranging from an "Obama Middle Eastern policy," to "The Kashmir Crisis in India/Pakistan," to "Islam, Sufism and Qur'anic Ethics," to "Oil Policy and the Middle East," to "U.S.-Kyrgyz Relations," to name only a few. Indeed, engaged in activities that signify its identity as much more than a cultural or religious institution, the Rumi Forum has cultivated relationships with dozens of U.S. members of Congress, has sponsored many visits to Turkey for powerful people, and has facilitated unofficial meetings between AKP deputies and ministers from Turkey with their counterparts in the U.S. power structure. Funding for all Rumi Forum events, as well as for its small administrative staff, is provided by himmet donations from the local DC GM community:

Fethullah Gülen's idea is that . . . is this . . . wherever there is an institution, there is supposed to be . . . ahh . . . funding by Turkish businessmen around that area. So he always motivates the Turkish businessmen to go everywhere to support the institutions in that local area. He does not support the idea of getting money from Turkey, for example. So, we are trying to reach out to Turkish people as well here, in order to be funded, you know. . . . We are not getting any funding from Texas, for example. We are not getting funds from Turkey. We are trying to reach out to all Turkish businessmen and trying to convince them to donate for our activities and events here. They donate because we are not the only people who are trying to motivate them to donate. But Fethullah Gülen makes it possible. . . . We have fund-raising. And, for example, we will have a Congress event now [2008] and we are trying to find some sponsors for that. . . . We gave an *Ifthar* dinner [Ramadan daily fast-breaking] on Capitol Hill last year. It was the first one, and now we are trying to, we are making the second one on the nineteenth of September on Capitol Hill, in the West Room. And twenty-one congressmen will come to this event. Last year, twenty-eight congressmen came to the event. And also we gave peace and dialogue awards to Congress at the Capitol Hill event. The turnout was very good. (Field Interview, Summer 2008)

Rumi Forum initiatives are supported by the efforts of the Mid-Atlantic Federation of Turkic Friends Association (MAFTAA) in Fairfax,

Virginia, an eastern U.S. umbrella organization that also consolidates the activities of the GM-affiliated outreach institutions in Delaware, Virginia, West Virginia, Kentucky, North Carolina, and Maryland (see http://www.maftaa.org/hakkinda/). Other noteworthy GM-affiliated organizations that engage in similar activities as that of the Rumi Forum include the Istanbul Center in Atlanta, the Turkish Cultural Center in New York City, and the Niagara Foundation in Chicago. These institutions, together with California's Pacifica Institute and Houston's Institute for Interfaith Dialogue, Raindrop Foundation, Turquoise Council, and the Gülen Institute, sit at the center of the GM's public relations network in the United States, and serve as models for new institutions in major cities and college towns throughout the country.

Adapting proven strategies to recruit sympathizers (yandaş) from the ranks of local, regional, and national leadership, among the activities of these organizations is the growing regularity of "award dinners," wherein members of the GM offer Ottoman/Turkish themed awards to specifically targeted recipients. For example, in early March 2007, the Rumi Forum held an event to offer the Turkish and Spanish prime ministers "Dialogue of Civilizations" awards in recognition of their 2006 agreement to lead European nations in dialogue. The Rumi Forum also extended awards to the high-profile Islamic studies academics John Esposito and John Voll, and well as to the director of the "Religion and Peace Initiative" at the U.S. Institute of Peace, John Smock. In a similar event, the Niagara Foundation in Chicago gave an award to Exelon Corporation CEO John Rowe for his environmental perspective on big industry. At that dinner, the importance of trade between the United States and Turkey as well as continued political friendship took precedence. In 2006 and 2007, the New York–based Turkish Cultural Center (TCC) hosted then senator, later U.S. secretary of state, Hillary Rodham Clinton, at its annual Ramadan Friendship Dinner. The event was also attended by Prime Minister Erdoğan. At the same event in 2008, former president Bill Clinton sent a video recording to praise the TCC's activities, and former senator and then New Jersey governor John Corzine gave the year's keynote address. In similar fashion, in the first year of its opening, former secretaries of state James Baker III and Madeline Albright both gave luncheon keynotes at the Gülen Institute in Houston. Other organizations regularly host similar events to offer awards to similarly powerful individuals throughout the country. At each award ceremony, Fethullah Gülen sends a letter of support and congratulations to award recipients. Highlighting the connectivity between GM institutions, I assisted an editor at the Akademi in Istanbul in translating and editing one such congratulatory note authored by Fethullah Gülen, which was written in Pennsylvania, e-mailed to Turkey, edited, and e-mailed back to the United States in time to be read to recipients of the "Fethullah Gülen Dialogue Award" at a Niagara Foundation in Chicago in July 2007 (Field Notes, Summer 2007).

Tied to the award dinners are "interfaith trips" to Turkey that are sponsored by GM benefactors, and that are arranged by GM dialogue and outreach institutions throughout the country (and the world). These tours are designed for groups to visit not only major cultural destinations in Turkey, but also a number of GM schools in Istanbul, GM luxury hospitals (e.g., SEMA Hastanesi), and perhaps *Zaman* headquarters. Upon their return, influential people are asked to write about their experience in Turkey, or to share with their communities or students their stories about the Turkish schools they visited and about the Turkish families who helped subsidize their trips. Many people who later present at GM-sponsored conferences (see below) are first introduced to the GM after they are recruited to participate in an "interfaith tour" to Turkey. Upon her return in 2007, a doctor in Boston was solicited to write an opinion column in *Today's Zaman* about her experience. She wrote as follows:

> I must confess, when I was first offered an all-expense paid trip to Turkey, I was filled with trepidation. And the source of my misgivings was actually a stereotype I was harboring—I thought of the Turks as an unbeatable and ferocious military power. . . . I discovered that Turkey is really at the vanguard of modernity in the Muslim world, and that Turkish scholars have already conceived of a truer representation of Islam. In books I was introduced to one of the founders of modern religious thought, Fethullah Gülen, who has described the essence of religious practice in these words: "Loving and respecting humanity merely because they are human is an expression of love and respect for the Almighty Creator." Whether secular or religious, I could think of no better ethos for the Muslims to follow. (Lahaj 2007)

A reputable professor of religious studies in the United States explained to me that on his trip in 2003, a colleague accompanied him from his campus department, as did a handful of academics from other universities in his U.S. state of residence and one state senator. Included in his itinerary were a number of dinners, cruises, and lunches that were all attended by different GM-affiliated businessmen, and by principals from a number of GISs in Istanbul. When his colleague broke his leg, this professor explained that they were taken to the GM's SEMA Hospital in Istanbul, where he excitedly informed me that he was "blown away by the luxury of the place" (Field Interview, Summer 2007). Moreover, his colleague's insurance was not billed for his treatment. From that point onward, this professor became a regular contributor to GM-sponsored conferences in the United States and elsewhere. On a similar trip in 2003, the GM's Institute for Interfaith Dialogue (IID) in Houston sponsored an interfaith trip that included a humanities and comparative religion professor from Rice University. Explaining that the GM immediately captivated her, this professor authored a book comparing Gülen's thought with that of European and Chinese philosophy as observed in the work of Plato, John Stuart Mill, Immanuel Kant, Jean-Paul Sartre, and Confucius. In the first month of its publication by The Light Publishing (a subsidiary of Kaynak Holding, now Tuğhra Books), a senior editor the Akademi informed me, Jill Carroll's *Dialogue of Civilizations* (2007) was a best seller under the "Islam" category on Amazon.com (Field Notes, Winter 2007). Carroll's book tour in 2007, like Helen Rose Ebaugh's tour in 2010 to promote her book *The Gülen Movement* (2010), consisted of a city-by-city schedule of visits to GM-cultural foundations throughout the United States. In Ebaugh's case, her connections to the IID and to the Gülen Institute in Houston allowed her to take advantage of connections abroad, which led to a continuation of her book tour in Turkey. In January 2011, thousands of GM loyalists flocked to ANKA Shopping Mall in Ankara to attend Professor Ebaugh's book signing. The event was well covered in GM media outlets in Turkey (e.g., *Zaman* and *TZ*), as well as by CNN Türk.[5]

In addition to lobbying initiatives, therefore, GM institutions in the United States have also initiated a process of reflexive intellectualization, whereby they strive to control, if not monopolize, the intellectual treatment of Fethullah Gülen by organizing and sponsoring conferences dedicated to the "contributions of the Gülen Movement," and by producing or commissioning academic analyses of the movement and its leader. The primary objective of these conferences is to recruit the intellectual support of scholars such as Carroll and Ebaugh and to facilitate their research on the GM. Indeed, my own first exposure to the GM occurred at an IID-sponsored conference in Houston at Rice University in November 2005, and at a follow-up conference in Dallas at Southern Methodist University in March 2006 (see http://fethullahgulenconference.org/). Unique to a typical academic forum, however, participants at these conferences include not only university professors and social science and humanities researchers, but also GM-connected teachers, editors, writers, and journalists from Turkey. Moreover, because they unfold more like one- to three-day promotions of the GM than they do as arenas for critical inquiry or theoretically informed discussion, their integrity as academic sites anchored on the intellectual traditions of skepticism, inquiry, and critique comes into question. Nonetheless, these conferences are typically cosponsored by institutions of higher learning, involve PhD-holding scholars in the humanities and social sciences, and typically result in a book publication.[6]

The first conference of this kind in the United States was held in Washington DC in 2002 and was sponsored by the Rumi Forum in conjunction with the Center for Muslim Christian Understanding at Georgetown University. This was followed in April 2005 and March 2006 by conferences at the University of Wisconsin, Madison (sponsored by the GM's Dialogue International), and by the aforementioned IID-sponsored 2005 and 2006 conferences in Houston and Dallas, followed by two more in November 2006 in San Antonio, Texas, and Norman, Oklahoma (in conjunction with the University of Texas, San Antonio, and the University of Oklahoma, respectively). The largest GM-affiliated conference to date took place in London and was cosponsored by the GM's London-based Dialogue Society in conjunction with the House of Lords, the English Parliament, the London School of Economics, the School of Oriental and African Studies (SOAS) at the University of London, the University of Sussex, and the Middle East Institute (see http://www.gulenconference.org.uk/). On the heels of the Dialogue Society's October 2007 conference in London was a follow-up in Rotterdam, Holland, and another in the United States sponsored by the TCC in New York City, which took place at the Middle East Institute at Columbia University, both held in November 2007. In 2008, the Rumi Forum hosted its second GM-sponsored conference about the GM in Washington DC, again in conjunction with Georgetown University (see http://fethullahgulen.org/). In March and December 2009, the Atlas Foundation in New Orleans (in conjunction with Louisiana State University) and the Pacifica Institute in California (in conjunction with the University of Southern California) sponsored two more GM-focused, GM-funded conferences about the GM's expansive impact in global education and interfaith/intercultural dialogue (see http://fethullahgulenconference.org/; http://www.gulenconference.net/).

Each of these conferences contributed to the GM's public emergence in the United States. Among the regular participants included recruited GM sympathizers (yandaşlar) in U.S. academia such as Jill Carroll and Helen Ebaugh, as well the regular participation of Father Thomas Michel, a Jesuit priest and scholar who developed a relationship with the GM in the late 1990s, and who became one of the community's most prolific recruited sympathizers. Indeed, by the end of 2009, the GM's efforts in the United States had proved quite effective. But to what end? Why do GM actors go to such lengths to affiliate themselves and their outreach institutions with institutions of higher learning in the United States and elsewhere? Field research suggests that they do so to establish legitimacy in the face of constant criticism in Turkey, to generate political capital to spend when affiliated actors and institutions are accused of infiltrating the Turkish police force, or when its critics chastise the GM's efforts to influence Turkey's national elections in the interests of AKP rule. It also proves useful when governments around the world accuse GM schools of hiding a "radical agenda," as they did in Holland in 2008,[7] and as some are starting to do in the United States (see below). As discussed previously, such accumulated political capital also proved useful when for the purposes of confronting a reluctant Bush administration, Fethullah Gülen was able to rely on the character witness support of twenty-seven noted scholars, intelligence officials, religious leaders, and political dignitaries (of whom many had attended a GM-sponsored "interfaith tour" of Turkey, had presented papers at GM-sponsored conference, or had received an award from a GM dialogue institute) to eventually receive his green card.

Although not mentioned in his immigration case file, Gülen's lawyers could have also discussed the "Fethullah Gülen Chair in Islam and in Muslim–Catholic Relations" at Australia's Catholic University (inaugurated in 2007), which was endowed via himmet collected and channeled through the Australian Intercultural Society in the amount of $560,000 a year for five years (Stokes 2008). By receiving a "chair" in his honor, Gülen increased his legitimacy as an educator, which would certainly have aided his case to become an "alien of extraordinary abilities in the field of education" in the United States. And although it did not happen for another two years, Gülen's lawyers were certainly pleased to learn of his official recognition from the State Senate of Texas in 2011, at which time Gülen was acknowledged for his "dedication to working toward a better world through education, service, tolerance, and the free exchange of ideas."[8] Although self-purportedly altruistic, the GM's collective efforts to lobby on behalf of Fethullah Gülen and the various initiatives credited to his inspiration have proved essential for the movement as a whole to continue its U.S. expansion in business and education.

The Opportunities of School Choice

The GM's education initiatives in the United States began as they did elsewhere, as private market-driven enterprises. Among the first GISs in the United States were the Science Academy of Chicago (est. 1997), the Brooklyn Amity School in New York (est. 1999), the Pioneer Academy of Science in New Jersey (est. 1999), and the Putnam Science Academy in Connecticut (est. 2000).[9] Despite these examples, however, as of November 2012 there were approximately 136 charter schools in twenty-six U.S. states whose majority board membership, administrative directors, principals, and a significant number of math and science teachers also appeared to be inspired by the teachings of Fethullah Gülen and connected to the GM network. Beginning in late 2009, however, many of these schools became targets of criticism for their administrators' repeated denials of affiliation to the GM, denials that started to baffle a number of recruited sympathizers in the U.S. academy. Many of these latter individuals had previously understood the Turkish-managed charter schools in their states to be noteworthy examples of the successful GIS model of education. Moreover, school administrators had, before 2009, been more than willing to discuss their relationships with GM-affiliated dialogue centers and business councils throughout the United States and the rest of the world (Field Notes, Winter 2010). That transparency ended, however, when a story broke in a local newspaper in Arizona in December 2009 (Vanderpool 2009), which was followed by two years of similar reporting at the local and national level. Since then, concerned teachers, parents, journalists, and county and city school board officials around the country have started to ask more pointed questions about the aims of alleged "Gülen-inspired" charter schools, and about their alleged connections to something called "the Gülen movement."

As of early 2012, denials of GM affiliation by charter administrators at GISs in the United States have become standard. In a brewing public relations catastrophe, the GM's proclivity for strategic ambiguity seems to have reached its limit in the context of public U.S. education, and thus provides an instructive case by which to observe the methods GM actors employ to adapt to diverse local contexts.

In the United States, "school choice" refers to the practice of creating alternatives for traditional K–12 public schooling. School choice includes home school (individual or small community), magnet school, private school, and charter school options. Although initiatives to expand such options began in the 1960s, according the U.S. Department of Education, it was not until the emergence of the charter school option in the early 1990s that school choice began to make a significant cross-class, cross-racial, cross-ethnic impact in the U.S. education system. Beginning in Minnesota in 1991, charter schools quickly became a viable option for families that desired an alternative to traditional public schooling. By 2003, thirty-five U.S. states and Washington DC had legislated in favor of charter school choice, and in that year 2,575 charter schools educated 1.4 percent of the total public school population (K–12). By 2007, those numbers increased to 4,132 charter schools in forty states, educating 2 percent of the total public school student population (Grady, Bielick, and Aud 2010, 4–10). The intention in introducing these statistics is not to make a politically charged assessment one way or the other regarding the effectiveness of charter school education. The purpose at hand, rather, is merely to introduce readers to a trend toward more "choices" in public primary and secondary education since the early 1990s, and to argue that the charter school system has inadvertently provided the GM with a unique opportunity space vis-à-vis its transnational affiliates.

If parents view their district's public schools as inadequate for whatever reason, publicly funded charter schools claim to provide an alternative. In order to attract students, however, charter schools must convince parents that they are able to provide a better education than that which is provided by a student's assigned public school. To this end, charter schools go to great lengths to advertise their students' achievements, and subsequently to cultivate a brand. In this way, although they are publicly funded, charter schools function much like private schools in a competitive marketplace. Successful charter schools are typically part of larger groups of schools that are managed by large or small nonprofit charter management organizations (CMOs) or by for-profit education management organizations (EMOs). The largest and most successful of such institutions in the United States are the CMOs Knowledge Is Power Program (KIPP) (125 schools in twenty states as of November 2012) and Imagine Schools (70 schools in twelve states and the District of Columbia as of November 2012). Despite the KIPP and Imagine Schools example, however, most CMOs manage a relatively small number of schools in specific cities or throughout one particular state. Among the most lauded and most recognized CMOs in the country are Cosmos Foundation and Harmony Schools (thirty-eight schools in Texas, one in Tennessee), Magnolia Schools and Willow Education Foundation (thirteen schools in California), Concept Schools (nineteen schools throughout Ohio, Illinois, Indiana, and Michigan), and the Daisy Education Corporation (nine schools in Arizona). Despite their organizational autonomy, however, what links KIPP's and Imagine Schools' above-mentioned competitors are the observable affiliations that their principals, board members, many of their teachers and, in many cases, their architects, educational materials suppliers, and management consultants have with the transnational network of Fethullah Gülen.

Worthy of praise, charter schools under the management of these CMOs regularly report higher-than-average standardized test scores, university acceptance rates, and student performance in state and national math and science competitions. The group of schools that constitutes Texas's Cosmos Foundation and Harmony Schools provides a useful example. As of August 2010, nineteen of the foundation's then thirty-seven schools received commendable recognition by the Texas State Education Agency, and eleven more were noted as "exemplary."[10] At the 2010 annual statewide science and engineering fair sponsored by ExxonMobil in Texas, twelve Harmony School students from across the state received the competition's top honors. According to the institution's press release, these twelve winners were selected from over 1,100 entrants.[11] For years, recruited sympathizers in the United States have understood the GM's move into charter school education as an organizational strategy without controversy. Indeed, at a GM-sponsored conference in Amsterdam in 2010, University of Houston Professor of Religion, Helen Rose Ebaugh, indicated that according to her understanding, Harmony Schools and their affiliates in Texas were not only "Gülen schools," but that their affiliation with the larger GM was something she saw as admirable.[12]

Applying Strategic Ambiguity

When Fethullah Gülen sought to overturn the Department of Homeland Security's (DHS) denial of his application for permanent residency in the United States, his legal team argued that Gülen deserved his green card because he was "an alien of extraordinary abilities in the field of education." In a move to overturn the DHS's initial decision, Gülen's advocacy team argued on his behalf (quoted at length), as follows:

> Plaintiff [Gülen] is the leader of the Gülen Movement. Plaintiff also has played a critical role in the Movement because *his work has served as the foundation for hundreds of schools across three continents.* Defendants [DHS] discount Plaintiff's leading and critical role for these educational institutions, and their denial was unsupported by substantial evidence in the record. . . . While Plaintiff [Gülen] may not have been involved in the business decisions that are involved in physically opening a school, *he nevertheless has played a critical role in establishing them. . . . In addition, Plaintiff's [Gülen's] methodologies are the basis of these schools. . . .* While Plaintiff may not be involved in the everyday management of these schools and the selection of specific curricula, *Plaintiff's [Gülen's] work*

serves as the basis of the educational philosophy at these schools. (Gülen v.
Chertoff, June 6, 2008; emphasis added)

Considering the above argument in support of Gülen's central role as
"the basis of the educational philosophy at these schools [i.e., GISs]," in
late 2009 and continuing through to the present, a number of parents of
students at GISs in the United States, together with a number of current
and former non-Turkish teachers at these schools, began to question
what they viewed to be a general lack of transparency regarding school
management, and a general pattern of denial from school administrators about observable connections between these institutions and
other GM-affiliated institutions throughout the country. According to
some parents and teachers, despite the above recognition that Gülen's
legal team demanded from the U.S. government, Gülen's "inspiration"
was not why they chose to send their children to schools managed by
Harmony, Horizon, Magnolia, Concept, and to other schools operated
by GM-affiliated CMOs. In fact, most of them had neither heard of
Fethullah Gülen, nor of the transnational social movement that bore
his name. In late 2009, news broke that in Tucson, Arizona, a number
of parents whose children attended the GM's Sonoran Science Academy (SSA, Daisy Education Corporation) had contacted a local newspaper to ask whether a reporter could find out more about the SSA's
alleged connections to the GM. The subsequent article started a divisive
local debate (Vanderpool 2009). Intrigued, another local paper wrote
a follow-up story four months later (Steller 2010). The first story questioned the apparent links between the SSA and the GM; the second
attempted to explain why so many teachers at SSA were (a) from Turkey, and (b) employed as foreign worker visa (H-1B) holders. Moreover,
just as allegations of discriminatory hiring and suspect connections to
a larger Turkish religious nationalist movement emerged in Arizona, in
Utah the GM-affiliated Beehive Science Academy (BSA) had its charter
revoked due to mismanagement of its charter funding (Stuart 2010a).
This decision, however, was later suspended and BSA was given a one-
year probation to respond to concerns raised by the Utah State Charter
School Board (Stuart 2010b).

Since they began, I have followed these events closely, as I view them
as instances of GM adaptation in diverse local contexts. I would be

remiss, however, if I did not indicate my surprise when in late 2009 (and continuing through to the publication of this manuscript), a number of self-identified "concerned parents," "former teachers," as well as county and city school board officials and journalists started to contact me from Illinois, Ohio, Maryland, Texas, Florida, Utah, Georgia, New York, and elsewhere. Indeed, despite the GM's self-projected identity as transparent and dialogic, what troubled the parents and teachers who contacted me was the insistence on the part of Turkish principals and administrators at Turkish-managed charter schools that connections to the GM were nonexistent. What troubled former teachers, school board officials, and labor union organizers were allegations of gender discrimination, charter funding mismanagement, and suspect hiring and retention practices at chartered GISs. What bothered parents was the curious responses and denials they received when they chose to probe about connections their children's teachers and principles had with something called the Gülen Movement.[13] I decided to treat this barrage of contacts from inquisitive and concerned parents, teachers, journalists, education officials, and labor organizers as an opportunity to continue my research on the unintended impacts of the GM's organizational strategies.

I had become accustomed to self-described "secularists" and "leftists" in Turkey expressing fears about the GM in regard to its association with Turkish Islamism and in regard to their fears about the withering of Turkish secularism; but why would a chemist from Louisiana, a grade school teacher from Georgia, a lawyer from Arizona, and a charter administrator from Ohio be concerned about a child's exposure to Turkish culture and language at a top-tier science- and math-based college prep school, or about a science teacher from Turkey sponsored by Turkish-managed CMO to teach physics to U.S. kids? If they were concerned parents, why not remove their children from these schools? If they were concerned school board officials, why not deny charter renewal? If they were current or former teachers, why not find a new place of employment?

Apparently, allegations of financial mismanagement, unfair hiring in favor of foreign Turkish teachers at the expense of unemployed U.S. teachers, and allegations of union busting and gender discrimination were too ubiquitous for some parents, teachers, and public education administrators to ignore. One of the first letters I received was from a self-identified "concerned parent." He explained that for the past two years his daughter had attended a charter school in the United States that he had only recently learned was affiliated with the movement of Fethullah Gülen. He wrote that he was a natural scientist, and that up until very recently he had been pleased with the math- and science-focused education his daughter was receiving. In the fall of 2009, however, this parent explained that he participated for the first time in a school board meeting, wherein he noticed that 100 percent of the board members were Turkish males. Thinking little of it at first, he started to attend meetings regularly. "Eventually," he said, he "began to feel concerned":

> What began to concern me was their reaction to any sort of questioning or disagreement with school policies—the degree to which they simply could not tolerate it, and the manipulative and forceful manner in which they responded struck me as distinctly abnormal. Formerly a staunch supporter of the school, I began to suspect that something just wasn't right. (Interview with "Concerned Parent 1," Winter 2010)

Eager to learn more about the GM, this parent explained that he became "alarmed" when he found so much contradictory material. He explained that, on the one hand, some Turkish and American commentators claimed that Fethullah Gülen was an exiled "radical Islamist" who commanded an expansive economic empire and who was determined to overthrow Turkey's secular republic. Other sources, however, insisted that Gülen was a noble, "Sufi-inspired" poet and orator, an "esteemed teacher" (hocaefendi) who had inspired two generations of inclusive social activism. This man explained that after months of research, he had come across my own work on the GM's organizational strategies (Hendrick 2009). He ended his e-mail with a number of questions. First and foremost, he wanted to know why, when asked, did the principal at his daughter's school deny affiliation with Fethullah Gülen or with the GM.

In an effort to alleviate this parent's concerns regarding what he expressed to be a fear of "Islamic indoctrination," I explained that such allegations were over thirty years old in Turkey, and that the conclusions reached by participant-observation researchers at schools around the world collectively indicated that involvement in the ideology of the Gülen Movement was (a) entirely voluntary, and (b) more focused on glorifying Turkey than it was on spreading Islam.

When another self-defined "concerned parent" contacted me in the early spring of 2010, he was in the midst of deciding whether he should let his son (and himself) go on a "dialogue trip" to Turkey that was to be subsidized by his son's school, and that was organized in conjunction with a local GM-affiliated dialogue center in his city. After his child's school principal denied GM affiliation, the parent contacted me to ask the following:

> Why doesn't the school acknowledge a link to the other schools? . . . If I had been told [school name omitted] was linked to a successful Turkish academic model, I think I would have been interested in looking at the other schools' accomplishments. Instead I feel uninformed and concerned. Why isn't there an open dialog about the Gülen influence on the academic model? Our tour of Turkey includes time at Coskun College and Fatih University. My guess is some of our administrators attended these schools, which from my limited research look directly related to the GM. ("Interview with Concerned Parent 4," Winter 2009)

This man explained that although his son received "a grant of three hundred dollars" from a GM-affiliated dialogue institute in his city, his school principal refused to acknowledge GM connectivity when he asked him about it before their trip. Instead, he was told, "our school works closely with our sister Turkish school in an effort to reduce costs" ("Interview with Concerned Parent 4," Spring 2010). Within a month, I received two more e-mails expressing similar concerns about organized trips to Turkey from parents whose children attended charter schools in two separate U.S. states. Before agreeing to take part in the trips/tours, or to allow their children to do so, each of these parents expressed concerns about what they observed to be a lack of transparency about these trips regarding chaperons, itineraries, hosts, lodging, and costs; about the Turkish identity of their children's schools in general, and about their recent realization that their school might be connected to something called the Gülen Movement. Considering the number of similar emails I was receiving, I decided to respond more uniformly to these and other queries as follows:

> The Gülen Movement (GM) is a controversial social movement in Turkey. In my opinion, this is why schools, businesses, and non-profits associated with the GM outside Turkey prefer to maintain a sense of ambiguity regarding their connectivity. Why [the principal] and principals at dozens of other charter schools around the U.S. insist upon maintaining their autonomy from the GM, in my opinion, needs to be contextualized in regard to the contemporary political situation in Turkey. Whether maintaining such ambiguity is "right" or "wrong" is in the eye of the beholder. My point is merely that there is indeed a reason behind it. (Correspondence with "Concerned Parents," Winter and Spring 2010)

In the most evenhanded way I could, I tried to explain that the GM's culture of ambiguity was innate to its organizational practice in Turkey, and that although I understood their frustration, it was necessary to consider the Turkish context, and the GM's history therein, to fully appreciate the rationale for such a practice.

Unfortunately, the GM's inclination for secrecy and denial has stirred up a public debate in the United States, and has incited a public relations scandal that receives national attention.[14] An unsigned document I received from a self-described "concerned parent" of a student at an alleged GIS charter school claimed to represent the concerns of nine families in one U.S. city, who claimed "to be in communication with some parents and former parents from other Gülen-associated charter schools in other states [who] have many of the same concerns that we do." A summary of the primary complaints listed by these "concerned families" were as follows:

- Denial of school affiliation with the broader GM network
- Concerns that the local school board does not have total authority over the school's administration
- Concerns about the allocation of the school's financial resources
- Apparent preferential treatment of Turkish teaching staff, and an apparent preference to hire Turkish and Central Asian Turkic teachers to teach science and math courses

- Apparent overcommitment of Turkish and Turkic teachers, who parents believe might not be aware of their civil rights as laborers in a public education system (e.g., right to overtime pay)
- Pressure for students to participate in GM-related academic events such as the Turkish Language Olympics
- Pressure for students to participate in Turkish-related events, festivals, and field trips
- A number of lavish, more xenophobic conspiracies that range from alleged "Islamic indoctrination" to "creating future sympathizers for Turkey," and to help "lobbying against the Armenian Genocide Resolution." (written correspondence with "Concerned Parent 1," Winter 2010)

According to his legal representative in the United States, Fethullah Gülen is (a) "the leader of the Gülen Movement," and (b) "the foundation for hundreds of schools across three continents." Nonetheless, in a recent news article that focused on the GM's emergence in U.S. education, the USA Today journalist Greg Toppo (2010) sent a list of questions to Fethullah Gülen. When asked about his leadership in the movement, Gülen responded in writing as follows:

First of all, I do not approve the title "Gülen Movement" given to the civil society movement that I call "volunteers' movement." I see myself [as] one of its participants. There might be some educators who have listened to or read my thoughts on humanity, peace, mutual respect, the culture of coexistence, and keeping the human values alive, and have come to the United States for various reasons and work at private or public schools. In fact, I have heard from the media that there are such educators. . . . It is well-known that I have no relation with any institution in the form of ownership, board membership, or any similar kind. . . . I do not approve that those who are familiar with and share these ideas and opinions to any extent, or the institutions they work at, should be viewed as connected with my person.

Echoing Gülen's strategic use of ambiguity regarding when GISs are to be labeled as such (i.e., when there is a clearly defined benefit from affiliation) and when they are to be designated as autonomous (when parents or journalists ask direct questions), the GM's Daisy Education

Corporation superintendent, Özkür Yıldız, responded to an Arizona journalist in similar fashion:

> We would like to stress and underline the fact that the establishment of Daisy Education Corp. was not, and is not, linked to any movement that can possibly have any substantive influence on [any] school's mission, vision, and operations. . . . DEC cannot, and does not, have any control over its employees' inspirations or beliefs. If any of DEC employees (administrators or teaching faculty) is inspired by Mr. Gülen, it does not suggest that DEC has an *institutional affiliation* or guidance from Mr. Gülen [emphasis in original].[15]

Soner Tarim, superintendent at the Cosmos Foundation in Texas, went on record with a similar denial of affiliation, as did the principal at Utah's Beehive Science Academy (Stuart 2010b).[16]

Why do leaders in the GM consistently deny affiliation when affiliation in clear? Because the employment of strategic ambiguity is central to the culture of the GM cemaat (community), a fact that only has meaning when understood in the context of the secular fortress of twentieth-century Turkey. It is within this context that Gülen advised his followers about the necessity of patience and keeping secrets:

> There are many important affairs regarding which secrets have to be protected. Often enough, when the representatives in such an affair do not keep certain matters secret, no progress is achieved and it produces serious risks for those involved, particularly if the affair relates to the delicate issues of national life and its continuation. . . . [A] person may explain as much as his duty demands, but must never give away all the secrets of his own job. It must never be forgotten that those who freely publicize the secrets of their hearts, will drag themselves and their nation to an unavoidable downfall. (Gülen 1998a, 68–69)

According to Gülen's teachings, to keep a secret is not a dishonest act; it is an attribute of strong will and national protection. Despite claims of transparency, therefore, keeping secrets about how institutions are connected, how individuals are linked through social networks, and how individuals and institutions mobilize for a common purpose, is a constitutive characteristic of the GM ethos. Nonetheless, evidence of connectivity between GM institutions is observable not only in terms of ideational cohesion, but also in terms of observable social networks that connect individuals, and observable patterns of organizational practice.

Social networks. Just as they do in Turkey, GM activists in the United States meet regularly in local reading circles, known internally as sohbetler, where they create community, collect donations, and organize effectively. Every city and town in the United States with a GM charter school or dialogue center plays host to an affiliated GM community. In addition to providing a social space where GM "volunteers" can create community, sohbet circles also function as spaces where connected individuals learn about activities happening in other nodes of the GM network, and where they associate with brothers who have spent time in different cities. Such connections provide individuals with access to other institutions, which facilitates extensive movement throughout the GM network. Someone whose H-1B foreign worker visa was sponsored by a GM school in Utah, for example, might find himself teaching in Texas a year later, and in Ohio a year after that. Similarly, a principal at a GM school in Chicago might find himself an opportunity to direct a "dialogue center" in Denver, or perhaps find a position at a GM-affiliated CMO in California. The problem is that while it functions as a very efficient and flexible organizational model, the movement of individuals from institution to institution is cited by a growing number of critics as evidence of dishonesty on the part of principals and administrators who insist that "there is no organic connection between these institutions."

Organizational practice. A regular criticism of the GM in the United States, Turkey, and elsewhere is that within the community, male privilege continues to dominate in positions of influence and power (Özdalga 2003; Turam 2004a, 2004b, 2006). In the United States, however, this common criticism is now extended to call attention not only to the all-male makeup of boards and administrations, but to their all-Turkish composition as well. Such allegations are compounded by specifically U.S. criticisms leveled against the GM that allege GISs to be mechanisms to collect public funding in an effort to sponsor the immigration of affiliated Turkish and Turkic GM "volunteers." According to the United States Citizenship and Immigration Services, the average

cost of sponsoring a foreign worker's H-1B visa ranges from approximately $1,500 to $3,500, depending on the worker's status as full- or
part-time. Between 2001 and 2010, the GM's Cosmos Foundation and
its subsidiary Harmony Schools (headquartered in Houston) submitted more H-1B visa applications than any other secondary school or
CMO in the country.[17] Over the same period, the GM-affiliated Riverwalk Education Foundation in San Antonio (now the School of Science
and Technology), Dove Science Academy in Oklahoma, Pelican Science
Academy in New Orleans, Lisa Science Academy in Little Rock, and
Sonoran Science Academy in Tucson joined Cosmos and Harmony
schools on the list of the top twenty-five secondary educational institutions that sponsored H-1B visas for foreign teachers.[18] At least nine
more GM-affiliated charter schools or related CMOs were represented
on the list of the top one hundred.

In addition to their complaint that GM-affiliated charter schools
hire foreign teachers at the expense of out-of-work American teachers,
critics of the GM in the United States claim that unlike county and state
public schools (and unlike most private schools) that sponsor large
numbers of work visas for foreign teachers, GM schools appear to hire
teachers only from Turkey or Turkic Central Asia. Moreover, most have
neither a degree in education nor certification to teach in the United
States. Nonetheless, Turkish principals at GM schools continually insist
that they hire from abroad to fill the void left by a lack of qualified math
and science teachers in U.S. labor markets. In the context of a penetrating economic downturn that deeply affected K–12 education, this argument on the part of GM-affiliated institutions has become increasingly
less viable. Indeed, considering the average cost of sponsoring an H-1B
visa, GISs (of which many have been, or continue to be, investigated
for financial mismanagement) spend tens of thousands of dollars from
their operating budget every year to sponsor foreign Turkish and Turkic
teachers in the U.S. Considering the public funding of charter schools,
this practice has led many parents, journalists, politicians, and state
education boards to focus more closely on the management of public
finances at GM-affiliated charter schools.[19]

Additional patterns of organizational parallels between GM-affiliated charter institutions include the near-verbatim use of language on
school websites,[20] the mutual participation of charter school students

in GM-sponsored math and science competitions and GM-sponsored Turkish Language Olympics, and an overlap in the use of the same GM-affiliated "educational research firms," such as the California-based Accord Institute, the Atlanta-based Grace Institute, or the DC-based Washington Education Foundation, among others.[21]

Conclusion

Because the GM's experience in the United States is (a) merely one example of the GM's transnational ventures, and (b) currently unfolding, we cannot claim it to be an exemplary case of the Movement as a whole, or to conclude how the GM's course of action there will affect the community's activities in Turkey or elsewhere. Notwithstanding, by insisting on the nonpolitical nature of the GM's lobbying and public relations efforts, by maintaining ambiguity regarding connectivity between individuals and institutions, by flatly denying suspect hiring and retention practices at affiliated charter schools, by allegedly engaging in gender discrimination at these schools, and by becoming the subjects of state and federal level investigations for financial mismanagement, the GM has opened itself up to intense criticism at best, and to potential criminal implications at worst.

Public officials cannot legally comment about ongoing state and federal investigations, but according to reports in U.S. media, the GM is currently the subject of at least five federal level inquiries as well as several more state-level investigations into its charter school practices.[22] Indeed, recalling the trend of rising Islamophobia in the United States, it is important to note that some critics point to the GM's ambiguous organizational strategies as "proof" of what they label "stealth jihad" in U.S. education. With minimal to zero understanding of the Turkish context, however, and often with very little regard to the diversity that exists within the symbolic world of Muslim politics, some critics have taken to the Internet to employ what is, in many cases, deeply xenophobic and often outlandish rhetoric to express their fears about Turkish Muslims "infiltrating the U.S. through our charter schools" (Rodgers 2010). Although alarmist such allegations have gained momentum. Notwithstanding, why does the GM maintain ambiguity concerning its mobilization strategies in the United States, and in so doing, why do its actors choose to contradict the Movement's stated identity as a collective advocate for dialogue?

According to this author, the GM is playing the U.S. political field as though it were Turkey in the 1990s (the last time the GM weathered a particular difficult media storm). If its activists continue to do so, however, the hundreds of teachers, administrators, businessmen, and students who constitute the GM network in the United States will find themselves the subject of more public scrutiny in an increasingly hostile, and an increasingly xenophobic, U.S. public sphere. Indeed, of perhaps greater concern to GM loyalists is that if associated actors in the United States do not begin to more effectively explain their organizational model to an increasingly critical U.S. public, more publicly funded GISs will likely become targets of more state and federal investigations, sites of more labor-related employment disputes, and subjects of more specifically focused external audits.

Conclusion

The Marketization of Muslim Politics in Turkey

> We have never jumped into politics; never discriminated between the political parties. We have always been at the same distance with the leaders of all political movements. We have shared our thoughts, which we have believed to be useful with them. We are standing in the same place today. . . . Our only wish is a Türkiye which is independent and an arbiter in the arena of global politics.
> —M. Fethullah Gülen

The development policies associated with Kemalist republicanism, institutional laicism, and limited democratization produced a unique sociopolitical context in late twentieth-century Turkey. During the formative years of the Republic, industrialization was administered unevenly between east and west, city and country; and at the same time, faith and youth were politicized and a particularly rigid form of secular nationalism sought to dominate Anatolia's collective consciousness. In addition to the social and political cleavages that positioned the country's Kurdish and Alevi populations against an ethnically defined Turkish state in two distinct battles for minority rights and recognition, Islam became a cultural point of contention that positioned state versus society in an epic battle for hearts and minds. But although Turkey's Islamic activists were consistent in voicing their longings for a societal-wide (re-)embrace of Islamic values, the symbolic authority of Islamic idioms rarely morphed into confrontational, revolutionary variations of religious fervor. Instead, Muslim politics in Turkey tended toward more passive forms of resistance via underground identity networks (e.g., the Nur) and, when possible, toward democratic participation (e.g., Milli Görüş). In practice, however, when Islam-identified politicians and public intellectuals lamented the demise of Turkey's Ottoman past, when they called for the implementation of Şeriat, and when they uniformly criticized Turkey's twentieth-century alliances with the United States, the European Community, and Israel, they rarely threatened the legitimacy of their national identity. Despite their discontent with the policies of Kemalist laicism, Islamic actors rarely sought to undermine the imagined community of the glorious Turkish nation.

In the 1960s and 1970s, Turkey's corporatist development model collapsed and a period of political economic liberalization ensued. In this context, new opportunities emerged for new actors to increase their share of social, economic, and political power. Following the 1980–1983 junta, the policies of the Turkish–Islamic Synthesis created opportunities for the emergence of "organic Muslim intellectuals" in media and publishing to exploit a state-led revival of Islamic identity. Increased access to wealth accumulation provided previously subordinated actors with the resources necessary to consolidate their once clandestine social networks into better-defined interest groups. This, coupled with advancements in information and communication technologies, made it increasingly more difficult for Turkey's long-entrenched managerial state class to maintain its monopoly over the institutions of social power. These transformations eventually led to the rise of the Islamist Refah Partisi (RP), whose leader, Necmettin Erbakan, became the country's first Islam-identified prime minster in 1996.

In 1997, Turkey's managerial state reacted alarmingly to these transformations by forcing Erbakan and the RP out of office during the infamous "February 28 Process," which led to a fissure in Turkish political Islam between old and young. After five years of reordering, a younger generation of Turkey's Islamic partisans managed to come to power in late 2002 as a single-party government under the heading of the AKP, a success they have since repeated twice (in 2007 and in 2011). Among the primary factors that contributed to the rather quick realignment of Turkish Muslim politics was that throughout the turbulent period of the 1990s, the communitarian base of support underneath Turkey's Islamic movement continued to expand its economic capacity through export, which contributed directly to its emergence as an alternative elite in the country's market system.

Guided by the inspiration of one or another faith leader and empowered by new access to material wealth, the latter years of the twentieth century bore witness to the rise of new collective of actors who became deeply effective players in Turkey's political economy. Falsifying the common, but simplistic, narrative that posits cultural incompatibility between "secularists" and "Islamists," however, this book illustrated how in Turkey, a war of position between entrenched and ascendant elites has never been a war between modernity and Islam. Quite the contrary, be they "Islamist" or "Kemalist," the Turkish war of position has long been one over the accursed share of social power in the market, in the state, and in civil society—an intra-elite struggle for the hearts and minds of the Turkish nation. Signified by the rise of the AKP in 2002, Turkey's Islamic activist movement distinguished itself within the world of twentieth-century Muslim politics when its leaders chose to drop "Islam is the solution" in favor of "conservative democracy." In an effort to interpret this transformation from the bottom up, this book introduced readers to conservative democracy's most ambiguous, and arguably, to its most effective organizational actor, Hocaefendi Fethullah Gülen.

Turkey's transformation to "conservative democracy" under the AKP is another way to say that Turkey's "Islamic alternative" has been co-opted into the fold of Turkey's ruling elite, or better still, into the fold of global neo-liberal market integration. Unlike twentieth-century "Islamists" who organized in the interests of state-directed social reform in accordance with Islamic law, however, Turkey's twenty-first-century "conservative democrats" realize that the Islamification of society does not require the Islamification of the state; quite the contrary, what is required is state decline. As newly competitive market actors in an export-led integration model, conservative democrats recognize that reform requires a liberated and competitive marketplace, and a social system that guarantees market access. In Turkey, greater access to global resources, wealth accumulation, and communication technologies has redirected "political Islam" toward an increasingly rationalized, post-political manifestation of something that might be termed "market Islam":

> Renouncing the vaguely leftist approach of the Islamists where the welfare state and nationalization are concerned, the new "Islamic" businessmen openly advocate the free market and see personal wealth as a

blessing from God, to the extent that the money has been made along halal lines or has been purified through *zakat* and alimony. In this sense, the growing development of Islamic NGOs and charities has more to do with the development of religious-minded middle-class entrepreneurs than with the call for *jihad*. (Roy 2004, 97)

Inspired by the teachings of Fethullah Gülen, "market Islam" in Turkey seeks to privatize religious revival, and subsequently to rationalize and institutionalize its mobilization as a profit-seeking and influence-peddling transnational advocacy network. GM schools have since become highly desired goods in a global education market. Its affiliated trade associations have taken the lead in expanding Turkey's export economy to nearly every country on earth. Its media has ascended to the top of Turkey's mainstream news market, and its leader has risen to the level of "extraordinary ability" and "most influential" in global recognition.

The Ambiguous Politics of Post-Political, Market Islam

The underlying effect of advocacy networks is "persuasion or socialization. . . . Since they are not powerful in the traditional sense of the word, they must use the power of their information, ideas, and strategies to alter the information and value contexts within which states make policies" (Keck and Sikkink 1998, 16). Such a "political process" approach to social movement studies, however, presupposes that by way of either revolution or reform, "the state" is the ultimate focus of social movement activity (McAdam, McCarthy, and Zald 1996; Tarrow 1994). But what if the state is not the primary target of social movement action? The "political process" approach isolates "the political" as that which is embodied in the state or that mobilizes against the state, and thus does not account for the "multi-institutional" nature of political mobilization. This is problematic because "not all [social movements] operate within a single polity, target one state, or seek policy change" (Armstrong and Bernstein 2008, 80). A multi-institutional approach to social movement research must adopt a perspective that privileges culture and that assumes social movements not to be "only those that directly address economic and political disenfranchisement" (82).

Although I am hesitant to refer to the GM as a social movement as such, I do agree, following Melucci (1996), that the GM's brand of collective action does seek to affect social power in ways that produce social change. The degree of social change that its activists call for, however, is less focused on state power than it is on social power in the marketplace of goods, services, and ideas. Moreover, as a faith-identified advocacy network, culture is central to the GM's collective identity and purpose. In anticipation of state suspicion and media slander, therefore, "strategic ambiguity" has proved a time-tested strategy employed by GM actors who seek to brand their leader as a scholar, poet, sage, and seer; and who long to present their community both as something more, and as something less, than it is.

According to his most devoted followers, Fethullah Gülen is second to none in an effort to cultivate "dialogue" between divisive Turkish political communities (e.g. secularist v. Islamist; Turk v. Kurd; Sunni v. Alevi). GM supporters insist that their aims are "nonpolitical" and thus constitute a collective identity as "advocates of dialogue" who are equidistant from all political agendas. More often than not, GM actors choose to downplay, if not to flatly deny, the profound impact their activities have in Turkey's political culture and in its political economy. Indeed, unless they have an opportunity to frame the discussion in their own terms, in accordance with their own timing, and in their own arenas (e.g., in internally produced media, at internally organized conferences), GM actors prefer a public persona that purports post-political populism. For example, although self-described as nonpolitical, according to an internal analysis of the GM's impact "the Gülen movement has been the most dominant factor [in the transformation of Turkey's Islamic movement]":

Most of the new elite's children and thus indirectly themselves have become acquainted with the movement and its worldview. As a matter of act, in most cases, the boundaries between these new elites and the Gülen movement supporters are blurred and it is the members of this Anatolian bourgeoisie who actually fund and establish Gülen schools, after seeing their success in other Anatolian towns and cities. These new middle classes have always been in close contact with center–right and Islamist parties, influencing center–right parties to be more Islamic and Islamist parties to be more center–right. Many provincial Islamist

politicians have also sent their children to Gülen schools. We must
also note that Gülen media is the largest in almost all Anatolian cities.
(Yilmaz 2008, 906–907)

The author of this quote, Ihsan Yilmaz, is an accomplished organic intellectual in the GM cemaat, a regular contributing columnist at the GM-
affiliated *Today's Zaman* newspaper, a onetime director of the GM-affiliated Dialogue Society in London, and a current faculty member of the
GM-affiliated Fatih University in Istanbul. In Yilmaz's view, the successes
of the AKP are anchored on the successes of Fethullah Gülen. Although
a nonpolitical movement, therefore, it is also the case that from a reflexive perspective, the GM sees itself as *the* motivating factor behind the
AKP's political success, and as *the* primary agent in the transformation of
Turkish Islamic activism in general. According to Yilmaz, GISs in Turkey
and the application of Gülen's teachings in media and outreach allow "a
younger generation of Islamists to be comfortable as far as Islam and their
minds and hearts are concerned" (914). In this way, the source (*kaynak*)
from which a new Turkey emerges is, in fact, Fethullah Gülen.

Interestingly, such an ambiguous and contradictory presentation
of political impact has proved both effective and damaging to its public persona in Turkey, the United States, and elsewhere.[1] Because they
define "the political" from a very narrow perspective, when organic
intellectuals affiliated with the GM insist on their nonpolitical identity (even though some simultaneously take pride in the their political
impact), they neglect to assess the political implications of the thousands of GM-affiliated businessmen who regularly traverse the world in
an effort to increase Turkey's export capacity, or their emergence as rising stars in Turkish finance. They prefer instead to present their leader
and his Movement as "modest" and "Sufi-inspired," and as focused
solely on spiritual frugality, education, peace cultivation, and democracy promotion. Simultaneously, however, its actors also control what is
now Turkey's most circulated print newspaper, three Turkish television
stations, the country's most influential newsmagazine, as well as dozens
of lobbying institutions in Washington DC and in other cities throughout the United States, western Europe, and elsewhere. This is all compounded by the fact that since 1991, this "nonpolitical movement" has
opened hundreds of educational institutions that double as unofficial

Turkish embassies and cultural centers in more than one hundred countries. These contradictions suggest that although nonpolitical in name, the GM has a dramatic political impact in practice.

Indeed, an ethnographic account of political mobilization measures the *stated purpose* of an advocacy/political campaign against the *practice* of campaign/movement actors (Eliasoph 1998; Lichterman 1996; White 2002; Wood 2002). In this way, it is necessary to study the ways in which personal accounts and observed lifestyles confirm "the lofty ideal," and the ways they complicate this ideal by illustrating the personal agency of rational individuals. In the case of the GM, the stated purpose of the core community (cemaat) is to train a totally devoted "golden generation" of "ideal humans" who will lead Turkey toward "the light" by revitalizing Islam as central to Turkish national identity, and by educating young Turks about their potential as world leaders in business, science, and statesmanship. The reality of participation, however, is that the cemaat also reproduces a system of social mobility, rational opportunism, and professional access that cannot go unnoticed or be trivialized as an after-effect of spiritual renewal.

GM actors mobilize as a strategically ambiguous network of ideas, people, and institutions that connect with one another in a graduated system of "applied Sufism" and market rationality. At the center of the GM network is a core cemaat, a charismatic community that includes Fethullah Gülen, his aristocrats, their staff at the Akademi, many teachers at GISs and volunteers at "dialogue" institutions around the world, as well as current and aspiring university students who illustrate interest in community participation at GM-affiliated "houses of light." Together, these actors constitute both Gülen's "ideal humans" *and* the "totally devoted" crusaders who Gülen's critics claim them to be. As an ambiguous network of people and institutions, the operation of GISs, dershaneler, dormitories, cultural centers, media centers, and other private places of business are autonomous. Collective identity is realized through shared practice, social networking, and the construction of intensive core ties and extensive weak ties in a complicated network of graduated affiliation. All members of the cemaat, as well as those who constitute the once-removed stratum of GM friends (arkadaşlar), meet regularly in sohbet circles to reaffirm their affiliation, to donate money (himmet), and to socialize in an alternative public sphere. At more removed strata are the sympathizers (yandaşlar) and unaware consumers. Yandaşlar are recruited to "support" the GM by providing its institutional actors with public legitimacy by granting them political and discursive support in media and academia; and in city, state, and national offices of political and economic power. The unaware consumer, by contrast, supports the GM in a globally competitive marketplace that showcases GM-affiliated products in education, media, printing and publishing, textiles, light manufacture, and trade.

In a developing country like Turkey, one with a highly competitive system of higher education, a historically volatile market economy, and a relatively weak social welfare system, affiliating oneself with a proven system of success is a rational option for personal fulfillment and economic advancement. Participation in "the community" (cemaat) or as a "friend" (arkadaş), in this regard, should be viewed as a hyper-rational decision on the part of upwardly mobile Turkish youth who must decide between limited opportunities for a prosperous future. GM loyalists in the cemaat can only passively acknowledge such rewards because to emphasize social mobility as primary would discursively undermine Gülen's supposed grace as a charismatic leader. Nonetheless, it would be grossly negligent not to acknowledge the "service" (hizmet) the GM provides for a Turkish youth population whose participants long for advantage in a competitive market system. Complementing and expanding on Turam's (2006) conclusions about the GM's impact as a contested but "engaged" political actor, this conclusion falsifies both the "lofty ideal" promoted by Gülen and his aristocrats, as well as the fears of "brainwashing" perpetuated by GM alarmists. Presented with a critical eye in regard to the GM's collective impact in the markets and hallways of social power, this conclusion offers a more nuanced understanding of the GM's mobilization than is to be found in most competing scholarly sources on the topic (e.g., Carroll 2007; Çetin 2010; Ebaugh 2010; Hunt and Aslandoğan 2007; Yavuz and Esposito 2003).

The Weight of Material Interests (Revisited)

The findings of this case study on the charisma and community of Fethullah Gülen suggest that rather than advocating the implementation of Islamic Law, the revival of the Ottoman Caliphate, or even an overhaul of Turkish secularism, *the GM is not the collective voice of Islamic revolution.* However threatening to a small sector of state oligarchs, media moguls, traditional capital holdings, and cultural "secularists," Fethullah Gülen is best defined as a collective voice of neoliberal social conservatism—free markets, pious nationalism, pluralist democracy, and civil dialogue. His variation is not that of antagonism or reactionary fundamentalism. Quite the contrary, more than developing a parallel system of social services, and more than creating a niche market in an Islamic sub-economy, the GM constitutes an effort to provide services for *everyone* who can afford the price of high quality. In this way, the community of Fethullah Gülen is best understood as a leader in a grand effort to increase "the Muslim share" in Turkey's political economy, and as spearheading an effort to rationalize (marketize) Turkish Islam. In so doing, the GM highlights the degree to which Turkey's goods and services market has been penetrated by the country's "religious market," and the degree to which free markets have the power to reframe traditional mores in their image.

Despite the insistence on the part of Gülen's most loyal supporters, therefore, the GM's organizational successes are not the result of Gülen's "God-given powers," nor does the GM "emerge from itself." The GM, rather, is a product of shifts in Turkey's development model that created opportunities for would-be antagonists to mobilize as powerful actors in a diversified capitalist class. The rise of the GM is tied to the rise of Turkey; and its future is dependent on Turkey's continued emergence as a regional and world power. Although nonpolitical in stated identity, the GM is among Turkey's most powerful political actors, and is best understood as a product of Turkey's globalization—a nonconfrontational, revivalist movement that focuses its efforts in the private marketplace of goods, services, and ideas, and that mobilizes in alliance with the party leaders of Turkey's "conservative democratic" transformation.

Contradicting the efforts of twentieth-century Islamic activism in general, the GM *does not* seek to generate a new civil society in Turkey; it merely seeks to reform Turkey's current civil society—to passively, and with minimal confrontation, stake its claim in Turkey's increasingly more diverse and pluralistic ruling class by increasing the Muslim share in the discursive production of bourgeois social hegemony.

In practice, when the GM expands materially, it expands numerically. The more schools it manages, the more contracts affiliated companies are awarded; the more countries TUSKON develops trade partnerships with, the more GISs are cited as effective "bridges" that link Turkey to the world; the longer *Zaman* and *Today's Zaman* remain as Turkey's most widely read Turkish and English language newspapers, the more the collective teachings of Fethullah Gülen are centralized as cornerstones of Turkish national discourse. Notwithstanding, the more GM actors insist on employing strategic ambiguity to explain their collective mobilization, the more they should anticipate criticism for nontransparency and for alleged ulterior motives. Despite these criticisms, however, the transnationally active charismatic community of Fethullah Gülen provides an empirical case to refute the assumptions of cultural incompatibility that posit essentialist narratives pitting "Islam" versus "modernity/the West" in an epic battle for cultural supremacy. The GM, rather, constitutes an economically motivated, rationally opportunistic advocacy community whose leader frames "this-worldly" objectives in terms of Islam. But as its collective impact deepens, the weight of material interests grows heavy.

Notes

NOTES TO THE INTRODUCTION

1. See "How Far They Have Traveled" (2008); "A Farm Boy on the World Stage" (2008); Amin (2010); Vurul (2008); Hudson (2008); Tavernise (2008).
2. See http://www.zaman.com.tr/ (Turkish); http://www.todayszaman.com/tz-web (English); http://www.stv.com.tr/ (Turkish); http://www.mehtap.tv/ (Turkish); http://www.ebru.tv/en (English); http://www.burcfm.com.tr/ (Turkish); http://www.aksiyon.com.tr/aksiyon (Turkish).
3. See http://www.tr.fgulen.com/ (Turkish); http://www.en.fgulen.com/ (English).
4. Member totals were accessed on September 21, 2011. Each of these e-mail groups is linked to extensive online social networks and social forums that are either loosely or tightly connected to the GM and to Fethullah Gülen. A non-exhaustive list is as follows: fethullah_gulen@yahoo.com, turk_okulları@yahoo.com, zaman_okurları@yahoo.com, adaletvekalkinma@yahoogroups.com, benimturkiyem@yahoogroups.com, hersey-konusulacaksa@yahoogroups.com, liberal-izmirliler@googlegroups.com, Liberal-Turkiye@yahoogroups.com, mefkure@yahoogroups.com, millikulturumuz@yahoogroups.com, NewJerseyTurk@yahoogroups.com, northjerseyturk@yahoogroups.com, NYTurkiye-Politika@yahoogroups.com, sanalsiyaset@yahoogroups.com, tbmm-milletve-killeri@yahoogroups.com, turkiyehaber@yahoogroups.com, turkkulturevi@yahoogroups.com, USA-Turkleri@yahoogroups.com, http://www.nurforum.org/, and http://www.antoloji.com/.
5. Krespin (2007). The full text and translation are widely published online. Video is available for viewing at YouTube (e.g., http://www.youtube.com/watch?v=oNi 3Z3qZ7Z4&mode=related&search).

NOTES TO CHAPTER 1

1. Al-Salaf (Salafiyya) itself refers to the original companions of the Prophet, and thus, to a time when sociopolitical organization was imagined to have been sustained in harmony with the teachings of Islam and the will of God. The grand narrative of twentieth-century Muslim politics stressed the necessity to "reopen the gates of *ijtihad*"(interpretation)—that is, to legitimate the practice of Qu'ranic and Hadith (sayings of the Prophet) interpretation so as

to assure Islamic society's ability to coalesce with modernity, to re-create the sense of social harmony that was imagined to have existed during the time of the Prophet and the Rashidun, the time of the "Rightly Guided Caliphs" that immediately followed the Muhammad's death.

2. There are numerous weblogs and other online forums whose authors are deeply critical of the GM's mobilization in the United States, concerning both its activities in charter school education, and its political lobbying and efforts to cultivate "dialogue." Among the most alarmist, and xenophobic, of these commentaries are published by local and national conservative activist organizations such as Act of America, Family Security Matters, *FrontPage Magazine*, and West Texas Patriots, to only name a few.

3. The events surrounding the longtime contributor to National Public Radio (NPR) and the Fox News Network (FNN) Juan Williams illustrate this phenomenon well. In the early fall of 2010, NPR fired Williams for defending his FNN colleague, Bill O'Reilly, whose views regarding the increasing visibility of Muslim identity in the United States often linked the events of 9/11 directly with the faith of Islam. When contributing to O'Reilly's program on FNN, Williams defended his host's opinions as follows:

   Look, Bill, I'm not a bigot. You know the kind of books I've written about the civil rights movement in this country. But when I get on the plane, I got to tell you, if I see people who are in Muslim garb and I think, you know, they are identifying themselves first and foremost as Muslims, I get worried. I get nervous. (Folkenflick 2010)

   Williams was fired from NPR the next day, but his comments had already stoked the flames of public debate regarding a perceived "Muslim challenge" to U.S. national identity.

4. As this manuscript goes to press in November 2012, the Turkish media is abuzz with regular stories and televised media reports about a growing rift between the AKP and the GM that has allegedly grown wider since the former's third national electoral success in June 2011.

5. Melucci (1996, 20) helps to clarify collective action as follows: "a set of social practices (i) involving simultaneously a number of individuals of groups, (ii) exhibiting similar morphological characteristics in contiguity of time and space, (iii) implying a social field of relationships and (iv) the capacity of the people involved in making sense of what they are doing." Such an open definition underlines the fact that social movements, advocacy networks, and other collective mobilizations are not necessarily synonymous. The analytical concept of collective action "must break down its subject according to orientations of action on the one hand and the system of social relationships affected by the action on the other . . . fighting for increased participation is different from rejecting the rules of the political game" (21).

6. According to some observers, both the GM and Opus Dei harbor ulterior agendas to infiltrate the state and to overturn secular republicanism in their

respective countries (Turkey and Spain). Both focus on the education of youth in a secular framework and both seek to convert by example and passive persuasion (*inandirma*), rather than by overt proselytizing. Both sets of leaders moved their organizations outside their native countries to countries that shared cultural and linguistic roots (Central Asian Republics and Latin America, respectively), and both found sanctuary and free movement in the United States. Finally, both the GM and Opus Dei found refuge and opportunity in the global marketplace where their sympathetic benefactors built fortunes based on an ethic of spiritually motivated accumulation. A more detailed comparison between these two organizations is a very worthy topic for future research.

Fethullah Gülen and Msgr. Jose Maria Escrivá de Balaguer, the founder of Opus Dei, bear a striking resemblance in how they are regarded by those who love and follow them. In her intellectual treatment of Opus Dei, Estruch (1995, 5) observes how his followers present Msgr. Escrivá in a similar fashion as Gülen's followers present their leader: "Whether because their emotional involvement is still very intense or because they were campaigning for his beautification—they wanted to make him into an individual made of a single piece, without any cracks or blind spots." While there is no official sainthood in Islam, followers of Fethullah Gülen have campaigned for his accreditation as an "alien of extraordinary ability in the field of education" in the United States, and for his being named "the world's most influential public intellectual" by *Prospect Magazine* and *Foreign Policy* (as discussed in the introduction). With regularity Fethullah Gülen is presented as a contemporary correlate of the eleventh-century Sufi saint Mawlana Jalal al-Din Muhammad Bakti (aka "Mevalana" or "Rumi," 1207–73 CE), and as a selfless leader equivalent to Mahatma Gandhi, Martin Luther King Jr., Nelson Mandela, and the Dali Lama.

NOTES TO CHAPTER 2

1. Kemalist reforms in line with the six arrows included but were not limited to the following: Islamic Caliphate abolished (1923), polygamy outlawed (1925), Sufi orders and shrine veneration of Sufi saints outlawed (1925), Swiss civil code adopted (1926), the fez and turban outlawed, brimmed hats mandated for males so as to assure a secular nature for all male headgear (1927), language reform implemented, Arabic script replaced with Latin (1927), and female voting rights and first female elected judges (1933–1934) (Zürcher 2004).

2. Immediately following the formation of the Republic of Turkey, an opposition party was formed, the Progressive Republican Party. This was quickly abolished, and until 1930 the CHP enjoyed single-party rule. In that year, Atatürk oversaw the development of another opposition party, the Serbest Cumhuriyet Partisi (Free Republican Party, SCP). To rival the growing power of the CHP and the cadre of bureaucrats and politicians loyal to Ismet Inönü, Atatürk gave his personal blessing to the formation of the SCP, which advocated for a return to liberal economic development. Despite winning thirty seats in the 1930

municipal elections, the SCP accused the CHP of electoral fraud. As president, Atatürk favored stability and backed the CHP in its denial of the accusations. The SCP closed the same year (Zürcher 2004, 178–179).

3. Both the DP in the 1950s and the AKP in the 2000s enjoyed wide support as a result of economic upswings, and both enjoyed repeat electoral victories. Both parties increased their margins between their first and second victorious elections, and during both second elections (1954 and 2007) the CHP relied on its connections with Istanbul-based capital, with an increasingly distressed civilian bureaucracy, and with a growing number of Kemalist revivalists (unlike the DP, however, which lost parliamentary seats in 1958, the AKP managed to increase its percentage of the electorate in its third national election to 49 percent in 2011). The tension between these two spheres in Turkey's political elite proved a precursor to contemporary social strife in Turkey between old and new elite power. Similar to the situation today, the opposition CHP in the 1950s appeared relatively inept in a lopsided competition with a socially conservative ruling party whose leaders mobilized in coalition with an export-driven ascendant upper class linked with religious brotherhoods and affiliated social networks. Also similar to the AKP in the 2000s, the DP in the 1950s came to power on a promise of political liberalization and democratization, which, at least in its initial years, earned its leaders the benefit of the doubt from liberal-minded intellectuals who advocated for democratic reform and world integration.

4. Discussed in more detail in chapter 7, in June 2007 Istanbul police forces raided an apartment in Istanbul that was filled with weapons and explosives. This event sparked an investigation into the sources from which these weapons were obtained. This led to a five-years-and-counting investigation into Ergenekon, the name given to an alleged network of retired and active military personnel, political leaders, and journalists who were accused of having conspired to instigate social/political tension in the interests of overthrowing the governing AKP. The Ergenekon trial began on October 21, 2008, when prosecutors started to read the 2,455-page first indictment. The now-four-indictment-long trial continues amid claims from all sides of conspiracy, scorn, praise, fabrication, ineptitude, and corruption.

5. Following the 1971 coup, a series of "caretaker governments" followed before a return to civil elections in October 1973. Between 1973 and 1980, Turkish citizens saw seven different governments rise and fall. First, Bülent Ecevit, head of a revived CHP, and the newly formed MGH-identified Milli Selamet Partisi (National Salvation Party, MSP) forged a coalition government in 1974 (January–November). Following this coalition's collapse was an interim caretaker government, followed by a right-wing coalition under the leadership of Süleyman Demirel's AP (March 1975–June 1977), followed by a two-week return of Ecevit, followed by a second government under Demirel, followed by a third Ecevit-led coalition between the CHP and the AP, and finally a third AP majority government led once again by Demirel (1979–September 1980).

6. Özal's pre-coup economic plan was as follows:

   1. Devaluation from TL35/$1 to TL70/$1, coupled with a decree that stated the exchange would change frequently to keep up with inflation.
   2. Authority granted to state economic enterprises to set prices according to their discretion. The Central Bank would no longer issue loans to SEEs.
   3. Lower tax rates (which fell from 11.7 percent GDP in 1980 to 6.5 percent in 1985). (Heper 1991; Krueger 1995; Rodrik 1990; Senses 1986)

7. Specifically, Section IV, Article 15 stipulated that in the event of "war, mobilization, or state of emergency, the exercise of fundamental rights and freedoms could be partially or entirely suspended." Article 301 of the Turkish Penal Code stipulated that "a person who denigrates 'Turkishness,' the Republic, or the Grand National Assembly shall be punishable by imprisonment of between six months and three years." Restrictions such as these are priority concerns for European officials negotiating Turkey's integration into the European Union.

8. *Voluntary organizations* include religious foundations, nonprofessional associations, and private firms. *Public professional organizations* refer to occupational associations such as the Chamber of Commerce and the Turkish Bar Association. *Trade unions* are viewed as somewhat akin to voluntary associations, but "because of their highly specialized characteristics . . . they [are] regulated by separate legislation" (Özbudun 1991, 44).

9. This point warrants a caveat to highlight the struggles of minority communities in Turkey whose twentieth-century experience with Kemalism was far from harmonious. Per the dictates of Lausanne (1923), Turkey has a confessional notion of citizenship. Jews, Greek Orthodox, and Armenian Orthodox are the only officially recognized minorities, although Kurdish, Arabic, and Zaza have recently been recognized as minority-spoken languages. Moreover, despite a confessional notion of citizenship, neither Turkey's Alevi population (approximately 12 percent of Turkey's total population) nor Christian Assyrians (a population of approximately five thousand) enjoy religious minority rights. The former are framed as Muslim, despite their divergent holidays, institutions, rituals, and history. Also, despite constituting approximately 20 percent of the total population, Turkey's Kurds are not a recognized minority. With the formation of modern Turkey, the country's Kurdish population was stripped of its ethno-linguistic identity, and until 2004 the use of Kurdish was restricted in the media. Kurdish continues to be restricted in public schools and in other public institutions. There are a small number of private Kurdish schools in Turkey's southeast, and satellite TV is broadcast in Kurdish from varying locations in Europe. In the July 2007 national elections, twenty candidates from the Kurdish-identified Demokratik Toplum Partisi (Democratic Society Party, DTP) managed to win seats in Parliament by taking advantage of a political loophole in Turkey's partisan system by running as independents. In 2008, Turkey's Constitutional Court shut down the DTP for its alleged connections to the

insurrectionary Partiya Karkerên Kurdistan (Kurdistan Worker's Party, PKK). Following its closure, DTP leaders reformed into the Barış ve Demokrasi Partisi (Peace and Democracy Party, BDP) in 2010, and again ran deputies as independents in the 2011 national elections. After briefly boycotting their thirty-five-seat victory, BDP deputies took the oath of office on October 1, 2011. On October 28, 2011, a BDP deputy and university professor, Büşra Ersanlı, was arrested in a party raid (along with seventy other BDP party members) for allegedly supporting the separatist movement led by the PKK.

10. FDI in Turkey was US$100 million in 1987, and rose to nearly US$800 million in 1993. Although relatively low numbers in relation to emerging markets globally (0.4 percent of total GDP), it was a sevenfold increase in FDI in six years (Economist Intelligence Unit 1997–1998).

NOTES TO CHAPTER 3

1. For a transcript of the complete June 11, 2001, testimony given in Newark, New Jersey, see http://en.fgulen.com/press-room/claims-and-answers/1050-fethullah-gulens-testimony.html.

2. Said Nursi is introduced to provide readers with an overview of the "Nur" tradition, with which Fethullah Gülen and the GM are affiliated. The *RNK* is published by a number of publishing houses in Turkey, most of which are affiliated with one of the several Nur communities. The *RNK* is divided into multiple volumes: *The Words*, *The Letters*, *The Rays*, and *The Flashes*, each of which are often found subdivided or abridged for easier access and publication. A complete e-copy of the *RNK* is available at http://www.nursistudies.com/. For a detailed account of Nursi's intellectual biography from a sympathetic perspective, see Vahide (2005). For a detailed account of his sociological impact on the formation and mobilization of Islamic political identity in Turkey, see Mardin (1989); and Yavuz (2000, 2003a, 2003b).

3. The primary divisions in the larger Nur Movement are as follows: Yeni Asya (New Asia), Yazıcılar (Scribes), Yeni Nesil (New Generation), Yeni Zemin (New Earth/Ground), the Abdullah Yeğin Grubu, followers of Mehmet Kırkıncı, and the community of Fethullah Gülen.

4. This is the work of an anonymous author who introduces the English edition of Gülen's *The Messenger of God Muhammad* (2005a, xv).

5. This is the work of an anonymous author who introduces the English edition of Gülen's *Key Concepts in the Practice of Sufism* (2004a, i).

NOTES TO CHAPTER 4

1. Not long after I left the Akademi in late 2007, I ran into a research participant with whom I had become friendly during my stay in residence at the Akademi. He told me that soon after my departure, holding company executives decided to make the Akademi "more comfortable for visitors" who were becoming more regular in recent years. He informed me that the carpet on the second and third floor at

the Akademi was replaced by marble tile, and that those who work and visit these floors no longer had to remove their shoes (Field Notes, November 2008).

2. Field Interview with a non-Turkish "recruited sympathizer" who was visiting Istanbul from the United States. Since the mid-1990s, this GM *yandaş* has worked with a number of GM institutions in education and cultural outreach.

NOTES TO CHAPTER 5

1. Officially proclaimed in 1839, the Tanzimat (1839–1876, "Restructuring") was the most profound state reform movement preceding the 1923 founding of the Turkish Republic. Its focus was grand and its impact, while not immediate, was penetrating in the long term. Beyond the creation of new schools, the Tanzimat initiated a state-led shift to secular education as a system, and subsequently to a restructuring of Turkey's educated classes. By slowly replacing the *ulema* and *medrese* system with a secular system, the late-Ottoman state laid the foundation on which Atatürk was able to envision his Republic. A central innovation in this period was the notion of *maârif*, "learning that which is not known." In late-Ottoman society, the "unknown" referred to knowledge of political and economic liberalism, industrial engineering, and technological innovation. It was on the basis of *maârif* that enrollments at secular schools boomed. The *medrese* was of little use to a student who sought knowledge in modern medicine, chemistry, and physics. The previously established Imperial Military College (Tıbbiye, est. 1827) and the Imperial Military College (Harbiye, est. 1833) were joined by newly constructed Schools Public Administration (est. 1877), Law (est. 1878), and Commerce and Fine Arts (est. 1882). Together they became intellectual beacons for a new Turkish elite (Berkeş 1998; Güvenç 1998).

2. By the mid-1930s, there were twenty-six imam-hatip schools throughout country, but later in the decade they were all closed. In 1946, Turkey pluralized its partisan system and allowed for the formation of rival political parties to compete with the CHP in municipal and national elections. The newly formed Demokrat Party (DP) comprised socially conservative, economically liberal CHP detractors. The DP enjoyed majority support in the conservative Anatolian countryside, as well as urban support from disenfranchised liberals and among religious communities. The DP won the 1950 national elections in a landslide, and in 1951 it revived the imam-hatip system. By 1962, there were again twenty-six such institutions in the country (Güvenç 1998, 3:4). Amid the political and economic turbulence of the 1970s, Islam quickly became a mechanism that was used to quell social tension. In 1974, the imam-hatip system was again revamped, and the seven-year institution that exists today was inaugurated. By 1977, there were 230 imam-hatip schools in Turkey, and by 1996, there were 561, teaching 492,000 students (Güvenç 1998, 3:4).

3. The ÖKS was terminated in 2007. Starting in 2009, the Ministry of Education began a new program of testing that was envisaged to span three years of middle school.

4. See the CIA World Factbook 2002 on Turkey, http://www.faqs.org/docs/factbook/print/tu.html.

5. See the CIA World Factbook 2005 on Turkey, http://www.umsl.edu/services/govdocs/wofact2005/geos/tu.html. In 2006, a Turkish blockbuster film, *Sinav* (*Exam*), earned millions at the box office by satirically depicting the plight of a group of high school friends preparing for the ÖSS. In their haste, the group of friends decided to enlist the aid of Jean-Claude Van Damme (playing an international mercenary named "Jean-Claude Van Damme") to help them steal the ÖSS questions days before the test was to be administered.

6. In Turkey "college" (*kolej*) designates secondary education, what in the United States is most often referred to as "high school." Universities are referred to as such.

7. This expression is used by Eyüp Can (1996) in his *Fethullah Gülen Hocaefendi ile Ufuk Turu* (*A Tour of New Horizons with Fethullah Gülen*). Yavuz cites this phrase when discussing the GM's emergence in the early 1980s following the coup and the return to a civilian government under Özal and the ANAP. I agree with Yavuz, who argues that while there was a community of devoted followers dedicated to the teachings and mission of Fethullah Gülen before this period, it was not until Turkey's structural transformation following the 1980 coup that the GM had the ability to accrue the resources necessary to mobilize into a national, and ultimately, a transnational advocacy movement (Yavuz 2003a, 184).

8. These and numerous other accolades are advertised in Turkish at http://www.yamanlar.k12.tr/.

9. At this time, FEM operated 45 branches in Istanbul, and another 118 branches, totaling 163 across the country. Anafen operated 43 branches in Istanbul and another 55, totaling 98 across the country. By November 2011, FEM had expanded to 185 branches throughout Turkey. See http://www.femdershaneleri.com.tr/BranchList.aspx

NOTES TO CHAPTER 6

1. Turkey's FDI in the period from 1963 to 1967 was $22 million. It was $40 million from 1968 to 1972, and $89 million from 1973 to 1977. In the same periods Mexico saw $162 million, $286 million, and $493 million of FDI, respectively. Even after Turkey's initial move to liberalize in the 1980s, in the period from 1983 to 1987, its FDI reached only $88.4 million, while Mexico's was over $1 billion (Buğra 1994, 67).

2. See Balcı (2003, 156). Although Balcı also lists eighteen schools in Uzbekistan, in 1999 the Uzbek government perpetrated a crackdown on the GM community, and as a result there are currently no schools in operation in that country.

3. As reported by the GM's *Zaman*, Samanyolu TV, and Ebru News, and on countless websites, the Çağ Educational Company in St. Petersburg was permitted to re-open its high school because the Russian 13th Court of Appeals found that

the charges laid against it—that its teachers were overworked, that its building was substandard, that it used textbooks imported from Turkey, and that its kitchen was unsanitary—were unsubstantiated.

4. The $12,000 figure is the 2007/2008 cost of tuition at the Silk Road International School, a subsidiary of the GM's Sebat Educational Institutions. See http://www.sris.com.kg/

5. Tuition rates and fees are published on school websites, usually under "admission information."

6. See http://www.kaynak.com.tr/.

7. In June 2011, the investigative journalist Stephanie Saul of the *New York Times* found a similar pattern of preferential client networks among GM-affiliated construction and contracting firms in the United States.

8. The Türkiye–Afrika Ülkeleri Kültürel, Sosyal, ve Ekonomik Iş Birliği (Turkish–African Cultural, Social, and Economic Business Association, AKSIAD) used to organize similar events and activities between GM-affiliated businesspeople and educational institutions across the continent of Africa. These services are now organized by TUSKON.

9. Ngarmbatna Carmel, trade minister of Chad, quoted in *Zaman*, May 11, 2006.

10. As of June 2009, there are four interest-free participation banks in Turkey: Bank Asya, Kuveyt Turk, Turkiye Finans, and Albaraka Turk. All are members of Turkey's Association of Participation Banks (Turkiye Katlim Bankalari Birliği), however, BA is the only institution that is majority-owned by Turkish shareholders (80 percent). In April 2008, Turkiye Finans sold 60 percent of its shares to Saudi Arabia's NCB. Kuveyt Turk originates from Kuwait, and Albaraka Bank is a member of Pakistan's Albaraka Banking Group. A fifth, Ilhas Bank, was a financial victim of the 2001 banking crisis.

11. The 2001 crisis resulted in the closure of twenty-five Turkish banks, including the first and largest interest-free bank, Ihlas Finans. BA is the primary sponsor of GM-related events, and is the bank of choice used by Kaynak Holding as well as all the GM affiliates who participated in my research in Istanbul for their personal banking needs (although some also had personal checking accounts with larger and more accessible Turkish banks).

12. In order to assure collectivity in the administration of BA, private shareholders are not permitted to own more than 9.99 percent shares in BA (Field Interview, Summer 2007).

13. After his time in Turkmenistan, Muhammad Cetin moved to England, where he attended the University of Leicester and the University of Derby, and where he received a PhD in sociology in 2009. While still working on his doctoral degree, Cetin moved to the United States, where he served the GM community as president of the GM-affiliated Institute for Interfaith Dialogue in Houston, and where he made a name for himself as a leader and spokesperson for the GM community in Texas. Cetin is now an adjunct faculty member in the Sociology Department at East Stroudsburg University in Pennsylvania, twelve

miles from Gülen's compound in exile. As a senior aristocrat in the GM cemaat, Cetin attempted to streamline his interpretation of the GM's collective purpose with the publication of *The Gülen Movement: Civic Service without Borders* (2009), a book that was published by the Kaynak subsidiary Blue Dome Press. It is important to reiterate that among Cetin's first major achievements outside the classroom was to translate Turkmenbashı's *Ruhama* into Turkish. Cetin's professional biography can be found at http://www.sierraf.org/activity_details. php?id=30.

14. See http://www.calikenerji.com/.

NOTES TO CHAPTER 7

1. This chapter expands on arguments and research data presented in Hendrick (2011a).

2. See "A Quick Primer on *Doğan v. Erdoğan*" (2008) as well as the extensive media coverage by Doğan Media Group newspapers beginning on September 4, 2008 in *Hürriyet*, *Hürriyet Daily News*, and *Milliyet*, as well as coverage by the non-Doğan news sources *Zaman*, *Today's Zaman*, *Yeni Şafak*, and *Sabah* beginning on September 5, 2008.

3. "Mole Claims in Fraud Case Decried as Pitiful by Turkish Prime Minister" (2011); "Turkish Deputy Prime Minister Mole in Fraud Case" (2011); "Turkish Deputy Prime Minister under Mounting Pressure to Quit Post" (2011); "CHP Leader to Follow Deniz Feneri Hearing" (2012).

4. Kanlı (2009). That is not to say that Doğan-owned media do not publish controversial stories about Ergenekon. One of its dailies, *Radikal*, was legally reprimanded by the Turkish Armed Forces and had its press accreditation suspended when it published the testimony of a former Istanbul police chief who is a defendant in the case.

5. See "The Ergenekon File," http://www.todayszaman.com/newsDetail_getNews-ById.action?load=detay&link=150458.
Between January 29, 2008, and January 27, 2009 (364 days), *TZ* published 580 stories related to the Ergenekon investigation or trial.

6. See http://www.byegm.gov.tr/; and "2,459 Newspapers, 258 TV Stations in Turkey" (2008).

7. Turkish Press Advertising Organization (2008). The average daily sales in June 2008 for Turkey's top five selling print dailies were as follows: (1) *Zaman*: 785,309, (2) *Posta*: 634,666, (3) *Hürriyet*: 521,100, (4) *Sabah*: 410,523, (5) *Milliyet*: 209,318. The tabloid magazine *Posta*, as well as both the *Hürriyet* and *Milliyet* dailies, are owned and operated by the Doğan Media Group. *Sabah* is owned by the AKP/GM-arkadaş Çalık Group, and *Zaman* is owned and operated by seniors in the GM cemaat.

8. See opinions and editorials in *Zaman* and *TZ* in the spring and summer of 2007 during the presidential nomination process of Abdullah Gül—specifically the piece by *TZ* editor in chief Bülent Keneş, "The Portrait of a Fascist Provocateur" (2007).

9. Circulation figures according to Turkey's Press Advertising Organization, reporting Turkey's English language print sales in June 2008.

10. For example, see the collection of defenses, counterattacks, and sympathetic responses dealing with Fethullah Gülen or the GM published in *Zaman* and *TZ* on Gülen's website, http://www.fgulen.org/press-room/columns.html. Incidentally, this website is published and managed by the Akademi.

11. A digital copy of Şik's banned manuscript is available for download in Turkish at http://theopinions.info/thearmyoftheimam.htm.

12. On March 12, 2012, the 16th High Criminal Court ordered Şik's and Şener's release from prison, pending the outcome of their legal proceedings. They both sat in prison for 375 days without trial. Two of their colleagues were also released, although six others who were arrested for overlapping charges were not.

13. See "Winners at Turkish Olympics Are Champions of Peace" (2007). Bank Asya is the TLO's primary sponsor. Smaller sponsors include several GM arkadaş companies based throughout the country. See http://www.turkceolimpiyatlari.org/.

NOTES TO CHAPTER 8

1. This chapter expands on arguments and research data presented in Hendrick (2011a).

2. In addition to writing as a columnist for the GM's *Zaman* and *Today's Zaman* newspapers in Turkey, Hüseyin Gülerce was once the editor in chief of *Zaman* and was a founding member of the GM's Journalists and Writers Foundation in Istanbul.

3. TABID first mobilized in New York City in coordination with the GM's Turkish Cultural Center (TCC), and now has branches in seven U.S. cities (see http://www.tabid.org/). In addition, there are a number of newly established Turkish chambers of commerce in U.S. cities whose members coordinate with regional GM cultural institutions to promote the expansion of Turkish–American trade relations. For an introduction to the activities of these institutions, see the Texas Turkish–American Chamber of Commerce (TTACC) website, http://www.ttacc.org/.

4. A complete organizational WATC member list can be found at http://watc.org/. The five other U.S. GM-affiliated culture and dialogue federations are as follows: Council of Turkic American Associations (CTAA, http://turkiccouncil.org/), Mid-Atlantic Federation of Turkic–American Associations (MAFTAA, http://www.maftaa.org/), Turquoise Council of Americans and Eurasians (TCAE, http://www.turquoisecouncil.org/), Turkic–American Federation of the Southeast (TAFS, http://www.turkicfederation.com/), and Turkish American Federation of the Midwest (TAFM, http://www.turkishfederation.org/).

5. See http://video.cnnturk.com/2011/yasam/1/16/gulen-hareketi-kitabina-buyuk-ilgi; "Author of Book on Gülen Movement Receives Much Interest in Ankara" (2011).

6. See, for example, Yavuz and Esposito (2003); Hunt and Aslandoğan (2007); Yurtsever (2008). Also, a compendium of conference papers is available at http://gulenlibrary.org/.

7. See http://www.nisnews.nl/public/110708_2.htm. The *NOVA* television program broadcasted a special report on the growing influence of the GM in Holland, and focused specifically on the alleged insincerity of the GM in terms of Turkish–Dutch integration. The program sparked an investigation into the funding and management of GM schools in that country, which led to considerable backlash that continues to unfold today.

8. This quotation is taken from Texas State Senate Resolution No. 85, adopted February 11, 2011. The full resolution can be read at http://www.legis.state.tx.us/tlodocs/82R/billtext/pdf/SR00085F.pdf#navpanes=0.

9. The more recently founded Pinnacle Academy in Oaktown, Virginia (est. 2005) follows this model as well.

10. See "Harmony Achievements," http://www.harmonytx.org/achievements/.

11. See "A Spirit of Achievement," http://www.harmonytx.org/news/12/a-spirit-achievement/.

12. During her presentation at a conference sponsored by the GM-affiliated Dialoog Acadieme in Amsterdam, titled "Mapping the Gülen Movement," Ebaugh explained that at that time there were "twenty-five Gülen schools in Texas . . . in the U.S. they are called charter schools." See a video of Ebaugh's paper presentation at http://www.youtube.com/watch?v=eJmldzfD884&feature=related (at minute 12:00).

13. See the Chicago Alliance of Charter Teachers and Staff/American Federation of Teachers press release "Charter School Fires Teacher Active in Union Organizing" at http://www.aftacts.org/charter-news/136-charter-school-fires-teacher-active-in-union-organizing. This document details the allegations made against the GM-affiliated Chicago Science and Math Academy (CSMA) by a female teacher who, although acknowledged by name and with a financial award for exemplary teaching and service to the institution, was fired for her efforts to organize CSMA teachers into a union. See also the 2001 Texas state discrimination suit *Couch v. Harmony Science Academy–El Paso, Fatih Ay, Cosmos Foundation Inc.* for an example of civil allegations against another GM-affiliated school for breach of implied covenant of good faith and fair dealing, breach of contract, unfair retaliatory actions, violations of the Equal Pay Act of 1963, and several violations of the Civil Rights Act of 1964.

14. See "Objectives of Charter Schools with Turkish Ties Questioned" (2010); Hansen (2010); Woodhall and Gatti (2011); Saul (2011).

15. E-mail correspondence between DEC Superintendent Yıldız and *Arizona Daily Star* reporter Tim Steller. Full correspondence available at "Superintendent's Main Responses," http://azstarnet.com/news/science/environment/article_dec199db-be3f-5519-be3d-f6ad970db1f8.html.

16. See also see Soner Tarım's denial of any affiliation between the Cosmos Foundation and the GM in remarks he made to a meeting of "concerned citizens" in Odessa, Texas, in "Harmony Schools Answer Claims" (2010).

17. Cosmos Foundation dba Harmony Science Academy and Cosmos Foundation Inc., 2001–2010: 1,418 visa/green card petitions; 10 H-1B denials; 1,327 H-1B visas issued (United States Citizenship and Immigration Services). Data can be located at http://www.myvisajobs.com/H1B_Visa.aspx.

18. 2001–2010: Riverwalk Education Foundation, 150 H-1B petitions, 149 H-1B visas issued, 1 denial; Dove Science Academy, 226 visa/green card petitions, 185 H-1B visas issued, 22 green cards issued, 3 H-1B denials, 9 green card denials; Pelican Education Foundation, 85 H-1B petitions, 8 denials, 77 H-1B visas issued, 0 denials; Lisa Academy, 96 visa/green card petitions, 87 H-1B visas issued, 9 green cards issued, 0 denials; Sonoran Science Academy, 89 visa/green card petitions, 87 H-1B visas issued, 2 green cards issued, 0 denials (United States Citizenship and Immigration Services). Data can be located at http://www. myvisajobs.com/H1B_Visa.aspx.

19. A GM-affiliated charter school in Louisiana recently had its charter revoked for an alleged bribery scandal and for alleged lapses in organizational governance. See "BESE Votes to Rescind Charter for Abramson Science and Technology School" (2011). The GM-affiliated Fulton Science Academy (FSA) in Georgia recently had its application for charter renewal revoked. Although the only national blue ribbon school in the state in 2011, FSA underwent a drawn-out renewal process that ended when Fulton County officials denied the renewal of its five-year-old charter in December 2011, a ruling that the state upheld six months later. See "State Recommends Denial of Fulton Charter School" (2012). The ruling was informed by long period of county-directed investigation into the management of the school, a process that culminated with, among other reports, a highly critical external audit of FSA finances. A copy of the audit is available at https://docs.google.com/ file/d/0B4ni2jH9ge1SYXBJUWx1WHROUXM/edit?pli=1.

20. See an evidentiary example of this practice on the following blog, which is now but one of many that keep a regular file on the GM's activities in the United States: http://gulencharterschools.weebly.com/tie-coordination-across-schools. html.

21. International Sustainable World Energy, Engineering, and Environment Project Olympiad, which is primarily sponsored by the GM's Cosmos Foundation in Texas, has hosted students from GM schools around the country since 2007. Similarly, statewide Turkish Language Olympics in states throughout the United States are connected to similar competitions throughout the world, which are all connected to an international event that has been ongoing in Turkey since 2002 (discussed in prior chapters). The Accord Institute is a GM-affiliated, self-described education research, training, and consulting group based in Westminster, California. Its clients include GM charter schools in California,

Nevada, Arizona, Utah, and elsewhere (see http://www.accordeducation.org/ website/index.php). Similarly, the Grace Institute is a self-described educational research and consultancy firm whose clientele consists of GM-affiliated charter schools throughout the Southeast region of the United States (see http://www.graceschools.us/). The Washington Education Foundation (WEDUF) established a name for itself by serving as an education consultancy and IT solutions provider for the Chesapeake Science Point Academy in Annapolis, Maryland, and for other schools operated by the Maryland-based, GM-affiliated Chesapeake Lighthouse Foundation. WEDUF was also cited as the intended provider for similar services on charter applications for GM-affiliated schools in Virginia, Delaware, and other states throughout the U.S. mid-Atlantic region (see http://www.weduf.org/).

22. See Woodhall and Gatti (2011); Woodhall (2011); Mahom (2011).

NOTE TO THE CONCLUSION

1. For a useful example of the ways in which GM intellectuals ambiguously and contradictorily present their political impact, consider first Yilmaz's comments presented in this chapter, followed by the exchange between Alp Aslandoğan (a senior GM intellectual in the United States) and Bulent Alriza in the Q&A transcript at the Center for Strategic and International Studies on June 17, 2009, available at http://csis.org/event/gulen-movement.

Bibliography

"2,459 Newspapers, 258 TV Stations in Turkey." *Today's Zaman* (October 3, 2008).

Adak, Hülya. "National Myths and Self Narrations: Mustafa Kemal's *Nutuk* and Halide Edib's *Memoirs* and the *Turkish Ordeal.*" *South Atlantic Quarterly* 102, nos. 2/3 (2003): 509–527.

Agai, Bekim. "The Gülen Movement's Islamic Ethic of Education." In *Turkish Islam and the Secular State: The Gülen Movement*, edited by John L. Esposito and M. Hakan Yavuz, 48–68. Syracuse: Syracuse University Press, 2003.

Akinoğlu, Hasan. "Primary Education Curriculum Reforms in Turkey." *World Applied Sciences Journal* 3, no. 2 (2008): 195–199.

Aksit, Necme. "Educational Reform in Turkey." *International Journal of Educational Development* (2006): 129–137.

Ali, Wajahat, Eli Clifton, Matthew Duss, Lee Fang, Scott Keyes, and Faiz Shakir. *Fear Inc.: The Roots of Islamophobia Network in America*. Washington, DC: Center for American Progress, 2011.

Amin, Khalid. "Kazbi Calls to Follow Thoughts of Iqbal, Rumi, and Gülen of Ideal Humanity." *Daily Mail* (February 3, 2010).

Aragonés, Enriqueta, and Zvika Neeman. "Strategic Ambiguity in Electoral Competition." *Journal of Theoretical Politics* 12 (2000): 183–204.

Aras, Bulent, and Omer Caha. "Fethullah Gülen and His Liberal Turkish Islam Movement." *MERIA* 4, no. 4 (2000): 30–42.

Arat, Yesim. "Politics and Big Business: Janus-Faced Link to the State." In *Strong State and Economic Interest Groups: The Post-1980 Turkish Experience*, edited by Metin Heper, 135–148. London: Walter de Gruyter, 1991.

Armstrong, Elizabeth, and Mary Bernstein. "Culture, Power, and Institutions: A Multi-institutional Politics Approach to Social Movements." *Sociological Theory* 26, no.1 (2008): 74–99.

Ata, Bahri. "The Influence of an American Educator (John Dewey) on the Turkish Education System." *Turkish Yearbook of International Relations* (*Milletlerarası Münasebetler Türk Yılığı*) 31 (2000): 119–130.

Atasoy, Yıldız. "The Islamic Ethic and the Spirit of Turkish Capitalism Today." *Socialist Register* 44 (2008): 48–69.

"Author of Book on Gülen Movement Receives Much Interest in Ankara." *Today's Zaman*, (January 19, 2011): http://www.todayszaman.com/news-232784-author-of-book-on-gulen-movement-receives-muchinterest-in-ankara.html.

"Aydin Dogan Says He Won't Back Down in Media Row with Turkish PM." *Hürriyet Daily News* (September 10, 2008): http://www.hurriyet.com.tr/english/home/9864991.asp.

Baiocchi, Gianpaolo, and Brian Connor. "The Ethnos in the Polis: Political Ethnography as a Mode of Inquiry." *Sociology Compass* 2, no. 1 (2008): 139–155.

Baker, Raymond William. *Islam without Fear: Egypt and the New Islamists*. Cambridge: Harvard University Press, 2003.

Balcı, Bayram. "Fethullah Gülen's Missionary Schools in Central Asia and Their Role in the Spreading of Turkism and Islam." *Religion, State, and Society* 31, no. 2 (2003): 151–177.

"Bank Asya Sees Increase in 2008 Profits despite Crisis." *Today's Zaman* (February 25, 2009).

Baskan, Filiz. "The Political Economy of Islamic Finance in Turkey: The Role of Fethullah Gülen and Asya Finans." In *The Politics of Islamic Finance*, edited by Clement Henry and Rodney Wilson, 216–239. Edinburgh: Edinburgh University Press, 2004.

Bayat, Asef. *Making Islam Democratic*. Stanford: Stanford University Press, 2007.

Beinin, Joel. "Political Islam and the New Global Economy: The Political Economy of an Egyptian Social Movement." *New Centennial Review* 5, no. 1 (2005): 111–139.

Beinin, Joel, and Joe Stork, eds. *Political Islam*. Berkeley: University of California Press, 1997.

Berkeş, Niyazı. *The Development of Secularism in Turkey*. New York: Routledge, 1998.

"BESE Votes to Rescind Charter for Abramson Science and Technology School." *Times Picayune* (August 4, 2011).

Biancchi, Robert. *Interest Groups and Political Development in Turkey*. Princeton: Princeton University Press, 1984.

Bourdieu, Pierre. *The Logic of Practice*. Cambridge: Polity, 1990.

Bray, Mark, and Percy Kwok. "Demand for Private Supplementary Tutoring: Conceptual Considerations and Socio-economic Patterns in Hong Kong." *Economics of Education Review* 22 (2003): 612–613.

Broadbent, J. "Movement in Context: Thick Network and Japanese Environmental Protest." In *Social Movements and Networks*, edited by M. Diani and D. McAdam, 204–229. Oxford: Oxford University Press.

"Brothers from Turkey, Africa Embrace on Trade Bridge." *Today's Zaman* (May 17, 2007).

Büdinenè, Virginija, et al. "Education in a Hidden Marketplace: Monitoring of Private Tutoring." Open Society Institute (2006): http://www.opensocietyfoundations.org/reports/education-hidden-marketplace-monitoring-private-tutoring.

Buğra, Ayse. *State and Business in Modern Turkey*. Albany: SUNY Press, 1994.

Can, Eyüp. *Fethullah Gülen Hocaefendi ile Ufuk Turu (A Tour of New Horizons with Fethullah Gülen)*. 13th ed. Istanbul: AD, 1996.

Carroll, Jill. *A Dialogue of Civilizations: Gülen's Islamic Ideals and Humanistic Discourse.* Somerset, NJ: The Light Publishing, 2007.

Castells, Manuel. *The Power of Identity: Economy, Society, and Culture, Volume 1.* 2nd ed. Malden, MA: Blackwell, 1997.

Çeçen, A. Aydin, A. Suut Dogruel, and Fatma Dogruel. "Economic Growth and Structural Change in Turkey: 1960–1988." *International Journal of Middle Eastern Studies* 26, no.1 (1994): 37–56.

Celâsun, Merih, and Dani Rodrik. "Debt, Adjustment, and Growth: Turkey." In *Developing Country Debt and Economic Performance,* edited by Jeffery Sachs and Susan Collins, 615–808. Chicago: University of Chicago Press, 1989.

Cetin, Muhammad. *The Gülen Movement: Civic Service without Borders.* New York: Blue Dome Press, 2010.

Çetinkaya, Hikmet. *Fethullah Gülen, ABD, ve AKP* (Fethullah Gülen, the USA, and the AKP). Istanbul: Gunizi Yayincilik, 2007.

"CHP to Follow Deniz Feneri Hearing." *Hurriyet Daily News* (November 16, 2012).

Clark, Janine. *Islam, Charity, and Activism: Middle-Class Networks and Social Welfare in Egypt, Jordan, and Yemen.* Bloomington: Indiana University Press, 2004.

Cooke, Miriam, and Bruce Lawrence, eds. *Muslim Networks: From Hajj to Hip Hop.* Chapel Hill: University of North Carolina Press, 2005.

Davenport, S., and S. Leitch. "Circuits of Power in Practice: Strategic Ambiguity as Delegation of Authority." *Organization Studies* 26, no. 11 (2005): 1603–1623.

Davie, Grace. "Europe: The Exception That Proves the Rule?" In *The Desecularization of the World,* edited by Peter Berger, 65–83. Washington, DC: Ethics and Public Policy Center, 1999.

Demir, Omer, Mustafa Açar, and Metin Toprak. "Anatolian Tigers of Islamic Capital: Prospects and Challenges." *Middle Eastern Studies* 40, no. 6 (2004): 166–188.

Ebaugh, Helen Rose. *The Gülen Movement: A Sociological Analysis of a Civic Movement Rooted in Moderate Islam.* New York: Springer, 2010.

Economist Intelligence Unit. *Turkey: Country Profiles.* London: Economist Intelligence Unit, 1995–2008.

Eickelman, Dale. "Qur'anic Commentary, Public Space, and Religious Intellectuals in the Writings of Said Nursi." *Muslim World* 89, nos. 3–4 (1999): 260–269.

Eickelman, Dale, and Jon Anderson, eds. *New Media in the Muslim World.* 2nd ed. Bloomington: Indiana University Press, 2003.

Eickelman, Dale, and James Piscatori. *Muslim Politics.* Princeton: Princeton University Press, 1996.

Eisenberg, E. M. "Ambiguity as a Strategy in Organizational Communication." *Communication Monographs* 51 (1984): 227–242.

Eliasoph, N. S. *Avoiding Politics: How Americans Produce Apathy in Everyday Life.* New York: Cambridge University Press, 1998.

Ergene, Enes. *Gülen Hareketinin Analizi Geleceğin Modern Çağa Tanıklığı* (*Tradition Witnessing the Modern Age: An Analysis of the Gülen Movement*). Istanbul: Kaynak Kültür Yayınları, 2005.

————. *Tradition Witnessing the Modern Age.* Somerset, NJ: Tuğhra Books, 2008.

Ertuğrul, Ahmet, and Faruk Selçuk. "A Brief Account of the Turkish Economy, 1980–2000." *Russian and East European Finance and Trade* 37, no. 6 (2001): 6–30.

Estruch, Joan. *Saints and Schemers: Opus Dei and Its Paradoxes.* New York: Oxford University Press, 1995.

Eustis, C. B. "Cry of the Nightingale: Fethullah Gülen: A Modern-Day Rumi?" Conference Proceedings. Islam and the Contemporary World: The Fethullah Gülen Movement in Though and Practice. Southern Methodist University, Dallas, TX (2006): 111–124.

Fagan, Gerladine. "Said Nursi Ban Brands Moderate Muslims as Extremists." *Forum* 18 (June 2007): http://wwrn.org/articles/25508/?&place=russia&section=church-state.

"A Farm Boy on the World Stage." *The Economist* (May 6, 2008).

Finkel, Andrew. "Who Guards the Turkish Press? A Perspective on Press Corruption in Turkey." *Journal of International Affairs* 54, no. 1 (2000): 144–166.

————. "A Dilemma." *Milliyet* (April 6, 2011): http://www.hurriyetdailynews.com/default.aspx?pageid=438&n=a-dilemma-2011-04-07.

Folkenflick, David. "NPR Ends Williams' Contract after Muslim Remarks." *National Public Radio Online* (October 25, 2010): http://www.npr.org/templates/story/story.php?storyId=130712737.

Fried, Daniel. "Testimony before the House Foreign Affairs Committee Subcommittee on Europe." Washington, DC, March 15, 2007: http://2001-2009.state.gov/p/eur/rls/rm/81790.htm.

Giddens, Anthony. *The Third Way: The Renewal of Social Democracy.* Malden, MA: Polity Press, 1999.

Gökçek, Mustafa. "Gülen and Sufism: A Historical Perspective." In *Muslim Citizens of the Globalized World: Contributions of the Gülen Movement,* edited by Robert Hunt and Aslandoğan, 183–193. Somerset, NJ: The Light Publishing, 2005.

Göle, Nilüfer. *The Forbidden Modern: Civilization and Veiling.* Ann Arbor: University of Michigan Press, 1997.

————. "'Islam in Public': New Visibilities and New Imaginaries." *Public Culture* 14, no. 1. (2002): 173–190.

Grady, Sarah, Stacey Bielick, and Susan Aud. *Trends in the Use of School Choice: 1993 to 2007.* Washington, DC: U.S. Department of Education, 2010.

Gramsci, Antonio. *Selections from the Prison Notebooks.* Edited by Quintin Hoare and Geoffrey Smith. New York: International Publishers, 1971.

Gülalp, Haldun. "Globalization and Political Islam: The Social Bases of Turkey's Welfare Party." *International Journal of Middle Eastern Studies* 33, no. 3 (2001): 433–448.

Gülen, Fethullah M. *Criteria; or, Lights of the Way.* Izmir, Turkey: Kaynak Publishing, 1998a.

————. *Prizma II.* Istanbul: Nil Yayınları, 1998b

————. *Towards a Lost Paradise.* Izmir, Turkey: Kaynak Publishing, 1998c.

————. *Pearls of Wisdom.* Fairfax, VA: The Fountain, 1999.

————. *Questions and Answers about Faith, Vol. 1.* Fairfax, VA: The Fountain, 2000.

————. *Key Concepts in the Practice of Sufism: Emerald Hills of the Heart, Vol. 1.* Somerset, NJ: The Fountain, 2004a.

————. *Toward a Civilization of Love and Tolerance.* Somerset, NJ: The Light Publishing, 2004b.

————. "Interview with Muhammad Gündem." *Milliyet Gazetesi* (January 19, 2005a).

————. *The Messenger of God Muhammad.* Somerset, NJ: The Light Publishing, 2005b.

————. *Statute of Our Souls.* Somerset, NJ: The Light Publishing, 2006.*Gülen v. Chertoff.* "Petition for Writ of Mandamus." Civil Action No. 07-2148, United States District Court, E.D. Pennsylvania. Filed May 27, 2007.

————. "Memorandum of Law in Support of Plaintiff's Motion for Summary Judgment." Case 2:07-cv-02148-SD. Doc 30. Filed June 4, 2008.

————. "Plaintiff's Motion for Summary Judgment." U.S. District Court, Eastern District of Pennsylvania. Case 2:2007-cv-02148–SD. Doc. 30. Filed June 6, 2008.

————. "Defendant's Response in Opposition to Plaintiff's Motion for Summary Judgment." Civil Action No. 07-2148. Case 2:07-cv-02148–SD. Doc. 31. Filed June 18, 2008.

————. "Order." Civil Action No. 07-2148. Judge Stewart Dalzell, J. United States District Court, E.D. Pennsylvania. Filed July 16, 2008.

————. "Memorandum of Judge Stewart Dalzell." 2:07-cv-02148-SD. Filed July 18, 2008.

"Gülen: The Law Judges Deeds Not Intentions." *Hürriyet Daily News* (June 24, 1999): http://www.hurriyetdailynews.com/default. aspx?pageid=438&n=gulen-the-law-judges-deeds-not-intentions-1999-06-24.

Gülerce, Hüseyin. "The Meaning of This Election." *Today's Zaman* (July 20, 2007a): http://www.todayszaman.com/columnist-117191-the-meaning-of-this-election.html.

————. "An *Iftar* Dinner in New York." *Today's Zaman* (October 5, 2007b): http://www.todayszaman.com/columnist-123869-an-iftar-dinner-in-new-york.html.

Güvenç, B. *History of Turkish Education.* Ankara: Turkish Education Association, 1998

Hall, Stuart. "On Postmodernism and Articulation: An Interview with Stuart Hall." In *Stuart Hall: Critical Dialogues in Culture Studies*, edited by David Morley and K. H. Chen, 131–150. New York: Routledge, 1996.

Hansen, Suzy. "Fethullah Gülen and International Islam." *New Republic* (November 10, 2010): http://www.tnr.com/article/world/magazine/79062/ global-turkey-imam-fethullah-gulen.

Harvey, David. "Time–Space Compression and the Postmodern Condition." In *The Global Transformations Reader*, edited by David Held and Anthony McGrew, 82–91. London: Polity Press, 2000.

"Harmony Schools Answer Claims." *Odessa America Online* (June 4, 2010): http://www.oaoa.com/news/harmony-48165-group-lot.html.

Hayward, Chloe. "Borrower Profile: Calik Builds Funding for Rapid Growth." *Euro-Money* (May 2007).

Hefner, Robert, ed. *Remaking Muslim Politics: Pluralism, Contestation, and Democratization.* Princeton: Princeton University Press, 2004.

Hendrick, Joshua D. "The Regulated Potential of Kinetic Islam: Antitheses in Global Islamic Activism." In *Muslim Citizens of the Globalized World: Contributions of the Gülen Movement*, edited by Robert Hunt and Alp Aslandoğan, 12–33. Houston: Tuğhra Books, 2007.

———. "Globalization, Islamic Activism, and Passive Revolution in Turkey: The Case of Fethullah Gülen." *Journal of Political Power* 2, no. 3 (2009): 343–368.

———. "Media Wars, Public Relations, and 'the Gülen Factor' in the New Turkey." *Middle East Report* 260 (2011a): 40–46.

———. "Neo-liberalism and 'Third-Way' Islamic Activism: Fethullah Gülen and Turkey's New Elite." In *The Sociology of Islam and Muslim Societies*, edited by Tuğrul Keskin, 61–90. New York: Garent/Ithaca Press, 2011b.

Heper, Metin, ed. *The State Tradition in Turkey*. Northgate: Eothen Press, 1985.

———. *The State and Public Bureaucracies: A Comparative Perspective*. New York: Greenwood Press, 1987.

———, ed. *Strong State and Economic Interest Groups: The Post-1980 Turkish Experience*. New York: Walter de Gruyter, 1991.

Herman, David. "Global Public Intellectuals Poll." *Prospect* (November 20, 2005): http://www.prospectmagazine.co.uk/2005/11/globalpublicintellectualspoll/.

Herman, Edward, and Noam Chomsky. *Manufacturing Consent: The Political Economy of the Mass Media*. 2nd ed. New York: Pantheon Press, 2002.

"The Highest Scores on the ÖSS Are Published." *Zaman* (July 13, 2007).

Hitchens, Christopher. "How to Be a Public Intellectual." *Prospect* (May 24, 2008): http://www.prospectmagazine.co.uk/2008/05/what-is-a-public-intellectual/.

"How Far They Have Traveled." *Economist*, March 12, 2008.

Hudson, Alexandra. "Turkish Islamic Preacher: Threat or Benefactor?" *Reuters UK* (May 13, 2008).

Human Rights Watch. "Human Rights Reform in Turkmenistan: Rhetoric or Reality" (2007): http://www.hrw.org/legacy/backgrounder/eca/turkmenistan1107/turkmenistan1107web.pdf.

Hunt, Robert, and Alp Aslandoğan, eds. *Muslim Citizens of the Globalized World*. Somerset, NJ: The Light Publishing, 2007.

Huntington, Samuel P. "A Clash of Civilizations?" *Foreign Affairs* 72, no. 3. (1993): 22–49.

———. *The Clash of Civilizations and the Remaking of World Order*. New York: Simon and Schuster, 1996.

Innaccone, Lawrence R. "An Introduction to the Economics of Religion." *Journal of Economic Literature* 46, no. 36 (1998): 1465–1496.

Introvigne, Massimo. "Turkish Religious Markets: A View Based on the Religious Economy Theory." In *The Emergence of a New Turkey*, edited by Hakan Yavuz, 23–48. Salt Lake City: University of Utah Press, 2006.

Jacoby, Tim. *Social Power and the Turkish State*. New York: Routledge, 2004.

Jarzabkowski, Paula A., John A. A. Sillince, and Duncan A. Shaw. "Strategic Ambiguity as a Rhetorical Resource for Enabling Multiple Interests." *Human Relations* 63, no. 2 (2010): 219–248.

Jelen, Ted, and Clyde Wilcox. "Religion and Politics in an Open Market." In *Religion and Politics in Comparative Perspective: The One, the Few, the Many*, edited by Ted Jelen and Clyde Wilcox, 289–313. New York: Cambridge University Press, 2002.

Kamrava, Mehran. "Pseudo-democratic Politics and Populist Possibilities: The Rise and Demise of Turkey's Refah Party." *British Journal of Middle Eastern Affairs* 25, no. 2 (1998): 275–301.

Kanlı, Yusuf. "Whose Turn Will Be Next?" *Hürriyet Daily and Economic News* (February 21, 2009): http://www.hurriyet.com.tr/english/opinion/11052132.asp.

Kaplan, Sam. *The Pedagogical State: Education and the Politics of National Culture in Post-1980 Turkey*. Stanford: Stanford University Press, 2006.

Kaya, M. K., and Svante Cornell. "Politics, Media, and Power in Turkey." *The Turkey Analyst* (Central Asia Caucus Institute and Silk Road Studies Joint Center, 2008).

Keck, Margaret, and Katheryn Sikkink. *Activists beyond Borders*. Ithaca: Cornell University Press, 1998.

Keneş, Bülent. "The Portrait of a Fascist Provoker." *Today's Zaman* (May 2, 2007): http://www.todayszaman.com/columnist-110062-a-portrait-of-a-fascist-provoker.html.

———. "The Media and the End of an Era of Impunity." *Today's Zaman* (February 13, 2009): http://www.todayszaman.com/columnists-166787-the-media-and-the-end-of-an-era-of-impunity.html.

Kepel, Giles. *Jihad: The Trail of Political Islam*. Cambridge: Harvard University Press, 2002.

Keyder, Cağlar. "Class and State Transformation in Modern Turkey." In *State and Ideology in the Middle East and Pakistan*, edited by Fred Halliday and Hamza Alavi, 191–221. New York: Monthly Review Press, 1988.

———. "The Turkish Bell Jar." *New Left Review* 28 (2004): 65–84.

Kim, H. C. "The Nature and Role of Sufism in Contemporary Islam." Unpublished diss. Philadelphia: Temple University, 2008.

Kramer, Heintz. *A Changing Turkey*. Washington, DC: Brookings Institution Press, 2000.

Krespin, R. "The Upcoming Elections in Turkey (2): The AKP's Political Power Base." MEMRI Inquiry and Analysis Series, no. 375 (July 2007).

———. "Fethullah Gülen's Grand Ambition: Turkey's Islamist Danger." *Middle East Quarterly* 16, no. 1 (2009): 55–66.

Krueger, Anne. "Partial Adjustment and Growth in the 1980s in Turkey." In *Reform, Recovery, and Growth: Latin America and the Middle East*, edited by Rudiger Dornbusch and Sebastian Edwards, 343–368. Chicago: University of Chicago Press, 1995.

Kuran, Timur. *Islam and Mammon*. Princeton: Princeton University Press, 2004.

Kuru, Ahmet T. "Search for a Middle Way." In *Turkish Islam and the Secular State: The Gülen Movement*, edited by John Esposito and Hakan Yavuz, 115–130. Syracuse: Syracuse University Press, 2003.

Kurzman, Charles, and Lynn Owens. "Sociology of Intellectuals." *Annual Review of Sociology* 28 (2002): 63–90.

Lahaj, Mary. "An Introduction to Istanbul." *Today's Zaman* (May 10, 2007).

Lewis, Bernard. *The Emergence of Modern Turkey.* New York: Oxford University Press, 1961.

———. *Islam and the West.* New York: Oxford University Press, 1993.

———. "The Roots of Muslim Rage." *Policy* 17, no. 4 (2002 [1990]): 17–26.

Lewis, Geoffrey. *The Turkish Language Reform: A Catastrophic Success.* Oxford: Oxford University Press, 1998.

Lichterman, Paul. *The Search for Political Community: American Activists Reinventing Commitment.* New York: Cambridge University Press, 1996.

Lin, Nan. "Building a Network Theory of Social Capital." *Connections* 22, no. 1 (1999): 28–51.

Lubeck, Paul. "The Islamic Revival." In *Global Social Movements*, edited by Robin Cohen and Shirin Rai, 146–164. London: Athlone Press, 2000.

Mahom, Ed. "Young Scholars Charter School Faces Scrutiny over Ties with Islamic Leader." *Center Daily News* (March 22, 2011): http://www.centredaily.com/2011/03/22/2597590/charter-school-faces-scrutiny.html.

Mamdani, Mahmood. "Good Muslim, Bad Muslim: A Political Perspective on Culture and Terrorism." *American Anthropologist* 104, no. 3 (2002): 766–775.

———. *Good Muslim, Bad Muslim: America, the Cold War, and the Roots of Terror.* New York: Pantheon Books, 2004.

Mamedov, Nazar. "Ethnocultural Practices in Post-Soviet Kyrgyzstan and Turkmenistan: A Comparative Perspective." MA diss. Budapest, Hungary: Central European University, 2005.

Mandaville, Peter. *Transnational Muslim Politics: Reimagining the Umma.* New York: Routledge, 2001.

———. *Global Political Islam.* New York: Routledge, 2006.

Mann, Michael. *The Sources of Social Power, Volume I.* New York: Cambridge University Press, 1986.

———. *The Dark Side of Democracy: Explaining Ethnic Cleansing.* New York: Cambridge University Press, 2004.

Mardin, Şerif. *Religion and Social Change in Modern Turkey: The Case of Bediüzzaman Said Nursi.* Albany: SUNY Press, 1989.

Maududi, Sayyid Abul A'la. *The Islamic Movement: Dynamics of Values, Power, and Social Change.* Leicester, UK: Islamic Foundation, 1984.

McAdam, Doug, John McCarthy, and Mayer Zald, eds. *Comparative Perspectives on Social Movements.* New York: Cambridge University Press, 1996.

McDowell, David. *A Modern History of the Kurds.* New York. I. B. Tauris, 1992.

Melucci, Alberto. *Challenging Codes: Collective Action in the Information Age.* New York: Cambridge University Press, 1996.

Michel, Thomas S. J. "Sufism and Modernity in the Thought of Fethullah Gülen." *Muslim World* 95 (2005): 341–358.

———. "Following in the Footsteps of Rumi." In *Peaceful Coexistence: Fethullah Gülen's Initiatives in the Contemporary World*, edited by Ihsan Yılmaz, 183–192. London: Leeds University Press, 2007.

Mitchell, Richard. *The Society of Muslim Brothers*. New York: Oxford University Press, 1969.

"Mole Claims in Fraud Case Decried as Pitiful by Turkish Prime Minister." *Hürriyet Daily News* (October 17, 2011).

Mouffe, Chantal. *On the Political*. New York: Routledge, 2005.

Nasr, Sayyed Hussein, ed. *Islamic Spirituality: Foundations, Volume 1*. New York: Crossroad Herder, 1997.

Nursi, Bediüzzaman Said. *The Letters 2*. London: Truestar, 1995

———. *The Risal-i Nur Külliyati Collection*. Istanbul: Sözler Nesriyat ve Sanayi AS, 1996.

Nuttall, Tom. "How Gülen Triumphed." *Prospect* (July 26, 2008): http://www.prospectmagazine.co.uk/2008/07/howglentriumphed/.

Olson, Robert. *The Emergence of Kurdish Nationalism and the Sheikh Said Rebellion*. Austin: University of Texas Press, 1989.

———. "The Kurdish Rebellions of Sheikh Said (1925), Mt. Ararat (1930), and Dersim (1937–8): Their Impact on the Development of the Turkish Air Force and on Kurdish and Turkish Nationalism." *Die Welt des Islams* 40, no. 1 (2000): 67–94.

Öniş, Ziya. "Political Economy of Turkey in the 1980s: Autonomy of Unorthodox Liberalism." In *Strong State and Economic Interest Groups: The Post 1980 Turkish Experience*, edited by Metin Heper, 27–40. New York: Walter de Gruyter, 1991.

———. "Conservative Globalism at the Crossroads: The Justice and Development Party and the Thorny Path to Democratic Consolidation in Turkey." *Mediterranean Politics* 14, no. 1 (2009): 21–40.

Öniş, Ziya, and Umut Turem. "Business, Globalization, and Democracy: A Comparative Analysis of Turkish Business Associations." *Turkish Studies* 2, no. 2 (2001): 94–120.

Open Source Center. "Turkey: Guide to Major Turkish Newspapers" (October 7, 2008): http://www.fas.org/irp/dni/osc/turkish-news.pdf.

Özbudun, Ergun. "The Post-1980 Legal Framework for Interest Group Associations." In *Strong State and Economic Interest Groups: The Post-1980 Turkish Experience*, edited by Metin Heper, 41–53. New York: Walter de Gruyter, 1991.

Özbüdün, Ergun, and Fuat Keymen. "Cultural Globalization in Turkey: Actors, Discourses, and Challenges." In *Many Globalizations*, edited by Peter Berger and Samuel Huntington, 296–320. New York: Oxford University Press, 2002.

Özcan, Gul Berna, and Murat Çokgezcen. "Limits to Alternative Forms of Capitalization: The Case of Anatolian Holding Companies." *World Development* 31, no. 12 (2003): 2061–2084.

———. "Trusted Markets: The Exchange of Islamic Companies." *Comparative Economic Studies* 48 (2006): 132–155.

Özdalga, Elisabeth. "Following in the Footsteps of Fethullah Gülen: Three Women Teachers Tell Their Stories." In *Turkish Islam and the Secular State: The Gülen Movement*, edited by John Esposito and Hakan Yavuz, 85–114. Syracuse: Syracuse University Press, 2003.

Palmer, Joe, and Howard Robinson. "BPA Audit Figures Reveal Turkish Newspaper as Having One of the Largest Subscriber Bases in Europe." BPA Worldwide (2007).

Park, Bill. "The Fethullah Gülen Movement." *Middle East Review of International Affairs* 12, no. 3 (2008): http://www.globalpolitician.com/print.asp?id=5355.

Parla, Taha, and Andrew Davidson. *Corporatist Ideology in Kemalist Turkey.* Syracuse: Syracuse University Press, 2004.

Passow, Sam. "Turkey Positioned for Growth." *Institutional Investor* 28 (February 1994): 4–9.

Passy, Florence. "Social Networks Matter: But How?" In *Social Movements and Networks*, edited by Mario Dani and Doug McAdam, 21–48. New York: Oxford University Press, 2003.

Pipes, Daniel. *In the Path of God: Islam and Political Power.* New Brunswick, NJ: Transaction, 2002.

"Platform Travels to N. Iraq." *Hürriyet Daily News* (January 29, 2009): http://www.hurriyet.com.tr/english/domestic/10878448.asp?scr=1.

"A Quick Primer on *Doğan v. Erdoğan.*" *Hürriyet Daily News* (September 9, 2008): http://www.hurriyetdailynews.com/default.aspx?pageid=438&n=a-quick-primer-on-dogan-vs-erdogan-2008-09-09.

Richards, Alan, and John Waterbury. *A Political Economy of the Middle East.* 2nd ed. Boulder, CO: Westview Press, 1998.

Roberts, John. "The Turkish Gate: Energy Transit and Security Issues." *Turkish Policy Quarterly* 3, no. 4 (2004): 97–125.

Rodgers, Guy. "Fethullah Gülen: Infiltrating the U.S. through Our Charter Schools?" (2010): http://www.campus-watch.org/article/id/7238.

Rodrik, Dani. "Premature Liberalization, Incomplete Stabilization: The Özal Decade in Turkey." Working Paper No. 3300. Cambridge, MA: National Bureau of Economic Research, 1990.

Roy, Olivier. *The Failure of Political Islam.* Cambridge: Harvard University Press, 1994.

———. *Globalized Islam: The Search for a New Ummah.* Cambridge: Harvard University Press, 2004.

Rubin, Michael. "Turkey Turning Point: Could There Be an Islamic Revolution in Turkey?" *National Review* (April 2008).

Sahin, Haluk, and Asu Aksoy. "Global Media and Cultural Identity in Turkey." *Journal of Communication* 43, no. 2 (1993): 31–41.

Sarıtoprak, Zeki. "An Islamic Approach to Peace and Nonviolence: A Turkish Experience." *The Muslim World Special Issue: Islam and in Contemporary Turkey: The Contributions of Fethullah Gülen*, edited by Zeki Sarıtoprak. 95, no. 3 (2005): 413–428.

Sarıtoprak, Zeki, and Sydney Griffith. "Fethullah Gülen and the 'People of the Book': A Voice from Turkey for Interfaith Dialogue." *Muslim World: Special Issue: Islam in Contemporary Turkey: The Contributions of Fethullah Gülen* 95, no. 3 (2005): 325–471.

Saul, Stephanie. "Charter Schools Tied to Turkey Grow in Texas." *New York Times* (June 6, 2011).

Sayyid, Bobby. *Fundamental Fear: Eurocentrism and the Emergence of Islamism.* London: Zed Books, 1997.

Schulze, Reinhardt. *A Modern History of the Islamic World*. New York: New York University Press, 2002.

Schwartz, Stephen. "The Real Fethullah Gülen." *Prospect* (July 26, 2008): http://www.prospectmagazine.co.uk/2008/07/therealfethullahglen/.

Şen, Mustafa. "Turkish Entrepreneurs in Central Asia: The Case of Kazakhstan and Kyrgyzstan." Unpublished diss. Ankara, Turkey: Middle East Technical University, 2001.

Senses, Fikret. "Short-Term Stabilization Policies in a Developing Economy: The Turkish Experience in 1980 in Long-Term Perspective." In *Turkey in the World Capitalist System*, edited by Huseyin Ramazanoglu, 130–160. Brookfield, VT: Gower, 1986.

Shamir, Boas, and Jane Howell. "Organizational and Contextual Influences on the Emergence and Effectiveness of Charismatic Leadership." *Leadership Quarterly* 10, no. 2 (1999): 257–283.

"Şık, Şener Appear before Judge as Court Begins Hearing OdaTV Case." *Today's Zaman* (November 21, 2011).

Şimşek, Hasan, and Ali Yildirim. "Turkey: Innovation and Tradition." In *Balancing Change and Tradition in Global Education Reform*, edited by Iris Rothberg. 153–185. Lanham, MD: Rowan and Littlefield, 2004.

"Small Enterprises Star in TUSKON's Trade Bridge with Pacific." *Today's Zaman* (April 9, 2007).

"State Recommends Denial of Fulton Charter School." *Atlanta Journal and Constitution* (May 4, 2012).

Steller, Tim. "Gülen Movement an Enigmatic Mix of Turkish Nationalism, Religion, and Education." *Arizona Daily Star* (April 25, 2010): http://azstarnet.com/news/local/education/precollegiate/article_41b354b0-6679-5b1e-8a73-4c51ec94b7ad.html.

Stokes, Jenny. "Submission into the Inquiry into Academic Freedom" Salt Shakers, Wantirna VIC Australia (2008).

Stuart, Elizabeth. "Islamic Links to Utah's Beehive Academy Probed." *Deseret News* (June 1, 2010a): http://www.deseretnews.com/article/700036619/Islamic-links-to-Utahs- Beehive-Academy-probed.html.

———. "Charter Board Reverses Decision to Close Beehive Academy." *Deseret News* (July 15, 2010): http://www.deseretnews.com/article/700039383/Charter-board-reverses-decision-to-close-Beehive-Academy.html.

Tanır, Ilhan. "Can Turkish and Armenian Diasporas Open the Channels of Dialogue?" *Hurriyet Daily and Economic News* (March 8, 2010): http://www.hurriyetdailynews.com/default.aspx?pageid=438&n=can-turkish-and-armenian-diasporas-open-the-channels-of-dialogue-2010-03-08.

Tansel, Aysit, and Fatma Bircan. "Private Tutoring Expenditures in Turkey." ERF Working Paper Series 0333. Ankara: Middle Eastern Technical University, 2003.

———. "Demand for Education in Turkey: A Tobit Analysis of Private Tutoring Expenditures." *Economics of Education Review* 25, no. 2 (2006): 303–313.

Tarrow, Sydney. *Power in Movement*. New York: Cambridge University Press, 1994.

Tavernise, Sabrina. "Turkish Schools Offer Pakistan a Gentler Vision of Islam." *New York Times* (May 4, 2008).

Tilly, Charles. *Social Movements, 1768–2004*. Boulder, CO: Paradigm, 2004.

Toksöz, Mina. "The Economy: Achievements and Prospects." In *Turkish Transformation: New Century, New Challenges*, edited by Brian W. Beeley, 141–164. Huntingdon: Eothen, 2002.

Toppo, Greg. "Objectives of Charter Schools with Turkish Ties Questioned." *USA Today* (August 17, 2010).

Tuğal, Cihan. *Passive Revolution*. Stanford: Stanford University Press, 2009.

Turam, Berna. "A Bargain between the Secular State and Turkish Islam: Politics of Ethnicity in Central Asia." *Nations and Nationalism* 10, no. 3 (2004a): 353–374.

——. "The Politics of Engagement between Islam and the Secular State: Ambivalences in 'Civil Society.'" *British Journal of Sociology* 55, no. 2 (2004b): 259–281.

——. *Between Islam and the State*. Stanford: Stanford University Press, 2006. "Turkish Deputy Prime Minister Mole in Fraud Case: CHP Head." *Hürriyet Daily News* (October 11, 2011).

"Turkish Deputy Prime Minister under Mounting Pressure to Quit Post." *Hürriyet Daily News* (October 14, 2011).

"Turkish PM Calls Party to Boycott Critical Media." *Reuters* (September 19, 2008).

"Turks Move to Ban Pro-Kurdish Party." *International Herald Tribune* (June 16, 2007).

"TUSKON Summit Initiates $300 Billion in Trade in Two Days." *Today's Zaman* (October 28, 2011).

Ünal, Ali. *Geçmişten Geleceğe Köprü: Fethullah Gülen* (*A Bridge from the Past to the Future: Fethullah Gülen*). Istanbul: Kaynak Kültür Yayınları, 2005.

Ünal, Ali, and Alphonse Williams, eds. *Advocate of Dialogue: Fethullah Gülen*. Fairfax, VA: The Fountain, 2000.

Ütkülü, Ütkü. "The Turkish Economy Past and Present." In *Turkey since 1970*, edited by Debbie Lovatt, 1–40. New York: Palgrave, 2001.

Vahide, Şükran. *Islam in Modern Turkey: An Intellectual Biography of Bediuzzaman Said Nursi*. Albany: SUNY Press, 2005.

Van Bruinessen, Martin. Forward to *New Voices of Islam*, edited by Farish A. Noor, vii–xi. Amsterdam: Institute for the Study of Islam in the Modern World, 2002.

Vanderpool, Tim. 2009. "Hidden Agenda? Parents Raise Concerns That a Tucson Charter School Has Ties to a Turkish Nationalist Movement." *Tucson Weekly* (December 31): http://www.tucsonweekly.com/tucson/hidden-agenda/Content?oid=1694764.

Vural, Fatih. "Turkish Schools World's Most Global Movement, Says Sociologist." *Today's Zaman* (June 10, 2008).

Wacquant, Loïc. "Ethnografeast: A Progress Report on the Practice and Promise of Ethnography." *Ethnography* 4 (2003): 5–14.

Weber, Max. *Economy and Society, Vols. 1 and 2*. Edited by Guenther Roth and Claus Wittich. Berkeley: University of California Press, 1978 [1922].

——. *The Protestant Ethic and the Spirit of Capitalism*. 3rd Roxbury ed. Translated and introduced by Stephen Kalberg. Los Angeles: Roxbury, 2002 [1905].

White, Jenny. *Islamist Mobilization in Turkey: A Study in Vernacular Politics.* Seattle: University of Washington Press, 2002.

———. "The End of Islamism: Turkey's Muslimhood Model." In *Remaking Muslim Politics: Pluralism, Contestation, and Democratization,* edited by Robert Hefner, 87–111. Princeton: Princeton University Press, 2004.

Wiktorowicz, Quintan. *Islamic Activism: A Social Movement Theory Approach.* Indianapolis: Indiana University Press, 2004.

"Winners at Turkish Olympics Are Champions of Peace." *Today's Zaman* (June 4, 2007): http://www.fethullahgulen.org/press-room/news/2352-winners-at-turkish-olympics-are-champions-of-peace.html.

Woodhall, Martha. "Philadelphia New Media's Charter School Contends It's Not a Public School." *Philadelphia Inquirer* (July 2, 2011): http://articles.philly.com/2011-07-02/news/29730728_1_science-academy-charter-school-public-school-charter-staff.

Woodhall, Martha, and Claudio Gatti. "U.S. Charter Network with Turkish Link Draws Federal Attention." *Philadelphia Inquirer* (March 20, 2011): http://articles.philly.com/2011-03-20/news/29148147_1_gulen-schools-gulen-followers-charter-schools.

Wood, Richard. *Faith in Action: Religion, Race, and Democratic Organizing in America.* Chicago: University of Chicago Press, 2002.

World Bank. "How Much Does Turkey Spend on Education? Development of National Education Accounts to Measure and Evaluate Education Expenditures." Working Paper, Report No. 41058. Washington, DC: 2005a.

———. "Turkey: Education Sector Study." Report No. 32450–TU. Washington, DC: 2005b.

"Yamanlar, Fatih, and Samanyolu Make Their Mark in Science Olympics." *Zaman* (December 13, 2007).

Yanardağ, Merdan. *Fethullah Gülen Hareketinin Perde Arkası: Turkiye Nasıl Kusatıldıı? (The Fethullah Gülen Movement's Hidden Plan: How Has Turkey Been Sieged?).* Istanbul: Siyah/Beyaz Yayincilik, 2006.

Yavuz, Hakan. "Search for a New Social Contract in Turkey: Fethullah Gülen, the Virtue Party, and the Kurds." *SAIS Review* 19, no. 1 (1999): 114–143.

———. "Being Modern the Nurcu Way." *ISIM Newsletter* 6 (2000): 7, 14.

———. *Islamic Political Identity in Turkey.* New York: Oxford University Press, 2003a.

———. "Islam in the Public Sphere." In *Turkish Islam and the Secular State,* edited by Hakan Yavuz and John Esposito, 1–19. Syracuse: Syracuse University Press, 2003b.

———, ed. *The Emergence of a New Turkey.* Salt Lake City: University of Utah Press, 2006.Yavuz, Hakan, and John Esposito, eds. *Turkish Islam and the Secular State.* Syracuse: Syracuse University Press, 2003.

Yeşilada, Birol. "Problems of Political Development in the Third Turkish Republic." *Polity* 21, no. 2 (1988): 345–372.

Yildiz, Cemil. "Niyasov Leaves Developing Country Behind." *Zaman* (December 22, 2006).

Yilmaz, Ihsan. "Beyond Post-Islamism: A Critical Analysis of the Turkish Islamism's Transformation toward Fethullah Gülen's Stateless Cosmopolitan Islam." In *Islam in the Age of Global Challenges: Alternative Perspectives of the Gülen Movement*, edited by Ali Yurtsever, 859–925. Washington, DC: Rumi Forum, 2008.

"Yobe Sends 595 Students to Turkish Schools." *Daily Champion* (Lagos, Nigeria) (September 17, 2008): http://allafrica.com/stories/200809170170.html.

Yurtsever, Ali, ed. *Islam in the Age of Global Challenges: Alternative Perspective of the Gülen Movement.* Washington, DC: Tuğhra Books, 2008.

Zürcher, Erik. *Turkey: A Modern History.* New York: I. B. Tauris, 2004.

Index

About the Author

Joshua D. Hendrick is Assistant Professor of Sociology and Global Studies at Loyola University Maryland in Baltimore. He received his PhD and MA degrees in sociology from the University of California, Santa Cruz, and his MA degree in cultural anthropology from Northern Arizona University.